BARBARIAN CURRENTS
HALF A CENTURY OF BRAZILIAN MEDIA ARTS

Gabriel Menotti and German Alfonso Nunez

The **MEDIA : ART : WRITE : NOW** series mobilises the medium of writing as a mode of critical enquiry and aesthetic expression. Its books capture the most original developments in technology-based arts and other forms of creative media: AI and computational arts, gaming, digital and post-digital productions, soft and wet media, interactive and participative arts, open platforms, photography, photomedia and, last but not least, amateur media practice. They convey the urgency of the project via their style, length and mode of engagement. In both length and tone, they sit somewhere between an extended essay and a monograph.

Series Editor: Joanna Zylinska

BARBARIAN CURRENTS
HALF A CENTURY OF BRAZILIAN MEDIA ARTS

Gabriel Menotti and German Alfonso Nunez

O
OPEN HUMANITIES PRESS

London 2025

First edition published by Open Humanities Press 2025
Copyright © 2025 Gabriel Menotti, German Alfonso Nunez
and respective authors

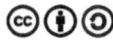

Freely available at:
http://openhumanitiespress.org/books/titles/barbarian-currents/

This is an open access book, licensed under Creative Commons By Attribution Share Alike license. Under this license, authors allow anyone to download, reuse, reprint, modify, distribute, and/or copy their work so long as the authors and source are cited and resulting derivative works are licensed under the same or similar license. No permission is required from the authors or the publisher. Statutory fair use and other rights are in no way affected by the above. Read more about the license at creativecommons.org/licenses/by-sa/4.0/

Cover Art, figures, and other media included with this book may be under different copyright restrictions.

Cover Image: Detail of Paulo Bruscky, *Xeroperformance*, 1980

Print ISBN 978-1-78542-143-3
PDF ISBN   978-1-78542-142-6

| Conseil de recherches en sciences humaines du Canada | Social Sciences and Humanities Research Council of Canada |

OPEN HUMANITIES PRESS

Open Humanities Press is an international, scholar-led open access publishing collective whose mission is to make works of contemporary critical thought freely available worldwide.
More at http://openhumanitiespress.org/

Contents

Acknowledgements   11

1. Technicised Barbarians   12
   Gabriel Menotti and German Alfonso Nunez

I Code and Language

2. Code and Language   38
   Gabriel Menotti and German Alfonso Nunez

3. Form, Function and General Project (1957)   43
   Décio Pignatari

4. Concrete Poetry – Language – Communication (1957)   46
   Haroldo de Campos

5. Poetry and Modernity:
   From the Death of Art to the Constellation.
   The Post-Utopian Poem (1997)   61
   Haroldo de Campos

6. Art and Technology, Part III (1967)   69
   Augusto de Campos

7. On Some Aspects of Concrete Poetry (1957)   74
   Haroldo de Campos

8. New Language, New Poetry (1964)   77
   Luis Ângelo Pinto and Décio Pignatari

9. The Three Sides of the Coin:
   Brazilian Poetry in the 1960s and 1970s (1983)   88
   Eduardo Kac

10. Two Lines of Contribution: Concretists
    in São Paulo / Neo-Concretists in Rio (1977)   101
    Aracy Amaral

11. The New Possibilities (1977)   111
    Walter Zanini

12. International Multimedia (1979)   113
    Walter Zanini

II Social Communication Systems

13. Social Communication Systems   116
    Gabriel Menotti and German Alfonso Nunez

14. Art in Hard Times (1964-c. 1980) (2004)   121
    Aracy Amaral

15. General Outline of the New Objectivity (1967)   132
    Hélio Oiticica

16. Mail Art: Art in Synchrony (1981)   141
    Julio Plaza

17. Mail Art and the Great Network:
    Art, Today, is this Statement (1977)   145
    Paulo Bruscky

18. Artistic Xerography: Art without an Original (from the Invention of the Machine to the Xero/graphic Process) (1985)   148
    Paulo Bruscky

19. Conversation with the Reader (1986)   153
    Júlio Plaza

20. By Way of Conclusion (1986)   159
    Júlio Plaza

21. Holopoetry and Perceptual Syntax (1986)   168
    Eduardo Kac

22. Pretext for an Intervention (1984) 171
    Annateresa Fabris

23. Museums and New Communication Media (1976) 176
    Walter Zanini

24. Introduction to the 17th São Paulo Biennial (1983) 179
    Walter Zanini

25. For a Creative Criticism / Curating
    Exhibitions as Creation (1989) 182
    Frederico Morais

26. From the Body to the Ground (2001) 189
    Frederico Morais

III Moving Images

27. Moving Images 200
    Gabriel Menotti and German Alfonso Nunez

28. Poets, Artists, Anarcho-Super8
    -Filmmakers (2001) 204
    Rubens Machado Jr.

29. Some Ideas around Expo-Projection 73 (1973) 210
    Aracy Amaral

30. (Audiovisuals) (1973) 218
    Frederico Morais

31. Block-Experiments in Cosmococa
    – Program in Progress (1973) 224
    Hélio Oiticica

32. The Early Days of Video Art in Brazil (2000) 235
    Fernando Cocchiarale

33. Testimonial: Regina Silveira (1984)   240
    Regina Silveira

34. Testimonial: Anna Bella Geiger (1984)   246
    Anna Bella Geiger

35. Videoart: The Brazilian Adventure (1996)   250
    Arlindo Machado

36. The Video Theatre Project (1985)   264
    Otávio Donasci

37. Video as a Utopian Television Project (2000)   271
    Yvana Fechine

38. Videobrasil and Video in Brazil:
    A Side-by-Side Journey (2000)   280
    Solange Farkas

39. Exploded Video and its Shards
    Hovering Above Us (2008)   288
    Lucas Bambozzi

IV Personal Computers

40. Personal Computers   296
    Gabriel Menotti and German Alfonso Nunez

41. Investigative Poetics (2005)   302
    Christine Mello

42. Time Capsule (1997)   311
    Eduardo Kac

43. Itaulab Research: Paulista 1919,
    Abadia Virtual and Policarpo (2008)   316
    Marcos Cuzziol

44. Technology and Contemporary Art:
    Bringing Politics Into the Conversation (2005)   322
    Arlindo Machado

45. Make Way for Tactical Media! (2003)   339
    Ricardo Rosas and Tatiana Wells

46. Gambiarra – Elements for a Reflection
    on Recombinant Technology (2006)   343
    Ricardo Rosas

47. Free Studios (2006)   355
    *Fabianne B. Balvedi, Guilherme R. Soares,
    Adriana Veloso and Flavio Soares*

48. re:combo Full Use Licence (2004)   365
    re:combo

49. Art Machines (1999)   376
    Frederico Morais

Notes   385

Original Sources   395

Works Cited   403

Acknowledgements

Barbarian Currents is an outcome of the project *Entangled Traditions: Mapping the Emergence of New Media and Computer Arts in Postwar Brazil*, funded by the Social Sciences and Humanities Research Council of Canada and the São Paulo Research Foundation (grant 17/13635-5). This publication has been made possible through the generous support of Queen's University Library Open Textbook Grant and the Vulnerable Media Lab.

Many people and institutions have collaborated on the arduous process of sourcing the documents, securing permissions, preparing translations and making sure all the pieces of this anthology came together. The editors would like to thank the authors, their families and, in particular, the following people: Isabella Altoé, Roberto Moreira S. Cruz, Associação Cultural Videobrasil, Alessandra Bergamaschi, Gabriel Moore Bevilacqua, Raíza Bruscky, Raquel de Campos, Lia Carreira, Vinicius Portella Castro, Sofia Fan, Ariane Figueiredo, Instituto Itaú Cultural, Susan Lord, Luciana Machado, Felix Mittelberger, Thiago Novaes, César Oiticica, Stefania Paiva, Diniz Pignatari, Anabela Plaza, Projeto HO, Daisy de Brito Rezende, Cristina Ribas, Juliano Ferreira da Silva, Vinicius Spricigo, Cristiana Tejo, Giseli Vasconcellos, ZKM Karlsruhe, Adriana Zanini and Joanna Zylinska.

Introduction

Technicised Barbarians

Gabriel Menotti and German Alfonso Nunez

Though familiar to many Brazilian art enthusiasts, this story remains relatively unknown outside of those Portuguese-speaking circles. It is about a strange artwork that unsettled the jury, critics and audiences of the very first São Paulo Art Biennial in 1951. At a distance, the piece looked very much like an abstract painting: multi-coloured blots on a canvas, stretched over a rectangular wooden frame and hanging from a wall. The blots, however, *shifted*. They moved and constantly changed over time, unlike anything that the public had ever seen before: an animated painting! A newspaper review called it 'magical' for the way it dazzled viewers with a 'parade of colours and shapes' (*Tribuna da Imprensa* 1951, 5). Magical indeed: these visual transformations were the main thing that caught people's attention. But hidden under the surface of the canvas was something equally impressive: a bespoke mechanism made with electric motors, gears, rods and lightbulbs. Not unlike the budding medium of television, the work presented viewers with a surface of live information. And, similar to TV, it did not function if it was not plugged in.

Was it a painting, a sculpture or something completely new? The artwork was initially rejected because the selection committee could not place it within any of the exhibition's categories.[1] But it made such a strong impression that the

Biennial jury decided to award it a special mention anyway. Perhaps it was a bittersweet prize for something so unique. Still, not a bad result for a piece that was admitted to the exhibition at the very last minute – and only because of some logistical missteps: it was there to replace Japanese artworks that did not arrive in São Paulo on time.

Titled *Azul e Roxo em Primeiro Movimento* [Blue and Purple in First Movement] (1951), the piece is one of the very first *cinecromáticos* conceived by a then young Abraham Palatnik (Natal, 1928-2020). In hindsight, it could be considered a textbook case of *kinetic art*, a visual arts genre that deploys movement as a central component of its poetic vocabulary. But within the Brazilian cultural context of the time, *Azul e Roxo...* meant much more. In its use of electricity and automation, it seemed to anticipate a post-war trend that had artists all over the West turn their attention to new media and technology.[2]

The following decade would see the emergence of Fluxus, an international movement that brought process, performance and electronic systems to the forefront of art practices (Higgins 2002). In 1965, the first gallery exhibitions of computer graphics took place in the USA and Germany (Taylor 2014). A year later, engineers Billy Klüver and Fred Waldhauer would partner with artists Robert Rauschenberg and Robert Whitman to form the non-profit *Experiments in Art and Technology*, in an attempt to promote collaborations across those areas (Klüver 1994). In that same year, John Whitney Sr., a pioneer in mechanical animation techniques, was awarded an artist-in-residence position at IBM, which led to the development of digital motion graphics (Kane 2014).

Eventually, a number of those new technological expressions were canonised under the umbrella of the late avant-gardes. Yet others were not. The creation of the British Computer Arts Society, already in 1968, testifies to the fact that some art forms emerging in that era were not fully accepted by the contemporary arts establishment.[3] Those art forms would be left to their own devices, leading to the constitution of a parallel institutional space featuring dedicated exhibition, discursive and funding mechanisms, hence the proliferation of specialised journals (*Leonardo*), academic associations (ISEA), awarding bodies (Ars Electronica) and thematic shows in the following decades. To this day, 'technological' or new media arts seem to thrive in a territory of their own, engaging in very little dialogue with the hegemonic artworlds (Shanken 2008, 2016; Nunez 2018; Taylor 2014.). This divide has often been described in adversarial terms, such as 'Duchampland *versus* Turingland' (Manovich 1996) and 'the World of Contemporary Art *versus* the World of New Media Art' (Kwastek 2015, 1; Shanken 2016, 464). Even in the 1980s, when a growing number of new media spaces sprung out of universities, associations and the like, critic Jack Burnham would proclaim 'art and technology' to be 'a panacea that failed' (Burnham 1980). However we want to interpret these tensions, it is clear that art and (new) media never had an easy relationship.

Palatnik, for his part, came to be celebrated as the forefather of Brazilian technological arts. In a comprehensive timeline of 'artistic experiments with technoscience in Brazil' from 1986, Eduardo Kac (Rio de Janeiro, 1962) mentions him as the first visual artist to engage with this practice in the country (Kac 1986). *Cinetico Digital* [Kinetic Digital], a retrospective exhibition held in 2005 at the Itaú Cultural Institute in São Paulo, would situate Palatnik's kinetic pieces as precursors of the computer art later developed by Waldemar Cordeiro. Indeed, like pioneering new media artworks elsewhere, the *cinecromáticos* represented a rupture. Their conspicuous use of technology broke away from established art practices in Brazil. If what happened in other Western countries was to be taken as a model, Palatnik would not have been easily admitted into the national arts canon. But the fact is that he was. The inclusion of *Azul e Roxo...* in the São Paulo Biennial might have been a product of chance, but its special mention revealed something else, namely the peculiar position new media had in Brazilian art.

Art and Technosciences in Brazil: Doubly Peripheral

From the standpoint of a global dichotomy between contemporary and new media arts, Palatnik's success seems highly unusual. Few technologically oriented artists in the Global North attained the same kind of importance as Palatnik did in Brazil. Rarely do German art historians, for instance, acknowledge the seminal contributions of computer artists Georg Nees and Frieder Nake. The same could be said of British or North American pioneers, who are only discussed within specialised circles. Palatnik, on the other hand, features heavily in many histories, exhibitions and events, partly due to his work and partly due to his close relationship with other heavyweights of Brazilian art (Asbury 2013; Kac 1996; Morais 2004; Pedrosa 1996; Scovino and Tjabbes 2013). Although primarily associated with kinetic rather than computer arts, he is often seen as a pivotal figure in the development of new media in the country.

As extraordinary a figure as Palatnik might have been in the Brazilian context, he was far from being a complete outlier. A quick glance at Kac's aforementioned timeline reveals multiple intersections between avant-gardes and 'experiments with technosciences' in the country since the 19th century. This document is relevant not only due to Kac's worldwide recognition as an accomplished media artist and scholar, but also due to his direct participation in many of these movements. Published in *Leonardo*, the field's main scholarly and artistic journal, the timeline is as close to an 'official history' of new media arts in Brazil as it gets. And this official history, as told by Kac, draws from the status of modern literature and concrete poetry. Moreover, it includes many thematic exhibitions that took place at institutions of undisputed renown, such as the Museum of Contemporary Art of São Paulo, the São Biennial and the Museum of Modern Art of Rio de Janeiro. Yet, unlike in other countries, there is a notable absence of venues, associations and recurrent events dedicated specifically to art and technology.[4]

Upon further consideration, the prominent connections between new media practices and the art establishment in Brazil make a lot of sense. Across the 20th century, industrial collaborations were instrumental in enabling technological artforms to thrive despite being rejected by the hegemonic artworld.[5] But the Brazilian industry, largely underdeveloped, was never able to provide the same kind of sponsorship as its Global North counterparts. As a result, an autonomous new media arts circuit, however marginal, did not take form in the country. For many practitioners interested in working with emerging technologies, the most viable solution was to rely on the meagre support they could get from high-profile art institutions, which could also broker eventual partnerships with the private sector. Thus, for decades, Brazilian new media arts did not have any spaces or institutions of their own. Instead, they thrived within pockets of the establishment itself.

Nevertheless, the Brazilian artistic field also had good reasons to embrace new media practices. Local cultural and economic elites, familiar with the European avant-garde, have always been self-conscious about the country's supposed backwardness.[6] The modernist movement that emerged in São Paulo in the 1920s, modelled by and large after foreign avant-gardes, championed the rupture from aesthetic traditions as part of a broader project for the country's socio-economic progress (Cavalcanti 2013). Written around that time, Oswald de Andrade's (São Paulo, 1890-1954) influential *Anthropophagic Manifesto* fostered an unapologetic appropriation of influences from abroad, framing the Americas – in opposition to Europe – as the privileged ground for a new society. The new people de Andrade foresaw to be inhabiting this utopia would be what he called *technicised barbarians* [*bárbaros tecnizados*].[7] The tone of 'cultural cannibalism' set by the *Manifesto* would infuse many Brazilian artistic movements throughout the 20th century with a decidedly postmodern sensibility. Consider, for instance, how Neoconcretism (1950), Tropicália (1960) and *mangue bit* (1990) navigated across different artforms, cultural references and techniques without observing rigid separations between them. Overall, the aspects of technological innovation inherent to new media work fitted nicely into the ambitions of the local avant-gardes. And these aspects would become even more relevant to the Brazilian cultural scenario after the 1950s, when the federal government fully committed to the project of the late modernisation of the country with the slogan '50 years in 5'. It is not surprising, then, that computer art in Brazil emerged from the concrete poetry movement and post-war avant-gardes. These genres were, at first, active proponents of the country's modernisation, advocating for a more cosmopolitan and universal – and even post-national – Brazilian culture (Arruda 2001).

Palatnik's award can be seen in this same light. In local art histories, the *cinecromáticos* came to be celebrated as an example of inventive and pioneering Brazilian efforts (Zanini 1997) – a development against all odds, given the country's socio-economic and technological underdevelopment. But it would not be fair to assume that this mobilisation of new media work resulted from official institutional agendas. It was rather the opposite. With modernity, well-positioned cultural agents were incited to perform curatorial gestures that boldly played into the country's cosmopolitan aspirations. In the case of the *cinecromáticos*, it is impossible to ignore the influence of cultural critic Mario Pedrosa (Timbaúba, 1900 – Rio de Janeiro, 1981). In a short newspaper article published upon the opening of the exhibition, Pedrosa gave special prominence to Palatinik's work, asserting that it 'will represent in this international show the cutting edge of the modern movement' (Pedrosa 1997). A closer look at many of the projects that endorsed new media within the Brazilian art establishment ever since reveals a similarly decisive role of other established critics/curators: Walter Zanini (São Paulo, 1925-2013), Aracy Amaral (São Paulo, 1930), Frederico Morais (Belo Horizonte, 1936), Christine Mello (Rio de Janeiro, 1966) and Lucas Bambozzi (São Paulo, 1965), to name but a few. These professionals' institutional role was instrumental for the success of new media practices in the country, even when they were not experts in the subject.

The lack of private industrial support, the institutional precarity and the participation of shrewd cultural agents all seem to have shaped the scenario for Brazilian new media arts. In the Global North, technological art forms came to occupy corporate-sponsored niches shunned by the art establishment. In Brazil, on the other hand, the situation was much fuzzier. There were not enough practitioners or resources to make similarly specialised communities sustainable. As Kac's timeline indicates, different approaches to art and technology were frequently clustered together, which enabled them to draw support from one another in an attempt to create a critical mass. Many artists that got involved in those practices were media-agnostic, experimenting with new technologies as opportunities arose. Oftentimes, this process was devised in collaboration with – or was even spearheaded by – those curators who could muster institutional solidarity (with Zanini being a prime example).[8]

The history of Brazilian new media arts thus seems to be characterised by a *double peripherality*. Technological artforms in the country were contingent on one-off efforts of the local arts establishment, which was in turn subaltern to the global artworld. How have these circumstances affected their formation? Did the continuing exchange of legitimacy and resources among different new media practices, as well as between them and the arts establishment, make these fields more permeable to one another? Has it shaped how Brazilian artists at large approach technology? Did it lead new media to play a more substantial role in other national cultural forms, socio-political issues and the formation of Brazil's identity?

Avant-Garde Ambitions, Opportunism and Institutional Support

As it should be clear by now, the development of art and technology practices in Brazil has been embedded in a very peculiar environment if contrasted with the situation found in the Global North. The few attempts to tell a comprehensive history of the field, such as Priscilla Arantes' (São Paulo, 1966) competent *Arte e Mídia: Perspectivas da Estética Digital* [Art & Media: Perspectives of Digital Aesthetics] (2005), tend to lose sight of these particularities while placing the Brazilian production against the backdrop of global media arts. In order to advance a critical understanding of new media arts in the country, it is not sufficient to look only into the aesthetics, creators or poetic-political projects of new media. Rather, one must also account for the (often messy) environments from which these art forms emerged – the external social factors that, as literary critic Antonio Candido once said, 'matter not as a cause, nor as a meaning, but as an element somewhat constitutive' of the structure of cultural expressions (Candido 1973, 4).

This book seeks to take a step in this direction by delving into the simultaneously multiple and fragmentary histories of Brazilian new media arts. Instead of proposing a unifying theory about these art forms, we intend to bring to light the conditions that made them possible and the discourses spawned along the way. This diachronic effort demonstrates how the social, economic and political context not only shaped Brazilian technological art forms but also allowed them *to be* in the first place. In doing so, we seek to reaffirm the idiosyncratic character of new media arts in the country as intrinsically and distinctively *Brazilian*. This was a phenomenon that emerged in the late 1960s in the periphery of capitalism, when globalisation had not fully affected the national scene, and remained situated in and shaped by local partnerships, disputes and opportunities for a good chunk of its history.

This is not to deny the existence of a post-war zeitgeist that celebrated the new technologies emerging in the second half of the 20th century. Perhaps best encapsulated by British Prime Minister Harold Wilson's 1963 'white heat of technology' speech, this techno-utopian zeitgeist was a powerful force behind the artistic push towards new technologies in Brazil, as it was in other places.[9] One just has to look at the reinforced concrete architecture of Brasilia for evidence of innovative aesthetics. However, given Brazil's challenging circumstances, one must acknowledge the decidedly unique contours this sentiment took on in the country. That said, this volume should not be mistaken for a defence of some kind of essential *Brazilianness* or, even worse, *Latinamericaness*. What it seeks to do instead is advance the rather straightforward argument that, in order to comprehend local art histories, one must first comprehend their own local dynamics. We believe that this attitude, coupled with a healthy distrust of reductive European or North American parallelisms, provides an honest, balanced and contextually rich account of the constituting factors behind Brazilian new media arts.

Brazil has always had a complicated relationship with the idea of progress. A major consideration is, of course, its history as a former exploitation colony. Under Portuguese rule until 1822, the country's occupation was primarily driven by natural resource extraction that led to the genocide of Indigenous populations, the abuse of slave labour, impoverished economic conditions and significant social inequality. This socioeconomic reality persisted even after independence, creating a difficult environment for its industrialisation. Reflecting the impacts of precarity, the discursive and production strategies of Brazilian modernity were marked by an acute geopolitical awareness. Bourgeois artists and intellectuals, conscious of the country's global subalternity, looked up to the former European metropolises as aspirational models. De Andrade's predominant notion of *anthropophagy* represents a particularly vindictive translation of this cosmopolitan appetite. Progress came to be trusted as a disruptive cultural force, capable of liberating Brazil from its colonial roots.[10] In that context, what the Brazilian avant-gardes articulated through concepts of nation-building and technological development could be interpreted as a decolonising impulse *avant la lettre*.

The interest in new media also had Brazilian postwar avant-gardes looking outwards, eager to engage with Western perspectives. This commitment, far from being a mere product of intellectual subordination, should be understood strategically. It not only allowed artists to participate in the global conversations deemed relevant but also empowered them to create a space for these conversations within the country. This attitude is represented in poet Augusto de Campos' (São Paulo, 1931) *Art and Technology* piece featured in the first section of this volume. This short essay, part of a weekly series originally published in 1967 in the *Estado de São Paulo* newspaper, reports on a Marshall McLuhan interview from the previous year. While it may not bring much novelty to the Anglophone audience already familiar with the subject, its ingenuity lies in its intervention into public discourses. One should bear in mind that, by the early 1960s, Brazilian concretists were already active abroad. By initiative of Max

Bense, the Noigandres group and the Campos brothers had works featured in the same publications as the German computer art pioneers (such as *Futura* magazine, published by Hansjörg Mayer,[11] and the *rot* book series, edited by Bense himself).[12] An essay such as de Campos' implies reciprocity. It promotes, among the newspaper's readership, specialised ideas that otherwise would not be accessible to them. In doing so, the essay upholds the significance of information technologies and provides emerging art forms (whether local or foreign) with established references to position themselves within Brazil's academic and cultural milieus. In sum, the article serves as a catalyst for the legitimacy, authority and, ultimately, political power of new media in the country.[13]

Ironically, the avant-gardes' enthusiasm for progress would falter at the very moment when material conditions aligned for the emergence of technological artforms worldwide (Goodyear 2008). In Brazil, this disappointment was coupled with a growing rejection of foreign influences. The military coup backed by the USA in 1964, followed by the economic crisis of the 1970s, decidedly changed the cultural mood. Brazil's developmental aspirations were transformed by its renewed attachment to Western powers, and progress became a value associated with the government's technocratic agenda. Very quickly, Brazilian voices would join a widespread counteraction against the naive perception of science and technology as utopian solutions. This tension was at the heart of early computer art in Europe and the USA (Taylor 2014). Once equated with an anti-establishment and anti-capitalist verve, the shift occurred as various social movements gained traction in the 1970s. Technology – and especially computers – came to be seen as proxies of an old order that was perceived as unfair, unequal and possibly catastrophic.

The work of critic and curator Frederico Morais illustrates this suspicion towards technology. In one of his texts included in this volume, *From the Body to the Ground*, which reflects on an exhibition project and manifesto from 1970, Morais expresses his reservations about new media arts. While not rejecting them altogether, he places greater value on art that challenges traditional boundaries and engages with political and social realities in a direct, often visceral way. He states: 'avant-garde is not to update materials; it is not technological art. It is a behaviour, a way of looking at things, people and materials; it is an attitude that defines itself against the world'. Morais' proposition suggests a move away from 'new media' as a formal category, embracing it instead as a set of protocols and institutional possibilities. This resonates with the artworks that emphasised the use of public spaces and resorted to the *détournement* of information channels as a form of aesthetic provocation. It also relates to the artistic use of consumer media such as slides, mail and photocopies, along with a broader interest in independent publishing as a vehicle for visual poetry.[14] Morais' own curatorial practice embodied experimental methods, dealing with art as a materially embedded form of social communication, operating among and within other systems. In Brazil, like in other Latin American countries, these approaches had a uniquely political character, associated with circumventing government censorship and challenging the regime.

In this adverse context, one of the continuing drivers of Brazilian media arts has been a certain degree of serendipity or, to put it more bluntly, *opportunism*. These dynamics evoke Michel de Certeau's notion of *tactics* as the method of the disadvantaged (De Certeau 2011). Lacking resources of their own, artists had to operate according to the support available from institutions and associations. Their needs emphasise the aforementioned importance of curators in being both propositional and inclusive. For instance, when organising the first exhibition in the country dedicated solely to audiovisual media, *Expo-projeção 1973*, curator Aracy Amaral made an effort to showcase a diverse range of formats, such as Super-8 and 16mm film, slide projection (audiovisuals) and phonograms. Amaral's correspondence with Suzanne Delehanty, then director of the University of Pennsylvania's Institute of Contemporary Art (ICA), reveals that this diversity, however accidental, had a political dimension.[15] In 1974, Delehanty had approached Amaral looking for Brazilian artists who could participate in a video art exhibition. In response, Amaral highlighted the challenges of the art scene in Brazil, citing the lack of economic conditions, an established art market (Durand 1989) and infrastructure for artists. She believed that a project focused on a single technology would overlook the rich variety of Brazilian culture and risk excluding artists not aligned with global standards. Worse, she expressed a concern that the appeal of initiatives like the ICA's could lead Brazilian artists to produce solely for foreign audiences, resulting in their disconnection from local communities. Amaral compares these demands from abroad to the religious art commissions from colonial times.

Amaral and Delehanty's exchange is perhaps one of the first documented occasions where the coherence of Brazilian media arts is placed in question. It is also revealing of the local avant-gardes' reliance on specialised international networks which were able to provide them with, if not direct support, then at least meaningful connections and opportunities to exhibit and experiment. Delehanty's invitation would, after all, lead to the production of some of the first Brazilian video art works. As explained in Fernando Cocchiarale's (Rio de Janeiro, 1951) testimonial on the *Early Days of Video Art in Brazil*, the prospect of participating in an event abroad was the necessary impetus for a group of Rio de Janeiro artists to start exploring the new medium. The actual production of the works could only happen, however, thanks to the assistance of a Brazilian filmmaker who owned a coveted camcorder, recently bought in the USA. This is when the country's traditional art institutions assumed a crucial role as the only entities with sufficient resources to equip artists with the tools and expertise required to produce new media art. For many of these institutions, too, foreign interest in Brazilian art represented a chance to foster the national scene and enhance its global profile. Over the years, institutions such as the São Paulo Biennial, the São Paulo University's Museum of Contemporary Arts (MAC-USP) and the Armando Alvares Penteado Foundation (FAAP) would promote activities dedicated to showcasing international artists working in new media and supporting Brazilian artists interested in the same pursuit. A memorable example is MAC-USP's video laboratory, created by Walter Zanini (who, perhaps unsurprisingly, also had been contacted by Delehanty about suggestions for the ICA exhibition). Active between 1977-78, the laboratory not only gave São Paulo artists access to a Sony portapak camera acquired by the museum but also offered training in equipment use and an exhibition space for their works.

Of course, there was only so much 'third world' art institutions could do. Throughout the latter half of the 20th century, Brazil remained largely underdeveloped, enduring an oppressive military regime, grappling with poverty and severe social inequalities. Equipment was not easy to come by. The ambition to explore the most cutting-edge technologies prompted artists to seek other kinds of support, whether institutional or corporate. Examples include Waldemar Cordeiro's (Roma, 1925 – São Paulo, 1973) early computer drawings (which relied on his collaborator Giorgio Moscati's [Gênova, 1934] access to an IBM mainframe at the Department of Nuclear Physics of the University of São Paulo), Eduardo Kac's first holopoems (created in partnership with Fernando Catta-Preta, who operated a commercial holography lab) and Julio Plaza's videotext exhibition (sponsored by public telecommunications company Telesp). It could be argued that the individual, relatively small-scale and extraordinary aspect of these initiatives contributed to their feasibility.

The connections artists were able to establish outside of the art world also played a significant role. However, none of these factors made technological arts sustainable in the long term. For a high-tech enthusiast like Kac, emigrating to the USA proved to be a more viable solution to building a career in the field.

In the 1990s, changes in trade policies would finally make personal computers readily available to the Brazilian middle class. The increased participation of Information and Communication Technology companies in the domestic market was accompanied by a more consistent support for technological art forms. This development allowed new media arts in Brazil to gain greater autonomy, with artists in the field working more independently from traditional art institutions. As a result, we can observe a cultural segmentation similar to that already established in the USA and Western Europe for a few decades, where one field operates separately from the other. Against this backdrop, the fourth and final section of the book delves into community initiatives and examines how tactical media and open-source software projects carried the modern avant-gardes' torch of social transformation into the first Workers' Party government of the country.

The Social History of a Messy Tradition

Overall, this volume yields two complementary results. Firstly, it demonstrates that the distinction between so-called 'technological' and 'traditional' art forms is largely one of *degree*, not of *kind*. In the Brazilian context, where those art forms emerged from the same established practices and discourses, it is abundantly clear how they also belong in the same art historical narratives. This is to say that Brazilian 'new media art' can be construed – at least in its origins – as just another modality of the broader set of activities one may call 'art'. Secondly, by delving into the history shared between media arts and other cultural practices, this book means to provide alternatives to a more generalist analysis of their development in the global periphery. In other words, it does not provide an account of Brazilian new media art as an appendix to European or North American art, but rather a *Brazilian* account of new media art as a product of its own environment.

It would be unfair to claim *Barbarian Currents* is not itself a product of Brazilian opportunism. Like other initiatives connected to new media arts in the country, our project has been enabled by resources and demands from abroad. Specifically, it responds to the growing efforts of liberal institutions to come to terms with the violence underlying their very existence. In academia, this movement has taken shape through attempts to unsettle traditional disciplines and diversify curricula. If we are to believe in the good faith of scientific pursuits, there should be no doubt about how this process benefits the Western canon. It provides an overdue chance to address a long history of knowledge extraction, historical negligence and other forms of epistemicide perpetuated along the North-South global axis. Accordingly, this book has been designed to add new information to the body of social sciences, cultural studies and art history available internationally. We are confident that these chapters will assist the interested reader in unlearning their own biases and achieving a richer understanding of what new media arts are – and how they come to be.

However, and perhaps more importantly, *Barbarian Currents* is committed to amplifying perspectives that have been consistently sidelined from global discourses. To be done appropriately, this process must be twofold: to the same extent that it elicits foreign curiosity, it rebuffs the exoticising gaze. Here, we attend to Arlindo Machado's (Pompéia, 1949 - São Paulo, 2020) calling in one of the pieces featured in our final section, *Technology and Contemporary Art: Bringing Politics into the Conversation.* For our own good, opportunism can only go so far. Decades of ambivalent relationship with Western hegemonies should not leave us complacent. We invite the reader to push back against any sense of condescension. It is crucial to cultivate an understanding of Brazilian new media that does not romanticise its complexities or downplay its contradictions. To acknowledge the effects of precariousness in Brazilian thought and cultural expression, for instance, should not be mistaken for a celebration of misery. To quote the magnificent carnival director Joãosinho Trinta (São Luis, 1933-2011), 'only intellectuals like poverty; the people like luxury'. As we hope to have shown so far, this is a story about intellectual elites and cosmopolitan avant-gardes as much as it is about a developing nation enduring a civil-military dictatorship. The many ways Brazilian artists managed to navigate the country's geopolitical circumstances and inhabit its violent history should not be trivialised as some generic kind of Latin American ingenuity. That is not to say their modes of working were not Latin American, or that they were not ingenious; only that we should take their *otherness* for what it is, fragmented and all, rather than reducing it to a convenient cliché.

The main tools we provide the reader with for this task are the words of the artists, critics and curators who, over the years, collaborated on the formation of Brazilian new media arts. The chapters of this book encompass newspaper articles, catalogue texts, book chapters, manifestos, journal essays and other documents that outline how the emergence of technological artforms was negotiated in Brazil. Most of this material is published here in English for the first time. In translating and preparing the English versions, we have attempted to make the texts as accessible as possible to a broad readership while preserving the authors' styles. Since they were not originally intended for academic audiences, many of these texts do not follow the scholarly standards of formatting and referencing. Whenever possible, we tried to remedy that and provide relevant notes. We have also provided new versions of some texts that had been translated previously. While we tried to cover the main subjects and voices featured in the country's specialist literature and therefore deemed central to the field, it is always a challenge to agree over a single, undisputed canon. Our intentions are nevertheless more modest. This selection of texts should serve, first and foremost, as an introduction. It offers a non-exhaustive guide that remediates the lack of availability of primary sources about Brazilian art abroad and that hopefully piques the curiosity of international readership, inviting further exploration.

In gathering these chapters, we have counted on the generosity of many authors, their relatives, friends and institutions committed to cultural preservation. Often, we have had the good fortune of finding precious material in recent publications and the well-maintained archives of institutions such as the Itaú Cultural Institute and the Videobrasil Cultural Association, which for decades have been an active part of this history. However, many texts had to be unearthed from used bookstores and personal storage spaces, indicating there is still much work to be done to keep this memory cohesive. It is a bit concerning, for instance, that online searches took us time and again to the repository of the Documents of Latin American and Latino Art of the International Centre for the Arts of the Americas at the Museum of Fine Arts, Houston (MFAH).[16] In 2007, the MFAH acquired the private Adolpho Leirner Collection of Brazilian Constructive Art, which features some of the most important post-war artists in the country (*MFAH Acquires* 2007). While we have nothing but praise for the museum's interest and wonderful preservation efforts, we lament that work of an equivalent breadth is not being carried out by Brazilian institutions. In our country, the burden of remembrance often falls on the shoulders of individuals, whether in the form of personal research projects[17] or disorganised piles of documents that would better be kept in an actual archive.[18] In a tale as old as time, the lack of infrastructure and care condemns the country to relinquish its identity and gradually give up on its heritage. We can only hope the diligence put into this collection might, by whatever tortuous routes, make a dent in the situation.

As with any editorial project involving archival research, authors from across many generations, dozens of copyright holders and translations from different textual genres, the making of *Barbarian Currents* was very resource- and labour-intensive. Sooner or later, contingencies forced us to make cuts against our personal preferences. The most glaring omissions are names with whom the reader might already be familiar, such as the critical work of Pedrosa (Ferreira 2015), manifestos by Cordeiro (1972) and filmmaker Glauber Rocha (Vitória da Conquista, 1939 -- Rio de Janeiro, 1981) (Rocha 1965) and more in-depth examinations of the work of Cildo Meireles (Rio de Janeiro, 1948) (Brett 2008). These represent, without a question, some of the most important pieces in the history of media arts in Brazil. And, precisely for this reason, even though our pride as editors may suffer, we do not feel completely uncomfortable for leaving them out. This material is readily accessible in English through many other competent sources; most of it can even be found online. We are confident their omission here does not compromise our objective of enriching the global conversation by presenting Brazilian new media art and discourses. It is a small sacrifice of comprehensiveness for the sake of diversity.

The reader might also be disappointed to find, amidst all this writing *about* and *around* Brazilian art, not that much on the artists and artworks themselves. This is primarily due, of course, to our emphasis on the *social* history of the arts over pure art history. *Barbarian Currents* gravitates towards the emerging socio-political circumstances of cultural expression rather than their formal characteristics. Moreover, it is important to bear in mind the scope of this book as a historical anthology. These texts have been originally written for the most diverse purposes and were never intended as an exhaustive record of the art of their time. If anything, they attempted to probe the future. Even in Brazil, it is only relatively recently that the particularities of new media arts became a subject of scholarly attention. Proper accounts of this history are still being pieced together and written.

As previously alluded to, this book mainly encompasses the second half of the 20th century. We have been a little flexible with dates to be able to cover the turn of the millennium as well. This period is significant because it encompasses the first strides of the Brazilian art world towards internationalisation, following the inauguration of the São Paulo Art Biennial. The next decades would see the country going through accelerated urbanisation, a long military dictatorship and a fragile stretch of redemocratisation. Brazil's entrance into the globalisation era in the mid-1990s would be characterised by increasingly neoliberal policies, including in the cultural sector. Our story ends with the arrival of the Internet in the country and the heavy privatisation of the telecommunications sector, which would finally provide local new media practices with mainstream relevance and necessary financial support.

The chapters are organised into four thematic sections, each roughly corresponding to a particular media phenomenon or technology: code and language; social communication systems; moving images; personal computers. Although not strictly chronological, the selected texts move alongside Brazil's history. This order helps provide a sense of the development of the arts discourse writ large in Brazil. Likewise, it makes it easier to frame each phenomenon within its context of emergence. For the benefit of international readership, likely unfamiliar with the country's turbulent history, each section opens with a short introduction that provides a summarised contextualisation. Hopefully, this arrangement will enable a clearer understanding of the driving concerns and wider implications of Brazilian media arts.

Barbarian Currents does not aspire to be more than a partial snapshot of a cultural niche during a short period in Brazilian history. Regardless, we believe that the material it presents allows for a situated and expansive perspective on the conditions of development of technological art forms worldwide. This selection of documents, inventories and ideas demonstrates that new media practices are not necessarily driven by technical or aesthetic innovation alone and that they have not existed in a completely segregated field either. In Brazil, at least, new media have always been part and parcel of established cultural debates and socio-political disputes, in tandem with other art and cultural products made in the country.

The book ends in a period of great optimism for technological art forms, when many places for them to thrive had taken shape in the country. Here, the international readership might feel like they are in a familiar territory. The Brazilian new media circuits of the early 2000s, though considerably smaller and more precarious, looked very similar to their counterparts in the Global North. Yet one should not lose sight of the fact that a certain 'technological consciousness' has underlaid the key artistic discourses and movements in the country up to that point. The peripherality of media arts in Brazil should not, in that sense, be compared to the relative isolation of the field in the USA or Western Europe. Rather than a field apart, Brazilian 'media arts' have historically been an undercurrent of the mainstream – often marginalised, but constitutive of the establishment nevertheless.

Fast-forward to the present – and this appears to be the global norm. As attested by the year-long installation of Refik Anadol's generative AI animation *Unsupervised* in the atrium of New York's Museum of Modern Art (2022-23) (MoMA 2022), the distance between the contemporary art world and the techno-arts ghetto has never seemed smaller. By bringing an influx of the capital and tastes of the Silicon Valley elites into the global art market, the 'cryptoart' boom of the Covid-19 pandemic had a noticeable impact on the agenda of many traditional art institutions.[19] Alongside these developments came a renewed interest in the history of technological art forms, providing this new wave of media arts with the canonical references they craved. Taking place amidst the collateral events of the 59th Venice Biennale, the *Icône 2020* exhibition of Hungarian computer arts pioneer Vera Molnár (2022) might have represented a turning point.[20] Twenty years after the Slovenian Pavilion hosted the controversial launch of the *biennale.py* virus, algorithmic art would now be found crystallised in Murano glass, standing comfortably under the umbrella of abstraction. One wonders how influential the Brazilian scene was in validating these changes, given that a lot of the early pushback against the environmental issues and speculative nature of cryptoart had been minimised by claims of its supposed benefits to Global South artists.[21] The fact that the first popular low-cost NFT marketplace, *Hic et Nunc*, was not only created and run by the Brazilian developer Rafael Lima but also teemed with Latin American users definitively added to the appeal of this argument (Smith 2021). We'd argue it is a situation where the opportunism runs mostly the other way round, with the cryptoart ecosystem drawing legitimacy from the affiliation of disadvantaged artists, which it compensates with hyperinflated tokens of questionable value.

The Brazilian artworld has been keeping up with those trends, however inconsistently. In 2022, MAC-USP accepted the first NFT into its collection: a piece by artist Gustavo Von Ha (Presidente Prudente, 1977) donated by a commercial cryptoart platform. On that occasion, the museum curator evoked MAC-USP's pioneering work with new media (*MAC*

USP é pioneiro 2022). Later in that same year, the Moreira Salles Institute awarded one of its competitive photography research fellowships to a generative AI project by artist and gallerist Igi Lola Ayedun (São Paulo, 1990).[22] But it wouldn't be reasonable to attribute these developments purely to the fascination that technology has historically exerted over Brazilian avant-gardes. The essential role that computers now play across society generates a lot of institutional anxiety over 'digital-born' artforms. Moreover, one must recognise that, in the last decade or so, the Brazilian cultural establishment has been coming to terms with more pressing forms of peripherality, namely of the country's marginalised populations. 2022 also symbolised the centennial of the Modern Art Week of 1922, widely regarded as the catalyst of Brazilian modernism. It represented an opportunity for a critical revision of the hegemonic avant-gardes, as well as for the redemption of other modernisms spread across the country. A number of recent large exhibitions revisited Brazilian history to testify to the systemic oppression of Indigenous and Black communities, and to uphold their cultural importance. To name a few: *Dja Guata Porã: Indigenous Rio de Janeiro* (Rio Museum of Art, Rio de Janeiro, 2017-2018), *Afro-Atlantic Histories* (Tomie Ohtake Institute and MASP, São Paulo, 2018), *Essays for the Museum of Origins* (Tomie Ohtake Institute and Itaú Cultural Institute, SP, 2023) and *Dos Brasis: Black Art, Black Thinking* (SESC Belenzinho, SP, 2023-24). Notably, the last two editions of the São Paulo Biennial (2021, 2023) have had a strong focus on Indigenous and Black artists respectively.[23]

Considering Brazil's tumultuous past, the avant-gardes' embrace of technology may seem like an improbable revolutionary urge. The study of its history can definitely teach us something about the resilience of arts in the face of economic and social adversity. It can also offer insights into how technoscientific advancements are acculturated differently across the world, against any universal norm. But perhaps the most important contribution this collection brings to the global narratives does not concern new *facts*, but rather a new *framing*. A serious analysis of Brazilian media arts and theories should challenge our assumptions about the autonomy of 'technologically oriented' art as a category. More crucially, the 'central peripherality' of their existence prompts us to rethink some other apparently subordinate relationships as co-constitutive – chiefly among those the relationship between a Global North and the Global Souths. It is a reminder of the fact that 'alternative' art histories – whether encompassing alternative techniques, aesthetics, ethnicities, groups or simply *the other* – are but the flipside of the dominant ones. They urge us to look beyond the prism of Western exceptionalism and contend with everything it overlooks, suppresses and – more often than not – plunders. As such, as so many other hard lessons have indicated, they tell us about the present as much as about the past. Hopefully they can also inform the future.

I

Code and Language

Chapter 1

Code and Language

Gabriel Menotti and German Alfonso Nunez

After the Second World War, artists in the West became increasingly interested in experimenting with the new media available. In Brazil, however, that push was extremely limited. The country's relative technological and industrial underdevelopment made the access to the latest innovations both expensive and restricted.[24] That was clear from an outsider's perspective: according to Edgar Carone, the Coke Mission report from 1942 described Brazilians as living in 'a primitive stage of industrialisation' (Ortiz 1988, 45).[25] That's also how the country saw itself: Brazilian economists referred to the Brazil's condition as one of 'restricted industrialisation', which means that the post-war industrial expansion took place only in certain sectors of society, but not across society as a whole. Accordingly, Brazilian cultural production, whether highbrow or lowbrow, was significantly limited. In the words of Renato Ortiz, 'despite the dynamism of Brazilian society in the post-war period', the country's emerging mass culture was still confined to 'well-defined boundaries'. Thus, at the time, Brazilian 'cultural industries' were characterised 'more by their incipience than by their breadth' (Ortiz 1988, 45).[26] It was not until the 1960s that Brazil began consolidating a relatively modern market of symbolic goods, connected to the emergence of an urban class with disposable income. This delay significantly affected how national artists would engage with newer technologies. Only in the 1970s would select Brazilian artists be able to get their hands on computers, plotters and the like (Zanini 1997), even though these tools were already beginning to constitute the basis of technological art forms elsewhere in the world.[27]

But the lack of direct access did not prevent local artists and critics from speculating. Before new media even arrived in the country, local avant-gardes were paying attention to them. By 1958, publications associated with the concrete poetry movement were already discussing developments in cybernetics and pondering over their implications for artists and poets (Barroso 1958). The fields of computing and electronic systems heavily inspired those avant-gardists' projects. In the absence of new media technologies, Brazilian artists were led to cultivate critical attitudes towards the technology and materiality proper to established art forms, such as painting and poetry. Though they were not easily available in the country, new technological advancements, especially computers, captivated the local arts discourse and imagination.

This first section of the book traces the early development of Brazilian art and technoscience as a history of *aspirations and ideas*. By presenting articles written between the early 1950s and the late 1960s, it covers a period of great social change, when the country went through late modernisation. In those two decades Brazil accelerated a process that would, by the late 1970s, transform the country from a largely rural society into a society with important urban centres (Santos 1993). Perhaps the most emblematic symbol of this transformation was Brasilia, a brand-new futuristic capital for the country, inaugurated deep within its territory.

This period was also characterised by the creation of important cultural institutions, which developed alongside Brazil's new urban bourgeoisie and industrial elites. Modern

Art Museums in both São Paulo and Rio de Janeiro, as well as the São Paulo Art Biennial, came to renew local artistic scenes and strengthen their international connections. Overall, the atmosphere was one of confidence and optimism. The country's momentum aligned with local artists' ambitions to assert themselves in the global artworld. Artists, elites and the country's government seemed to be chasing a common project: the construction of a modern, technologically and culturally advanced Brazil, which could break away from its agricultural past as a colony and claim its position as a developed Western nation.[28]

Concretism, the movement that spearheaded this modernising drive, was mostly composed of poets and painters. The movement's prominent figures, including Haroldo (São Paulo, 1929-2003) and Augusto de Campos (São Paulo, 1931), Décio Pignatari (Jundiaí, 1927 – São Paulo, 2012) and Ferreira Gullar (São Luis, 1936 – Rio de Janeiro, 2016), were also cultural theorists attuned to international debates surrounding new technologies. Drawing inspiration from semiotics, they developed novel approaches to art and language that were more attentive to information systems. Although the group coalesced around the magazine *Noigandres* (1952-1962), they contributed extensively to public discourse by publishing in other newspapers and magazines, notably *Arquitetura e Decoração*. They would, in time, become recognised as forerunners of Brazilian media arts and theory.

Concretism urged artists to embrace the new world of industrial production and break away from any romanticised attachment to the past. A more rational and universal mode of expression could be attained by engaging with the objective attributes of the medium, be it text or canvas. In painting, this translated into a self-proclaimed *rupture* from figuration, as expressed in a manifesto and a pioneering group show held at the São Paulo Museum of Modern Art in 1952 (in which Waldemar Cordeiro played a central role). In poetry, it entailed a radical shift from the signified to the signifier: a more structural understanding of the text, in which the arrangement and characteristics of words on a page became at least as important as the absent meaning they conventionally evoke.

Concrete poetry's affiliation with Brazil's rapid development is evident in its late manifesto, *Plano Piloto para a Poesia Concreta* [Pilot Plan for Concrete Poetry] (1958), whose title is borrowed from Brasília's distinctive urban plan, drawn in the shape of an airplane. As a result of architecture's pivotal role in the country's modernisation, it became the perfect model for the more functional and 'scientific' art form that concrete poetry aspired to be. The movement's aspiration towards objectivity led to a host of formal innovations underpinned by the exploration of the spatial, technical and material affordances of various media. Concrete poets believed that these other dimensions of textual expression tapped into the virtualities of language. One of their earliest and most straightforward techniques was to deploy typography characters as a modular visual system, inspired by the logic of the Chinese ideogram. This technique renders the poem as an image as much as a text and anticipates some of the pioneering, lo-fi computational works that would be developed in Brazil almost two decades later, such as Cordeiro's *A Mulher que Não é B.B.* [The Woman who isn't B.B.] (1973) and Erthos Albino de Souza's (Ubá, 1932 – Juiz de Fora, 2000) *Machine Gun Nest* (1976).

While computers were an object of interest for concrete poets from the outset, it's crucial to remark that their sphere of influence was not limited to a local 'ghetto' of art and technoscience. Instead, the movement's impact on Brazilian postwar culture was far-reaching and extensive. Concrete poetry's focus on objectivity and objectiveness fuelled multimedia explorations that brought experimental literature and pop culture closer together. As Walter Zanini's pieces featured in this section demonstrate, the robust conceptual framework created by concretism also allowed for an institutional convergence between visual arts and mass media. In the art world, the movement triggered a *neo-concrete* trend that brought its medial concerns beyond sheer rationality and into the realm of embodiment and sensation. In later years, the impact of concretism would still be felt in Brazil's particular take on the ideas of the dematerialisation of the art object (Mário Pedrosa) and the aesthetic potentials of electronic media (Waldemar Cordeiro).

Chapter 2

Form, Function and General Project (1957)

Décio Pignatari

The already classic postulate that 'form follows function', which suggests that beauty is something useful and utilitarian, represents the artist's poetic as well as productive consciousness as they face the new world of industrial mass production. In this world, artisanal production has been taken out of the picture for it is inefficient, anachronistic, incompatible and incapable of communicating with an impersonal, collective and rational world that now depends entirely on design in every sense, on every level and across every scale.

In the face of the big antagonistic contradictions between industrial and artisanal artistic production – an opposition that has opened an immense gap between art and its audience – the attempt at a conjunction between the useful and the beautiful became imperative for two reasons: first, to appeal to a new kind of consumer, the 'consumer of physical design', in the words of Richard Neutra; and, second, to overcome the individualistic stage of critical rebellion against the machine, which has only led to the design of 'beautiful' yet useless (i.e. purely literary) Picabian machines. The Bauhaus school marks the turning point of that newly acquired awareness, in a positive-constructivist sense: beautiful useful machines.

In the formal treatment given to this new reality, it was clear that Architecture and Urban Planning should take the lead in proposing solutions to problems big and small concerning modern art. These fields of knowledge possess a physical, dynamic and perpetual presence in society. Always necessary, they imply the highest and most complex functions of artistic objects, which should be experienced both individually and collectively.

Visual Arts was inspired by the fields of Architecture and Urban Planning, Industrial Design, Film and Advertising to expand into a larger field of possible applications, while our era headed towards a greater prevalence of non-verbal signs, due to the urgent need for faster, more precise and efficient communication. New electronic music began to appear in film, television and radio under the guise of sound design. The young concrete poetry movement, so recent, finds its own utility in advertising, in graphic arts, in journalism.

The useful or utilitarian object whose *form*, however creative, merely paraphrases a certain *function* (another word for *content* in fields such as Architecture), cannot absorb art's entire creative capacity. Art still finds the most consequential and profound of its manifestations in the autonomous object-idea.

This is why painting, sculpture, poems and novels continue and will continue to be produced, as objects valid in themselves, objects that formally create their own function by expressing the sensible idea that constitutes them. These objects are consumer goods in the realm of thought and sensibility, for they are irreducible to mere utilitarian values. These artworks are goods rooted in universal culture and spirit. Their likewise universal function is to embody the general layout or formal configurations of a given era. As such, they provide generic and concrete laws of form, laws which consubstantiate themselves in countless particular objects and manifestations, thus contributing to the *foundations* of the common language and style of their time. An obvious example is Mondrian's neoplasticism, which influenced building facades and interior design, proposing a new *forma mentis*: a new formal sensibility and attitude for the people. In the last few years, we have been seeing concretism, in its many manifestations, experiment with a new general form, one that doesn't deny the previous ones, but rather tries to absorb them in a critical way.

Only from a totalising historical perspective can the binary opposition between *form* and *function* contribute to the value judgement of artworks in and on themselves, as pure formal structures pertaining to the cultural organism as a whole. The more objectively general and impersonal, the more objectively universal – the more beautiful artworks are.

One can therefore see that the difference in problems involving the terms *form-function* and *general project* is not ontological but rather hierarchical, concerning different cultural configurations or ideograms.

Chapter 3

Concrete Poetry – Language – Communication (1957)

Haroldo de Campos

For [Alfred] Korzybski, founder of 'general semantics' – a new pedagogical discipline defined as an 'empirical science of humans' based on the study of language, communication and their effects on human behaviour – the Aristotelian principle of identity 'tends to obscure the difference between words and things' (Hayakawa 1948).[29] When we say: 'this is a pencil', we tend to unconditionally identify the object with its verbal expression; but (says Korzybski) 'since words aren't the objects they represent, the structure becomes the vehicle for connecting our verbal processes to the empirical data'. Transformations in traditional thinking habits and the cosmovision offered by the present state of the sciences (non-Euclidean geometry, Einstein's physics) require a similar revolution in the structure of language to make for more precise descriptions of the world of objects. Instead of the 'metaphysical, pre-scientific and animist' dualisms insisted upon by common linguistic structure, which 'obscures and erases functional relations' – for example, barren and oppressive concepts of individuated space and time (a process Korzybski terms *elementalism*) – a linguistic structure closer to reality would allow for the notion of *'espaçotempo'* (space-time, which we can find in Joyce's *Finnegans Wake*, where the Bergsonian *durée*, devoid of any spatial structure, is overcome and ironically rendered) (Obradovic 1934, 10). In order to renew language, in addition to this terminological *non-elementalism*, Korzybski advances the 'mathematical method': 'a system of propositional functions, deliberately emptied of content and thus able to receive any content'.

A fascinating perspective arises when such formulations meet the challenges posed by concrete poetry. Concrete poetry questions, from the outset, the logical structure of traditional discursive language, which inherently hinders access to the world of objects. Teleologically, the position of the poet differs fundamentally from that of the semanticist. The former aims to communicate forms, while the latter seeks to communicate content. Nevertheless, both want communication to be carried out in the most straightforward and effective manner and both reject structures incapable of achieving that straightforwardness.

In the past sixty years (after Mallarmé), a culturomorphology more inclined to a synthetical-ideogrammatic rather than to analytical-discursive composing technique arose in the artistic domain. It armed poets with linguistic tools that were closer to the real structure of things, tools that prophetically 'situated' poets in relation to the modern creations of scientific thought. The concrete poem, with its spacetime structure producing optical, acoustic and signifying stimuli in its field of relations, is an entity which possesses an isomorphic kinship (in the Gestalt psychology sense of the term) to 'the whole world of objective actuality'. This world, according to Trigant Burrow, has been subtracted from modern humans since their childhood, locking them 'in a field of nominative symbols'.

Concrete poetry searches for an instrument to bring poetry closer to things, for a language that incorporates, in addition to the temporal structure of verbal-discursive poetry, a spatial (visual) dimension or, more precisely, a dimension that operates in a *spacetemporal* way. In doing so, however, concrete poetry doesn't aim at the precise description of objects, nor at developing a system of signs structurally able to transmit, without deformations, a worldview rectified by modern scientific thought.

Rather, concrete poetry wants to put such a rich and flexible intellectual instrument – malleable, close to the real form of things – at the service of an unusual purpose: that of creating an object of its own. For the first time, it doesn't matter that words are not a given object [*um dado objeto*], for within the special domain of the poem, they will always be the object that is given [*o objeto dado*]. Concrete poetry aims at a language that communicates the world of things as quickly, clearly and effectively as possible by exchanging this world with a structurally isomorphic system of signs. Thanks to a sudden change in its field of operation language lends the power of its arsenal of virtualities to a new enterprise, creating a form with its own materials, a world corresponding to the world of things: the poem. This reflowing of the virtualities of language into itself mirrors and explains the special verbal process it unleashes into the poetical realm, making it clear how, though they may intersect up to a certain point, the paths of the language scientist and the artist will ultimately reject each other in pursuit of their respective goals. We must now attempt to describe these processes and their many modern requirements, even if briefly, so that we can arrive at a basic clarification about how they operate in the mind.

[Samuel Ichiye] Hayakawa, commenting on the theory preconised by Korzybski that 'new physical-mathematical languages must be developed to structurally correspond to the structure of human individual and social behaviour', suggests two areas where 'such programs began to be carried out: mathematical biology and cybernetics' (Hayakawa 1954). Oliver Bloodstein, facing the same problem, adds that modern art – just like mathematics – 'is a non-Aristotelian system' and thus rejects, among other things, the principle of identity (art = imitation of nature) (Bloodstein 1943).

ra terra ter
rat erra ter
rate rra ter
rater ra ter
raterr a ter
raterra terr
araterra ter
raraterra te
rraraterra t
erraraterra
terraraterra

If we apply these notions to concrete poetry's field of operation, we can affirm without a doubt that the concrete poem follows these assessments in a surprisingly radical way. The concrete poem, according to an observation by [Eugen] Gomringer about 'Constellation', 'is a reality in itself, not a poem about something else'. Since the poem doesn't mean to communicate any content, and since it employs the word (as sound, visual form, content) as compositional material instead of as means to interpret the objective world, its structure is its true content. Only in the cultural-historic plane is there a connection between the concrete object-poem and an external content: a connection which will remain, however, as a relationship between structures. Thus, 'the physiognomy of our era' (the industrial revolution, marketing and journalistic techniques, the cosmovision granted by revolutions in scientific and philosophical thought, communication theory cleaved by cybernetics, etc.) will be the 'content' structure that stands in relation to the structure-content of concrete poetry, rather than such and such object, or such and such subjective feeling extracted from the interior or exterior world of the poet. Such contents, through the usual semantic affinities involved in the manipulation of words, leave traces on the magnetic field of the poem, to which readers and even critics always and unconsciously cling in the last hope of salvation. Those traces of content are undeniably present in poetry, whose instrument – the word, different from colour or sound – cannot be regarded as an entirely neutral element; rather, the word carries immediately aprioristic meanings. The function of concrete poetry is not, as one might expect, to void the word of its content, but rather to make such content into a material as valid as any other tool at one's disposal. Words are employed in their totality instead of being mutilated by unilateral reductions that turn them into descriptive music (*lettrism*) or decorative pictography (*calligram*, or any other graphic-hedonistic arrangement). The simple act of putting the word *terra* [earth, soil] onto paper can imply an entire georgic. What the reader of concrete poetry needs to know is that any one connotation will be valid (and to some extent unavoidable) exclusively on a material level, as long as it reinforces and confirms the other elements employed – to the extent that this connotation participates, with its peculiar effects (a quantitative- and qualitative-determined semantic relation), in the content-structure that constitutes the poem. Any cathartic *démarrage,* any subjectivistic detours, are alien to the poem and exist only due to a tendency towards nomenclature, i.e. the subsumption of artistic objects by vague nominative tags, as keenly noted by Hayawaka in the following ludicrous anecdote:

A trivial but revealing example of such naming adjustments came to me recently while I was at my own house. I own an abstract painting, a late-period Moholy-Nagy. A lady who was visiting us could not concentrate on the conversation; she kept turning to the picture. It seemed to disturb her. Finally, she rose and came close to it and found a thin paper label containing the words: 'space modulator, 1941'. 'Oh, so this is a space modulator, isn't it?', she said. 'Isn't it pretty?!'. Then she sat again, relieved. After that she wouldn't bother to take another single look at the painting.

The word *'terra'* functions as an excellent way of understanding not only the treatment language undergoes in a concrete poem but also how the question of content can be presented within it. The Dadaists, says André Gide (quoted in Mondrian's 'Neoplasticism') wanted

> to free the word from thought by arranging words side by side with one another without any connection ...; each word-isle [*vocábulo-ilha*] must show abrupt contours on the page.
>
> The word will be put here (or there, as long as it's good) as pure sound tonality; other pure sounds will vibrate not far from it, but through a lack of relations that won't authorise any mental association. Thus the word will be finally devoid of any previous meaning, of any past evocation.

That is the exact opposite of the procedure chosen by concrete poetry, in which the poem is a 'material relationship' and in which the question of poetry is the question of relations. Décio Pignatari proposes to make a poem built upon a single word (an experience that, in concrete music, was attempted by Pierre Boulez in his 'Study about a Sound') (Schaeffer 1952,

191). The word *terra* serves as the generating core of the set of relations which constitutes the following poem:

Terra [earth, soil] – *erra* [to make a mistake, to wander] – *ara terra* [to plough the earth] – *rara terra* [rare earth or soil] – *erra ara terra* [mistake ploughs soil] – *terra ara terra* [soil ploughs soil]: those are the thematic components originating from the core of the poem, in addition to the statement '*terra a terra*' [earth to earth; to cover with earth] tacitly accompanying the poem as a virtual phonetic chorus. In the poem, Pignatari makes use of the 'feedback' process borrowed from cybernetics as a structural tool. W. Sluckin writes:

> The machines that most impress us aren't those that are simply capable of complex calculations, but rather the ones that work in such a way as to strongly evoke human or animal behaviour. Such machines embody some form of automatic self-regulation or, as it's called today, automatic control. This is achieved by a mechanism sometimes called 'servomechanism'. The servomechanism regulates the functioning of a machine at any given moment according to the previous results it produced. In other words, the performance of the machine always controls its operation, so that it won't exceed or fail to achieve certain values. ... Any device that makes use of negative feedback, whether it's called servomechanism or not, can be regarded as 'moved by error' and 'self-correcting' (or 'error-compensating'). That's because the device operates when the performance deviates from a certain given level or errs from it; a negative feedback operation compensates for the mistake and corrects the performance. (Sluckin 1954)

In the seventh limb-line [*linha-membro*] of the poem *terra* – which up until then had consisted only in this single word, phrasing and rephrasing itself as if running on a teletype tape or a scrolling news sign – a new component is suddenly introduced, generated from the initial core of the poem: the syllable *ra*, which forms *ara* by connecting itself to what was discarded from the word 'terra' in the previous limb-line. This new component (an error from the reader's perspective, who might have been expecting the simple word 'terra' to keep repeating and reforming itself, rather than the duplication of its final syllable) is 'memorised' by the poem and starts driving its development, correcting it and unleashing another unexpected component entailed by the process – *rara* – until it reaches the climax – *terraraterra* – which controls and corrects the operational field of the poem. This structure, regulated by feedback, is corroborated by the thematic components of the poem in the most efficient way. The word *erra*, already produced in the second line of the poem and constantly insinuating itself through the body of the piece, makes explicit the underlying content-structure: at the same time, the way the poem operates through the *'errata* glance'[30] of the poet, who succeeds by wandering [*acerta errando*] or who transforms mistakes into successes within the semantic field on which he labours, resulting in an isomorphic structure: an *ideoforma* [ideal form or form of idea]. At the verbal and procedural levels, the mistake expresses a self-correction to which the poem is subjected, coerced by the poet's structural operation. One could invoke here a correlated theme in cybernetics: the problem-solving method of 'trial and error', which is also of interest to Gestalt psychologists. As W. Sluckin points out, 'trial and error' behaviour can be described in terms of 'negative feedback':

> The solution to the problem can be regarded as an immediate target or as a creature's state of equilibrium. Information – the distance needed to reach the target – is fed back to the controlling centre. One could say that this flow of information controls the steady march of the creature until it reaches the target.

This system explains the labyrinth-deciphering mechanisms built by [Claude] Shannon, I. P. Howard and J. A. Deutsch in the past five or six years. Similarly, the poem *terra* concretely deciphers itself.

The other thematic components also constitute lines of force that guide the content-structure: the poem generating itself, the active mistake – *errar arar* – as a soil that self-ploughs (*terra ara terra*), a rare soil and in spite of that a down-to-earth, earthly, elemental operation, as characteristic of the productive and grounded human condition as the act of ploughing performed by the labourers of the earth. A concrete painting has a certain *chromatic number* that defines both quantitatively and qualitatively the number of colours needed to solve a particular problem. The concrete poem, meanwhile, has a *thematic number*: which is to say that words, from a material standpoint, only allow for a certain number of implied meanings, which are precisely those that act as the poem's structural vectors and that participate in its gestalt. There is no space for 'decorativism', for intimate effects of subjectivistic pyrotechnics.

Here we must differentiate the concrete poem from the surrealist poem. Surrealism, battling against traditional logical barriers, didn't try to develop a language to surpass logic; on the contrary, it installed itself inside logic's headquarters to live within the curse of discursive-logical language that produces 'admirable ideas, like a spotted tail ape is not a legitimate convention' (Fenollosa 1953). Breton's 'white-haired revolver' rules over the absurd kingdom unleashed from within the Aristotelian system of language when this system is taken to its ultimate consequences. It's the realm of paradox, of nonsense, whose law is the 'mixing up of abstraction levels'. Although it rebels against logic, Surrealism is nothing more than logic's bastard son. Hayawaka, expounding on Korzybski, writes:

Traditional Aristotelian language structure and its corresponding semantic reactions tend to ignore a fundamental fact regarding the human nervous system: that we make an indefinite number of abstractions – we abstract abstractions, abstractions of abstractions of abstractions etc. In maths, the process of symbol manipulation is such that, when orders of abstraction are mixed up, the system will immediately call attention to it by communicating a contradiction. In that regard, mathematics' efficiency is demonstrated by the simplicity with which many traditional logical paradoxes, in which everyday language hides the transition between abstraction levels, are solved by mathematical methods.

Concrete poetry (which, like mathematics, is a special non-Aristotelian language system) also has, in its thematic number, a control mechanism to search for and eliminate all components that contradict its rigid structure. Thus, in the poem 'terra', words such as the noun *'era'* [age, epoch] and the interjection *'arre'* [dammit!],[31] for example, would be immediately rejected as alien bodies by the regulating mechanism of the piece's content-structure, even though they may be part of its phonetic arrangement. Concrete poems repel traditional logic as well as its half-brother, 'mental automatism':

> Logic has abused the language that has been left at its mercy. Poetry agrees with science, not with logic. (Fenollosa 1953)

Graphically and visually, the poem *terra* addresses its own structure. The generation of the poem, beginning with the syllable *ra*, which then forms *terra* and moves on, grabbing 'erra' from its core, creates its own movement in space based on proximity and similitude. The sector dwindling from *terra* to *a* (upper centre, in a triangle-rectangle) is connected by one of its corners to another triangle, which shrinks from *terr* to *t*. To the right (upper-lateral sector), the reiteration of the component *ter* forms an orthogonal column. Finally, a larger triangle-rectangle appears, encompassing all of the previously described elements, with the smallest side in *terra ter* and one of its corners in *t*. On the opposite side, one can distinguish another large triangular sector, with its smaller side in *terraraterra* and one of its corners in *ra* (truncated). Inside it, pushed by a furrow running between the *aa* and *tt* lines, there is a truncated triangle (from *ra* to *raterra*), a rectangle (the orthogonal column formed by the sixfold repetition of *ra*) and a trapezoid (sides marked by the *tt* line, by *terra* in the 11th limb-line, and by a straight line running from *t* to *a*, which forms its largest base). The trapezoid in turn creates a small triangle-rectangle (corner in *t*, smallest side in *terr*) and a parallelogram (*terr* repeated six times). The blank of the page operates in the narrow furrow, as well as in the other larger furrows (one separating the two big opposing triangles, the other separating the upper-centre triangular sector – from *terra* to *a* – from the *ter* column). A large triangle frames the total area of the poem and sets limits on the game. The conflicting orientation of the main triangular elements; the perceptual production of forms within other forms; the two parallel furrows and the other two perpendicular to them, whose injunction creates a kind of visual curve on the reading path; sectors that dwindle from words to letters: all of these impose a graphic-spatiotemporal structure to the poem, suddenly disrupting its verbal flow, straightening and directing it through its climax-development by means of feedback, self-correcting mistakes. There is a movement from *physiognomy* (white furrows = furrows on the ploughed earth) to *isomorphism* (visual structure = verbal structure). However, one should be aware that the in-depth analysis we have just provided is only a pedagogical way of describing the whole process. The poem does not offer any challenges at the perceptual level, in which our ocular geometry acts, simply and naturally, on sensorial data.

Acoustically, we have a similar phenomenon. The poem's internal dialectics, the cuts and coagulations of the phonetic elements – starting from the source-word *terra*, which produces *erra, rara, ara* – synergise with the desired content-structure and call for utterance (timbre-play, pauses, etc). The words require a human voice to emphasise them and to express, through creative vocalisation, their movement. Only those averse to the techniques employed in modern music for the activation of the voice (the *Sprechgesang*, for example, used by Schoenberg in his *Pierrot Lunaire* and in *Ode to Napoleon*) would question the aurality of a concrete poem. A silent, mental reading will be richer the more it sounds out the effects of such vocalisations.

In passing: a critic once noted that E. E. Cummings' poetry (one of the most important poets for the concrete movement), being predominantly visual, would be 'impossible to hear' (Monteiro 1957). Susanne Langer seems to think otherwise in her study of the role of sound in poetic creation: 'There is a kind of poetry that benefits from real vocalisation or even demands it. E. E. Cummings, for example, profits tremendously when read out loud' (Langer 1953).

Since the poem *terra* is no georgic, it presents no narrative that could indulge the kind of imagination prone to discourses on nature or to pastoris eclogues. Its content, like in a concrete painting, is its structure, and only on a cultural-historical level can one find a structural connection with any exterior subject – such as *feedback*, as it is currently studied by cybernetics – ingrained in today's cosmovision. The content of words and the word sequences required by *terra*'s *thematic number* won't lead to the catharsis expected by some of its readers, for those contents are inseparable from the poem's structure. Only in this structure can they find their resolution. Thus, the key to understanding a concrete poem is to learn how to see and listen to structures.

For a scholar of general semantics like Bloodstein, however, modern art is also a non-Aristotelian system precisely because modern art 'regards structures, relationships and order as art's single content'. This entails a reassessment of the reader's usual semantic reactions, for readers are used to looking in a poem for objects that are not the poem's objects, and to using the work of art as an excuse for meta-artistic digressions. Korzybski (quoted by Bloodstein): 'Any fundamental new system involves new semantic reactions. That's the greatest difficulty we face when we try to master a new system. We need to reeducate or change our old semantic reactions'. This warning applies even more to concrete poetry, whose structural concerns aren't transitive (that is, destined to transmit another structure, that of reality, as is the case with others non-Aristotelian systems) but self-sufficient, exhausting themselves as they materialise. Herein lies the problem of communication.

It has been said, perhaps for the sake of simplification, that the pioneers of the concrete poetry movement (the São Paulo group) 'believe that the efficiency and validity of a work of art is determined by how fast or slow it affects its spectators' (Bastos 1957). This is a trifling scholastic postulation, whose mere enunciation obscures the problem in question.

What was actually said by the concrete poetry pioneers is that the concrete poem has among its virtues the ability to perform swift communication, a communication of forms, of structures, rather than of verbal content. Supported textually, orally and visually [*verbivocovisualmente*] by components integrated into structural consonance, the concrete poem attacks from all sides the field of perception of any reader who is looking for what the poem contains: a structure-content. The concrete poem, by regarding the word as a material object, achieves the difficult task of bringing the potential of non-verbal communication to the realm of poetic communication without renouncing the singular nature of the (written) word. To put it differently, since the concrete poem seeks to communicate its structure, the content of the manipulated words (a feature that would supposedly include the poem among other modalities of verbal communication) is controlled by the thematic number in benefit of this structure. The content load thus does not exclude, but rather appeals to the reader's non-verbal level of understanding.[32] Jurgen Ruesch and Weldon Kees, in their recent work (Ruesch and Kess 1956), make the following distinction between verbal and nonverbal communication: the former relies on the digital codification of information, of which the main examples are the phonetic alphabet and the numeral system ('information transmitted through such channels is of course coded through combinations of letters and digits'); the latter relies on analogue codification ('different kinds of actions, paintings and material objects represent analogical kinds of denotation').

> In terms of codification ... digital stands in opposition to analogue; in terms of language, discursive stands in opposition to non-discursive. ... Discursive language is founded on logic and is made of a set of artificial, generally accepted rules, expressed in verbal terms around a certain kind of work. Logic rejects analogue codifications even though a good part of our thinking and communication processes relies as much on the non-verbal as on the verbal aspect. (Ruesch and Kess 1956)

By rejecting the logical-discursive order and by opening itself up to suggestions offered by an ideogrammic method of composition (which is analogue rather than digital), concrete poetry advances in its fascinating adventure of creating a non-discursive linguistic space with digits and with phonetic systems. This non-discursive space partakes in the advantages of non-verbal communication (standing closer to things and objects, maintaining the continuity between action and perception) without mutilating its main instrument – the word – whose special ability for 'expressing abstractions, communicating inter- and extrapolations, and making possible the framing of different kinds of events and ideas in understandable terms' is not neglected, but rather used in favour of a communicative totality. The idea of metacommunication describes, according to specialists, 'the relations between verbal and nonverbal codification':

> [M]essages can be regarded as having two sides: the statement itself and the explanations provided by its interpretation. The nature of interpersonal communication requires that these sides meet in time, which can only be achieved by taking another path. Thus, when a statement is verbally phrased, non-verbal instructions tend to be necessary. The effect is similar to a musical arrangement for two instruments, where the voices move independently while modifying and supplementing each other, thus remaining integrated into a functional and organic unity. (Ruesch and Kess 1956)

To a certain extent, a phenomenon similar to metacommunication takes place in the concrete poem, with the significant difference that the poem doesn't entertain communicating external messages or contents, but rather deploys those resources to communicate forms, to create and corroborate, *verbivocovisualmente*, a content-structure....

Chapter 4

Poetry and Modernity: From the Death of Art to the Constellation. The Post-Utopian Poem (1997)

Haroldo de Campos

...

The Mallarméan Lineage in Brazil

It's possible to summarise, to 'reconstruct' a corresponding itinerary [of the Mallarméan tradition] in Brazil in an indirect or explicit way. Oswald de Andrade's instantaneous, almost-haiku-like blitzing montage poetry of the last 20 years; a number of self-reflecting poems by Carlos Drummond de Andrade, himself part of the 1930s generation; the unrestricted image and the later substantive thinking diction of Murilo Mendes, also part of the 1930s; João Cabral, the 'engineer' and 'psychologist' of composition, in the 1940s and in the evolution of his poetry's metalinguistic line. But it's in Drummond, in his poem *Isso é Aquilo* [This is That] from the 1962 book *Lição de Coisas* [Lesson of Things], a lucid and visual poem already under the clear influence of concrete poetry, that the debt to the Mallarméan lineage becomes explicit, even emblematic, thanks to the ironic game Drummond plays with the word *ptyx*. Not to mention Manuel Bandeira, forerunner and master of the Brazilian modernist movement, whose intimacy with *Coup de Dés* was evident in the beautiful talk he gave in 1942, during the 100th birthday celebration of Mallarmé. Bandeira, who tried to practice concrete poetry in some of his later poems, hailed the movement with openness and youthfulness during the controversial moment of its debut.

Brazilian concrete poetry was the totalizing moment of this process. In a way, it was also the last poetic, collective and international avant-garde movement, with ramifications that reached even Japan through the VOU Group, led by Kitasono Katue. It accomplished, not only in isolated poems but also in its entire poetics, the confluence of East and West: from the poetic ideography attempted in alphabetic-digital languages to the re-exportation of concrete poetry's typographical techniques to a language written with ideograms (the Japanese language) in a sort of supplemental-reverse tropism. Exhausting all possibilities and taking a 'verbo-vocal-visual' radicalisation to its limits, concrete poetry, in a collective, anonymous and plural gesture, took upon itself to bring the project initiated by Mallarmé to its logical conclusions. It broke the residual links with discourse (I here refer to the poems of the minimalist period that have a geometrically controlled structure, corresponding to the 1958 *Pilot Plan*) and converted itself, monad-like, into a 'conflict between word-things in space-time'. Thus, concrete poetry also produced (even without the intention of doing so) a model at once provocative and intensified, instantised, for the exercise of 'poetic function' (a projection of the paradigm into the syntagm) as posited by [Roman] Jakobson. Concrete poetry's structure is both its content and its metaphor, an 'epistemological metaphor' (in the words of Umberto Eco) of the 'produced', autonomous and self-conscious world of the poem, which has taken the place of nature and of the *état de naïveté* already dethroned in Baudelaire's urban poetry. On the other hand, while trying to temporarily abolish chance, concrete poetry integrated this world in the fleetingness of the poetic construction at the very useful moment of its dynamic balance just as, in Mallarmé, 'every thought throws a dice...' In Baudelaire: a negative-critical function, in Mallarmé: a utopian-critical function; the former, a conclusion to the history of Modernity, the latter, the appearance of the postmodern space... If Walter Benjamin regards Baudelaire as the modern poet *par excellence*, Octavio Paz adds (in a key that Benjamin, who saw in the *Coup de Dés* the future of poetry, wouldn't disapprove) that

> Baudelaire puts analogy at the centre of his poetic creation. An ever-oscillating centre, always disturbed by irony. ... But the core of the analogy is itself empty: the plurality of texts implies that there's no original. The emptiness makes the reality of the world and the meaning of language simultaneously appear and disappear. However, it's not Baudelaire, but Mallarmé who dares to contemplate such emptiness and who then transforms this act of contemplation into the stuff of his poetry.[33]

Postmodern and Post-Utopian

I understand that the moment we now live in – a moment we are living in since at least the end of the 1960s, when concrete poetry's process as collective movement and an *in progress* experiment emerged – is not actually a post-modern moment, but rather a post-utopian one. Mallarmé flirted with the project of designing a permutating book (*Bloc*) that would become the one and only Work, of which the *Coup de Dés* would have represented only an initial tentative version. He imagined a spectacle-book, the kind that could take part in theatre, liturgical service or concert; a book conceived at first to be 'private' but, in the long run, made into a communal celebration. This multibook, according to the poet, was to be 'modernised', that is, made available for everyone. For that, Mallarmé considered all practical details of such a modern *Bible*, from the organisation of public readings up to the details of funding and printing (aiming at nothing less than 480,000 copies...), according to what we now know based on the drafts of the project published in 1957 by Jacques Scherer. It's clear that, behind such a dream (where, as noted by Maurice Blanchot, the 'restrictive' economy of the book corresponds to history and political economy, whereas the poet's singular intervention corresponds to general action), lies a 'hope-principle' (to borrow Ernst Bloch's expression). This programmatic hope allows us to catch a future glimpse of the postponed present, which animates the assumption that, ultimately, 'universal progressive poetry' can still occupy the social place of the newspaper – a popular fantasy, like the encyclopaedic poem produced for the masses, 'as indispensable as bread and salt'. In the utopic horizon of his 'ideal commune', free from bureaucrats, while arguing against criticisms that his poetry would be hermetic, Mayakovsky would echo that yearning for a book whose clarity derives from its necessity and whose condition of possibility arises from the increasing cultural literacy of the people, rather than from the lowering of the levels of poetic innovation (all this is already present in his 1927 poem *Incomprehensible for the Masses*).

The Avant-Garde and the 'Hope-Principle'

Without this 'hope-principle', not as a vague abstraction but as a real expectation nurtured by a prospective practice, there can be no avant-garde as a movement. Teamwork, rejecting the individual in favour of the collective struggle and the anonymous result, is something that can only be put into motion by this 'elpidic' engine – from the Greek *elpis* (expectation, hope). In their rehearsal of totalisation, the avant-garde provisionally erases all differences looking for the utopian identity. It alienates the *singularity* of each poet into the *sameness* of a collectively aspired poetics in order to, in its final stage, un-alienate itself as it reaches an optimal point in history, reserved for its culmination or for the rescue of its undifferentiating and progressive enterprise. The avant-garde, as a movement, is the quest for a new common language, a new *koiné*, for language reconciled at the horizon of a transformed world.

During the 1950s, Brazilian concrete poetry was able to entertain the project of an ecumenic language: the new barbarians from a peripheral country rethinking the legacy of universal poetry and usurping it under the 'decentralised' (because 'ex-centric') banner of 'anthropophagic reason' (an analogy for the 'excluded third'), both deconstructive and transconstructive of this legacy, now in a devouring form. It's the project of summoning the totality of the code and re-operating it through the expropriative perspective resulting from the evolution of Brazilian poetry, which would, from that point on, formulate the terms of a new, universally accessible *lingua franca*.

Brasília and Concrete Poetry

The circumstances were favourable. The city of Brasília was being erected: Brazil's futurological capital, simultaneously baroque and constructivist, designed by Lúcio Costa and Oscar Niemeyer. The 'engineer' João Cabral de Melo Neto was our closest forerunner; the conservative generation of 1945 and its florid games were our natural enemy. Then president Juscelino Kubitschek ruled, with statesmanlike attitude, over the Brazilian political-administrative moment, and succeeded, with his economic and industrializing 'Target Plan', in balancing conflicting forces, thus producing one of the rarest *interregnum*s of democratic plenitude that my generation has ever lived. Celso Lafer, in his basilar analysis of the Kubitschek administration, helps us understand how the president, attentive to the increasing popular participation in politics, 'acknowledged the system's dynamics and foresaw the need to consider the future, rather than the past, as a framework for governmental action' (Lafer 1970).

The main artform of the Juscelinian Age was architecture and its most important artist was the Marxist architect Oscar Niemeyer. In this regard, the liberal-progressive Juscelino displayed high aesthetic sensibility and the ability to respect ideological differences. The then young concrete poetry movement, although circumscribed to literary and artistic fields far from the political decision-making circles, couldn't avoid reflecting on the optimism of this generous moment. Like Brasília's development plan [*Plano Diretor*], our 1958 manifesto was entitled *Pilot Plan*, and proposed 'total responsibility before language. Thorough realism. Against a poetry of expression, subjective and hedonistic. To create precise problems and to solve them in terms of sensible language. A general art of the word. The poem-product: useful object'.

Utopian Crisis, Ideological Crisis

Later, in the 1960s, there were the alluring beginnings of the Cuban Revolution, the sharpening of the political debate and the restoration of a fascinating historical perspective. Poetic renovation once again had the opportunity to (as Octavio Paz used to say) 'embody itself' in social transformations – as it had happened in the beginning of the Russian Revolution, during the feverish years of Cubo-Futurism, constructivism, the *LEF* magazine, the 'ROSTA Windows', the poster-poem and combative experimental typography. We translated Mayakovsky, recreating the technical complexity of his poems. We once again put his motto into circulation: 'without a revolutionary form, there can be no revolutionary art'. We intervened in the national cultural debate of the time, making a stand against the narrow proposals made by the Brazilian partisans of the Jdanovist realism, as we proposed an alternative 'critical nationalism' open to the universal: a *poetry-towards* [*poesia para*] that was able, from the standpoint of *engagement*, to make use of the technical achievements of *pure poetry* [*poesia pura*].

Then came the 1964 coup, the 1968 dictatorial calcification, the long years of nation-wide authoritarianism and frustrated expectations: poetry in times of hardship. Internationally, the ideological crisis pressed on. On the one side, imperial capitalism, savage and predatory; on the other, the bureaucratic State, repressive and uniformizing, turning yesterday's revolutionaries into today's *apparátchki*, turning art into a space of servitude for party dogmas. Poetry's utopian function dried out (even though, paradoxically, new electronic media promised poetry's unexpected possibilities which seemed to fulfill Walter Benjamin's and Mallarmé's prophecy of an iconographic universal writing).

Post-Utopia: Poetry of the Nowness

Without a utopian perspective, the avant-garde movement loses its meaning. In that sense, the only viable poetry for the present is post-avant-garde poetry. Not because it is post-modern or anti-modern, but because it is post-utopian. After the totalizing avant-garde project – which, ideally, can only be supported by a redeeming utopia – comes the pluralisation of possible poetics. After the hope-principle, turned towards the future, comes the reality-principle, firmly grounded in the present. I agree with Octavio Paz when he writes, in the last pages of *Los Hijos del Limo*, that today's poetry is a poetry of the 'now' (I'd rather use the word 'nowness' [*agoridade*] / *Jetztzeit*, a term dear to Walter Benjamin): a poetry of 'another present' and of 'plural history', which implies a 'critique of the future' and of its systematic paradises. Against the monological pretence of the single and last word – against the absolutism of a 'final interpreter' that stagnates the 'infinite semiosis' natural to all signifying processes and which hypostatises itself in a messianic future yet to come – the present can only deal with temporary synthesis. The only utopian trace that can and shall remain within this poetry is the critical and dialogical dimension inherent to utopia. This poetry of the now, as I see it, should not stand as pretence for a poetics of abdication, nor serve as alibi for regressive eclecticism or for lazy work. Instead, if we are to admit that such a 'plural history' exists, we should be inspired to critically seize any 'plurality of pasts' without having first to make exclusive predeterminations about the future. I've been saying, on more than one occasion, that the 'concrete poetry' of the 1950s and 1960s, as an 'experience of limits', didn't confine itself nor myself. On the contrary, it has taught me to see what is concrete in poetry and to transcend the particularizing 'ism' of 'concretism' in order to consider poetry as trans-temporal, as a global and open process of signifying concretion that always updates itself in different ways and in different times of literary history, in the various opportunities for the materialisation of language (of languages). Sappho and Basho, Dante and Camões, Sá de Miranda and Fernando Pessoa, Hölderlin and Celan, Góngora and Mallarmé: all of them are, for me, in the most fundamental sense, concrete poets (an 'ism' here wouldn't make any sense). Therefore, the 'post-utopian' poetry of the present no longer needs to appeal to a 'dominant opposition' in order to define itself, be it something in the past or even itself, as required by the self-affirming, evolutive-historical processes characteristic of modernity. As a poetry of nowness, it has at its disposal an indispensable critical device in the act of translation. The translator, writes Novalis, 'is the poet of the poet', the poet of poetry. Translation – regarded as the practice of reading tradition in a reflexive way – allows us to recombine the plurality of possible pasts and make them present as difference, in the *hic et nunc* individuality of the post-utopian poem.

Chapter 5

Art and Technology, Part III (1967)

Augusto de Campos

In an interview with Eli Bornstein for the Canadian magazine *The Structurist* on the topic of art and technology, the popular critic Marshall McLuhan states that the conscious role of art in our time is to explore and produce a consciousness appropriate for the new context created by new media.

McLuhan says that in primitive (non-mechanical, non-literate and non-technical) societies, the artist had a different function: they connected society to cosmic powers. The artist played a religious role. Today, however, in the age of Malraux's 'imaginary museum', the role of the artist is to reveal the kind of world humans have technologically created for themselves. Every communication medium, such as the alphabet, creates a new context, a new extension of sensorial life that reshapes every sensibility. The medium is the message.

According to McLuhan, new contexts are always invisible at first. It's the artist's duty to reveal what would otherwise go unseen, thus producing new forms of perception. Besides the invisibility of the new contexts, there is also an intense obsession with older ones. This happens in art as well. Thus, when the electric circuit entered the picture at the end of the 19th century, it transcended the world of the machine and transformed machinery into a form of art. Then came the futurists and the Russians, with their constructivism and their awareness of the machine as an artistic form. With the rise of the electric circuit, the machine suddenly became obsolete, even before it could reach its full potential. The circuit remains, however, invisible, and everyone is becoming increasingly obsessed with the machine precisely when it's about to leave the stage. The electric circuit produces a field of simultaneity, which is intensely engaging and totally invisible in how it affects our psychic functions. It produces what is now known as a 'happening:' a world in which everything happens all at once, a world in which there's no sequence or progression of events.

How should the artist react to this electric world in which everything happens at once? The artist should make the existence of this world clear; they shouldn't get themselves lost in the general interest in old, industrial-age machinery. Additionally, the artist should react by demonstrating that this context of simultaneity has become a work of art in itself. For the first time in the history of humankind, we have the power, the energy and the capacity to program every human context as a work of art. The artist has already begun such an enterprise through all sorts of 'crazy stuff' and comedy shows – some of which are mere 'pop art' spectacles. If we take a fragment of the context and put it inside an art gallery, that's a way of stating that, from now on, the context itself is a work of art; the 'pop art' movement should perhaps be praised for having demonstrated that. Satellites and electric information spinning around the planet are transforming human habitats themselves into art, into a kind of old 'camping site'. The planet itself is an art form.

For McLuhan, over in the last centuries artists have focused their power on trying to perceive hidden contexts that were created in quick succession by new technologies. Evoking Burrough's *Naked Lunch*, McLuhan asserts that the new contexts are literally cannibalistic: they lay us bare and eat us alive (which is reminiscent of the fantastically current doctrine of 'anthropophagy' posited by Oswald de Andrade, the greatest and most slandered figure in Brazilian modernism). Only the artist can warn us of such powers and teach us to defend ourselves against them. The artist is a sort of 'catcher in the rye', someone always training their perception within the yet unperceived invisible context. The artist's aim today is much larger in scope: not just to give form to objects, but to program the human context as a whole. Art should therefore be regarded as an attempt to extend human consciousness. The task of art today is to expand consciousness into the context; to create a context that is, itself, totally conscious. This is the most exciting enterprise ever experienced by artists. In the past, since at least the Renaissance, art was a distillation of essences, a repository of privileged moments and perceptions for the benefit of a select few. This kind of art, McLuhan assures us, although in many aspects valuable (including in the negative sense), is simply over. Now, in Malraux's 'museum without walls', it's the exterior world that becomes art; art will no longer be something that can only be found inside galleries and museums. It's possible to begin formulating our very earthly and celestial context as an artistic object. It's possible to program the human senses in order to resist the 'cannibalistic attack of new technologies'.

Very few people, according to McLuhan, are prepared to accept modern painting, poetry and music as exploration probes, as instruments devised for those investigating an era, as a means of active participation in the making of one's own era. Though many still cling to their role as consumers, this new form of art requires the audience to become a producer rather than a consumer! It requires a great deal of energy and entrepreneurship from the spectator.

Contrary to those who see advertising from an exclusively negative angle, as a 'destructive form of mass propaganda and brainwashing that creates conformity and cultural homogeneity', McLuhan has a rather positive view of it. 'Why can't we look at advertising simply as art? The constructivists have taught us how to see machines as art'. Since the advent of television, old silent movies have already become artistic forms. By putting old movies into a new televised context, those movies are converted into artistic forms. And if one regards advertisements as artistic forms, one should also accept them as evidence of the context. And advertisements can be very efficient at that. They are quickly evolving from products to pure information. People are increasingly reading advertisements not to buy products but to enjoy them for their own sake. Art itself is heading towards a world of pure information. Art is becoming pure programmed information.

For McLuhan, there have been too few studies and attempts aimed at understanding the meaning of advertising in our age. Propaganda, McLuhan argues, following Jacques Ellul, is society's entire way of life. Naturally, people from all cultures suffer brainwashing from their own cultures, but propaganda ends where dialogue begins. In other words, if one is not ready to face one's own culture by means of dialogue or self-conscious discourse, one cannot 're-wash' their own brainwashed brain.

Though we might ascribe brainwashing to far-away regions of the universe, we never think about applying this notion to our own cultural practices. Nevertheless, our own native language operates within us as a form of brainwashing since it shapes our sensorial life and means of perception. One could say that every concept brainwashes us, that they are pernicious until confronted with dialogue. And, in McLuhan's perspective, only the artist can provide terms for the counter-dialogue needed to counterbalance the mental effects of the surrounding contexts. Only the artist can preserve consciousness and create consciousness within a technological society.

Electric technology should be regarded not as an outsider or intruder, but as part of our own nervous system, stimulating and extending beyond us into space. In other words, the world of technology, no matter at which layer, is nothing but a legitimate enlargement of our physical human powers. Every technology is therefore humanistic, in the sense that it fully belongs to the human organism. Thus, artists must dedicate themselves today to tasks that are as fantastically unusual as the technologies that have created them.

McLuhan observes that Buckminster Fuller noted that the space capsule was the first completely planned human-made context, since humans needed to take the planet along with them into the capsule. Since the beginning of the 20th century, there have been more technological mutations and more new technological contexts than in all the pre-historical and previous ages of humankind. Under those conditions, the function of art should not be to produce dated residues and fossilised encrustations, but to move as fast as guerrillas through new fields of action – and to collectively challenge new kinds of contexts, creating new kinds of space and new time capsules in which humankind can survive despite its own fantastical inventions.

Chapter 6

On Some Aspects of Concrete Poetry (1957)

Haroldo de Campos

Would *you say that the concrete poets are heading towards the notion of 'machine poetry', not unlike Ramon Llull's combinatory art?*

Concrete poetry is a poetry 'in situation'. Unlike Rilke's ninth 'Duino Elegy', it does not refrain from surrendering to the machine and its products. It keeps its distance from handcrafted mysticism. Firstly, the concrete poem – just like the concrete painting made with a revolver – is composed entirely on the machine: the fixed spacings and the standardisation of typefaces, characteristic of the modern tool, allow for greater control over these elements than handwriting does. Concrete poetry is an art of the present, but that doesn't mean that it cannot prepare us for other forms of written communication that would benefit from existing yet still creatively unexplored media. (Augusto de Campos, in *noigandres*, already considered the possibility of using illuminated ads or *filmletras* [filmletters] for the colour poems in 'poetamenos', having come so far as to have written a letter to Abraham Palatnik.) The possibilities presented by combinatorial art achieved through electronic means, cybernetics, etc., are of great interest to the concrete poet since they represent new ways of organising poematic [*poemático*] material. The most creative music of today, for instance, is represented by composers who use as their basic element the sine wave provided by electronic frequency generators, which allows them to achieve a total and synthetic serial organisation (Stockhausen). But that doesn't mean that the path of modern music should be called mechanistic or that it is fated to replace the composer with a 'thinking machine'. Such accusations have been made against the serial, chromatic twelve-tone technique itself, to which Michel Fano objected as follows:

> Just as dodecaphonic writing does not imply the simultaneous presence of all twelve notes, the dialectical power of serialisation cannot result in a statistical totality of structures. For that to happen, it would be better to trust the electronic thinking machines with the creation of all future music. Then there wouldn't be any mistakes or omissions! On the contrary, we propose that, if a series is chosen out of all possible functions it allows, then only the creative act puts the composer in charge of reacting to the material he arranges, which allows him to twist the intentional element in the very moment of creation, thus respecting the rules of unpredictability. ... This permanent emerging of the creative will is one of the most extreme consequences of serialisation, whose unpredictable power it defines.

Something analogous can be seen in the ideogramic method of composition on which concrete poetry relies. As for the future tools and instrument that the creative artist will have at their disposal, heed Pierre Shaeffer's sharp words (*À la Recherche d'une Musique Concrète*):

> Machines capable of reading, that is, of translating graphism into sound, are beginning to be conceived and built. They are really the first talking machines. In

a similar vein, in the future we might have machines that are able to translate the realm of space into the realm of duration. Let's refer to a previous example: machines that can translate pictorial compositions into sounds. Those confined to fake spiritualism will be offended by this kind of idea and shall soon utter (somewhat robotically) the word 'robot'. It's not about expecting those machines to produce some automatic symphony; it's about acknowledging the limited means of a regular symphony produced deliberately. Everything will depend on which paintings will be read and what relational functions technical artists will establish between values of space and time....

Chapter 7

New Language, New Poetry (1964)

Luis Ângelo Pinto and Décio Pignatari

Semiotics

Before we move on to what we want to say, it's important to briefly discuss some of the fundamental concepts of semiotics, or the theory of signs, founded by the American philosopher and mathematician Charles Sanders Piece and further developed by Charles W. Morris.

Let's give the name *SIGN* to a thing that stands for another thing in order to produce the same set of reactions as the thing it stands for.

A sign, insofar as it stands for an object to which the sign refers, can be categorised as:

- *INDEX*, when the sign is directly connected to the object. For example: wet ground indicates that it has rained; footprints indicate that a person or animal has passed through.

- *ICON*, when the sign possesses an analogical relation to the object. For example, a photograph, a diagram, a plan, a pictogram, etc.

- *SYMBOL*, when the relationship between the sign and the object is arbitrary and conventional. For example, the word 'table' in relation to the referred physical object of a table.

It's also possible to attest to the existence of mixed signs; for example, signs that are in part analogical, in part arbitrary.

A signifying process can be broken down into three levels in order to be studied:

- *SYNTACTIC*, or the relationship between signs and other signs;
- *SEMANTIC*, or the relationship between the sign and the object;
- *PRAGMATIC*, or a level indicating the relationship between the sign and the interpreter, the user of signs.

Language

By *language* we mean any set of signs and their usage, that is, the ways in which signs can be brought into a relation with one another (syntax) and with objects (semantics) by an interpreter (pragmatics).

In this definition we include not only all languages but also any traffic signalling processes (road, naval, air, space); schematic and diagrammatic languages (block diagrams, Venn diagrams, etc.); electronic computer languages; mathematical and symbolic logic languages; audiovisual languages such as film, etc.

Every object must be designed and built according to the needs and functions it will serve or respond to. This basic principle of modern industry is not limited to what we traditionally consider an object but can also be extended to other 'objects' such as languages. In that sense the poet is a designer, a language planner and deviser.

Languages tend to be built or transformed in order to fulfil certain goals. In specific languages, the most frequently used words are the shortest ones (so as to achieve an economy of time and labour); in tachygraphic languages, which aim to achieve the speed of phonetic transcription, signs are conveniently designed to enable quick drawing; a traffic language employs a set of signs immediately visible and audible from a distance; symbolic logic establishes a set of signs and rules to produce, among other things, greater clarity and precision.

Towards New Languages

Relying on this concept of language, we propose the creation of new languages.

The problem of creating new contents is closely related to the problem of creating new linguistic forms, new languages. Every language, as encompassing as it might be, is limited; it has a restricted set of signs and syntactic affinities. Therefore, when we think or communicate with one another through language, we cannot refer to anything or make any connections that were not first subordinated to the form of the language employed.

In that sense, we propose the creation of languages designed and constructed according to each situation and need. This means: 1) designing and building new sets of (visual, acoustic etc) signs; and 2) designing and building new syntactical rules that can be applied to the new set of signs. Note that neither of these items is independent from each other; rather, they are mutually dependent. The resulting syntax must derive from, or relate to, these signs' very form.

Letters, words and other grammatical elements are signs suited to the syntax of a linear written language. These signs can in many cases be useful to a non-linear language, though with more limitations than possibilities.

Traditional written language employs the same syntax as oral language. Concrete poetry, according to its 1958 *Pilot Plan*, 'begins to explore the [bi-dimensional] graphic space'. It thus achieves the creation of a new syntax and new linguistic structures, thus freeing itself as much as possible from an oral, purely linear syntax. Concrete poetry's planar language, however, still employs signs from oral languages whose form is better adapted to linear writing processes. This in turn imposes limits on its possibilities as a new language. Concrete poetry thus allows for juxtapositions, dismemberings, the use of words of different lengths and forms, and a kind of 'simultaneity' based on *juxtaposition*. Possibilities of *superpositioning* (like in Augusto de Campos' poem *greve* [strike]) or *intrapositioning* (like in certain montage-words) are, however, more limited. In some cases, from concrete poetry up until now, it has been possible to create writing with syntax derived from the very graphic design of the signs employed, as in the last parts of the poem *organismo* [organism] and especially in the poem *LIFE*, both by Décio Pignatari.

Such cases were only possible due to the virtualities within the signs' own design. In this process of creating new languages, our forerunner was the series *SOLIDA* [solid] (1962) by Wlademir Dias-Pino.

Hence the idea of a language in which the form of the signs determines its syntax, thus granting us new communication possibilities.

To do so, a set of signs (and the signs themselves) must be dynamic and malleable, so it can undergo transformations according to the needs of each text.

There are clear connections between visual texts and Chinese ideograms: analogical syntax, the use of graphic signs representing the object regardless of phonetic elements (non-verbal language). However, in this new language, ideograms must be intentionally designed and built. This doesn't mean that a new language needs to be necessarily visual or only visual. It can also be acoustic, audiovisual, etc., depending on the situation.

It's clear that, at first, any new language will be tied to one or more existing languages to a certain degree. As it develops, however, the new language will gradually become autonomous. The autonomy and singularity of a language in relation to others, but also of each individual work of art, are the *sine qua non* condition for an artwork to be considered as such. In other words, the work of art is irreducible.

The value of a language lies in what it has of the untranslatable, its unbridgeable aspects, its irreducibility to other languages. Likewise, the value of a piece of writing is defined by what it has that cannot be reduced to other writings in any language. It's meaningless to attempt to express a certain reality with elements alien to its nature – for example, to translate into linear language a text made on a plane, using planar syntax. That is precisely why the goal of creating a new language is not simply to produce another representation of realities or contents already existing in other languages, but rather to create new realities, new content-forms.

However, we don't mean to suggest that all creative resources of existing languages have dried up. Rather, we want to show how it's possible to create new sets of signs, new syntaxes; in sum: new languages designed and built in accordance with what each situation imposes. Now, more than ever, as already stated in the *Pilot Plan for Concrete Poetry*,

> *il faut que nôtre intelligence s'habitue à comprendre synthético-idéographiquement au lieu de analytico-discursivement* (Apollinaire).[34]

Finally, it seems very clear to us that even the most radical aspects of this new poetry remain connected to the basic principles of concrete poetry. That's why we will continue to call such poetry 'concrete'. Let us now give some examples of it:

two poems by décio pignatari

lexical key

☐ now!

□ maybe

■ never!

New Language, New Poetry (1964)

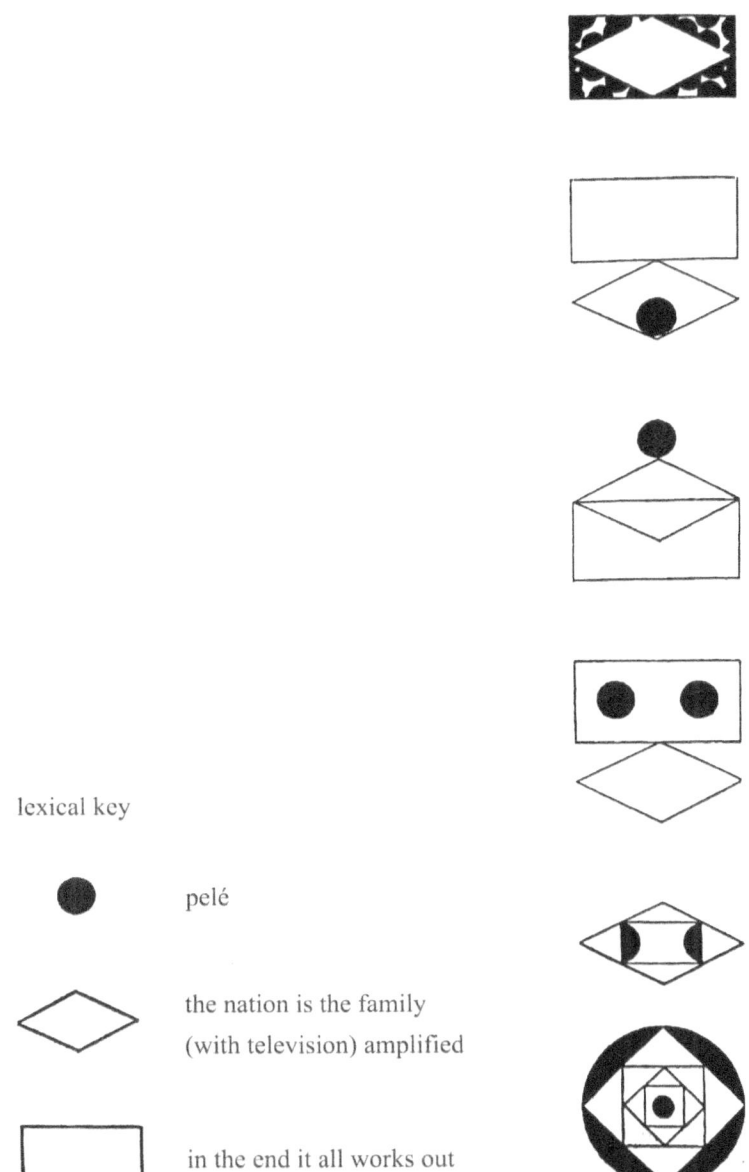

lexical key

● pelé

◇ the nation is the family (with television) amplified

▭ in the end it all works out

four poems by luis ângelo pinto

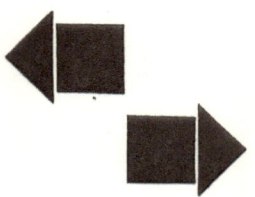

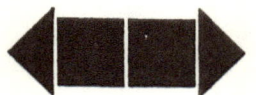

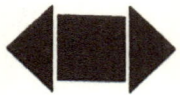

lexical key

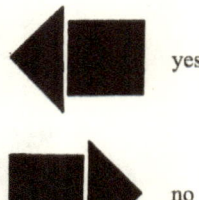 yes

no

New Language, New Poetry (1964)

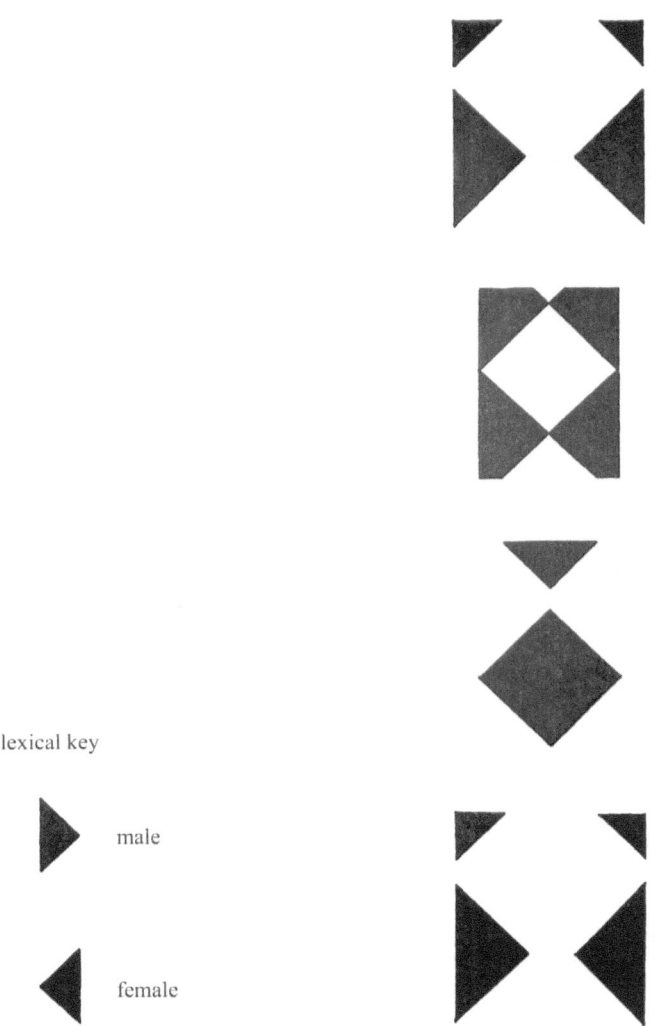

lexical key

male

female

Luis Ângelo Pinto and Décio Pignatari

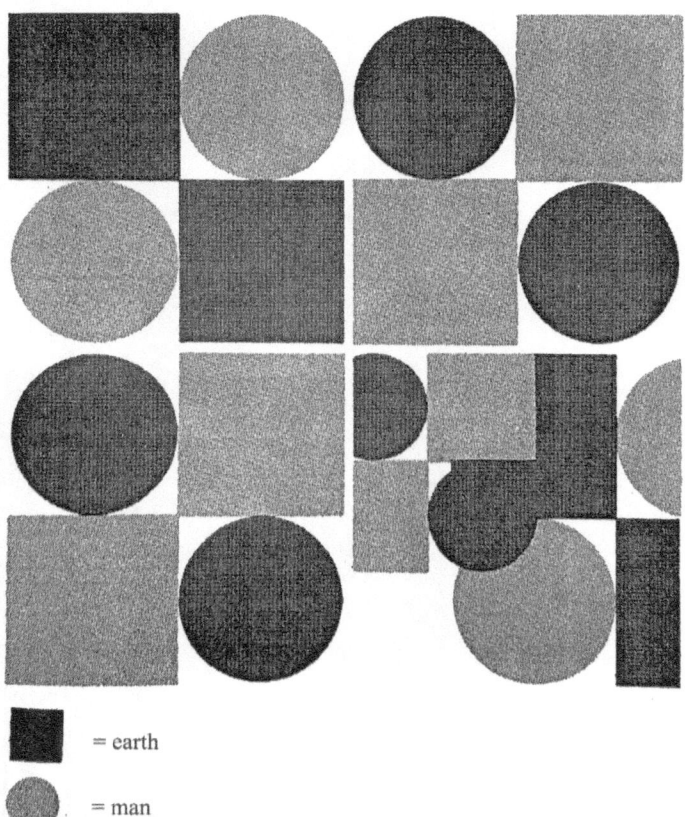

■ = earth
● = man

New Language, New Poetry (1964)

lexical key

mineral and/or vegetable

vegetable and/or animal

Chapter 8

The Three Sides of the Coin: Brazilian Poetry in the 1960s and 1970s (1983)

Eduardo Kac

...

The Joyous Revelry of the Avant-Garde

In the final years of the 1950s, after the previous decade's developmentalist boom, Brazilian society had become inflated with a *frisson nouveau*. The mixture of technological innovations and national consciousness resulted in a tense and fertile environment for the discussion of art and its political consequences. One of the main landmarks of such an environment was the 1956 National Exhibition of Concrete Art, which took place at the Museum of Modern Art in São Paulo and then, in 1957, at the Ministry of Education, in Rio de Janeiro.

The National Exhibition of Concrete Art gathered visual artists and poets such as Wlademir Dias-Pino, Ferreira Gullar, Décio Pignatari, Ronaldo Azeredo, Haroldo de Campos and Augusto de Campos. It didn't actually present a collective manifesto for concrete poetry. It was the news media that, in a reaction to the exhibition, assembled individual testimonies and presented them as a group. Therefore, in a sense, the first actual collective manifesto for concrete poetry – or, at least, the movement's first collective statements and political manifestations – appeared in the article 'Poetry's Rock and Roll' by Luís Edgar de Andrade, published in the *O Cruzeiro* newspaper on March 2, 1957, as well as in testimonies collected and published by Reynaldo Jardim in the Sunday edition of the *Jornal do Brasil* newspaper during the exhibition's first anniversary celebrations. The collective manifesto, 'Pilot Plan for Concrete Poetry' – which echoed both the announcement of the Contest for the Creation of the Pilot Plan for Brasilia that appeared in the Official Gazette of Brazil on September 30, 1956, and the 'Pilot Plan for Brasilia Report', published by Lúcio Costa in the 8th edition of the *Módulo* magazine in 1957 – would only appear in 1958 as a way to distance Décio Pignatari, Haroldo de Campos and Augusto de Campos from the other founders of the movement. Ronaldo Azeredo, although supportive of the group, did not sign the 'Pilot Plan'.

While most of the poems exhibited at the National Exhibition of Concrete Art were composed exclusively with words, Wlademir Dias-Pino exhibited his ultra-radical work *Solida*, a codified poem with many different versions, ranging from the typographic-verbal to the statistic-graphical, and employing new intersemiotic procedures, renouncing even words themselves. In *A ave* [The bird] (1953-1956), available for purchase at the Rio de Janeiro exhibition, Dias-Pino also employed an intersemiotic procedure: the poem's syntax derived from an ordinal numeral sequence. Dias-Pino's new composing processes – syntaxes derived from non-verbal coding, manipulable poems, the production of different versions and series, the use of boxes (and other forms) as alternative to books, wordless poems, the use of silkscreen and other printing processes for the making of non-typographical poems – had a profound influence on Brazilian experimental poetry. Years later, they would serve as theoretical foundation for his 1968 *poema/processo* [poem/process] movement.

At the end of the 1950s, however, the first new movement to arise from the split within the concrete poetry founders

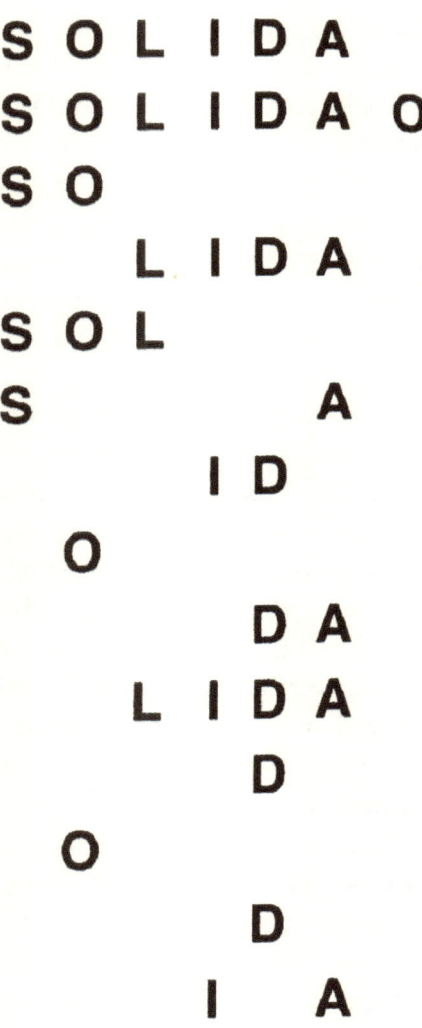

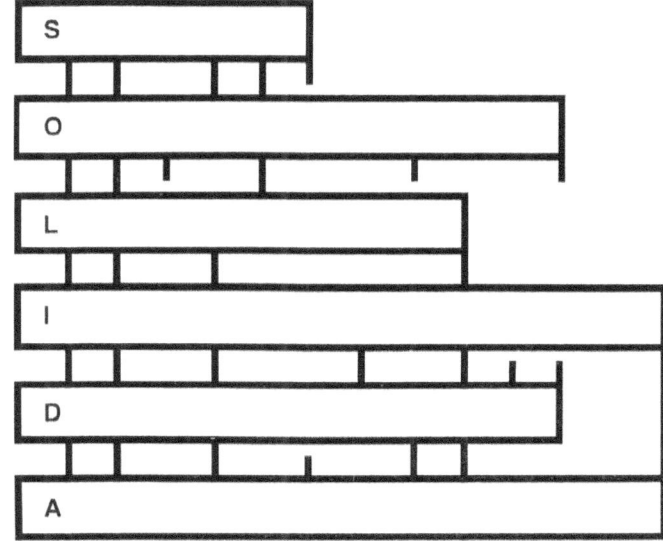

was Neoconcretism in 1959. Led by poets Ferreira Gullar e Reynaldo Jardim and by visual artists such as Hélio Oiticica and Lygia Clark, Neoconcretism engaged in a productive conversation with literature and the visual arts. Between 1959 and 1962, Gullar produced a number of poems that were also tridimensional objects. Requiring the reader's active involvement, they had been labelled 'non-objects' [*não-objetos*] by Gullar. These poems had to be activated by the participant in a physical and tactile way in order to be read. For example, his neo-concrete poem *Lembra* [Remember] (1959) consists of a square wooden plate in the centre of which rests a cube, partially contained inside a square hole. By taking out the cube, the reader sees the word *lembra* at the bottom. The act of putting the cube back into its place and consequently losing visual access to the word, an act of uncovering and covering again, receives a semantic charge and a linguistic function, indicative of the acts of remembering and forgetting. This revolutionary interactive poetry would undergo further evolutions through the neo-concrete movement, for example, in the 1962 electric poem by Albertus Marques in which electrical devices must be activated by the reader to reveal, through a light source, words inscribed on a surface.

One of the first book-poems dates as far back as 1960: the poem *Organismo* [Organism] by Décio Pignatari (1977). The poem represents a rupture with the usual form of simply putting a poem on a page; instead, the poem is activated by the act of manipulation, the consecutive turning of the pages. The poem only happens if the reader skims the book's eight pages, through which Pignatari highlights the visual potential of letters and words, charging them with a strong erotic connotation by repeating the letter 'O', which becomes bigger and bigger until it exceeds the boundaries of the paper.

In the 4th edition of *Invenção* magazine from December 1964, Pignatari and Luis A. Pinto published a manifesto for 'semiotic poetry'. The progress thus achieved by the poets – carrying forth the intersemiotic poetics inaugurated by Wlademar Dias-Pino's *Solida* and *A ave* – was of foremost importance, as it made possible for poetry produced with new codes or even unconnected to any specific idiom to become autonomous. For the poets, it wasn't about decreeing the end of poetic explorations in already existing languages, but rather about asserting their continuous preoccupation with inventing new forms of poetic production, since new contents are always forcefully tied to new forms of expression. They are inseparable. In their manifesto, the poets didn't fail to mention the pioneering influence of Dias-Pino's *Solida*, who later in the decade would affirm himself as one of the most innovative Brazilian poets ever.

In 1962, Dias-Pino, together with Manuel Bandeira, published the box-poem *Solida*, which, just as in its 1950 instances, required the reader's physical manipulation. Augusto de Campos, in an article published in the literature section of *O Estado de S. Paulo* newspaper in 1966, stands by

Décio Pignatari's words published in *Invenção,* highlighting the poem's revolutionary elements:

> The *Poema Espacional* [Spational Poem] consists of nine words extracted from a single word-core ('solida') [solid]: 1) 'solidão' [solitude], 2) 'só' [alone], 3) 'lida' [past tense of read], 4) 'sol' [the sun], 5) 'saído' [left], 6) 'da' [from, feminine], 7) 'lida' [day-to-day labour], 8) 'do' [from, masculine], 9) 'dia' [day]. As we can see, the words are connected by a syntactical link. In the first version, after being presented as a set, the words were replaced letter by letter with punched or drawn holes and circles, connected by dashes. In the second version, published as an unfolding poem-pamphlet in 1957, the words were exchanged with punctuation signs (commas) throughout the poem. The third and final version of *Poema Espacional* would then result in the group of texts named 'solida' by Wlademir. Its presentation is revolutionary. Instead of a book, it is a box containing forty cards. Words were used only in the first two. In the first card, the word 'solida' and its nine derivations appear in the same structural order as the previous versions (the same letters aligned in vertical stripes). In the second card, only the core word appears; the letters of the other words were replaced with commas (as in the poem's second version); in the third and fourth versions, traces, curves and circles substitute for the words. This is followed by five series of nine cards each, each card reserved for a single word; the circles and traces, in blue or in red, gradually free themselves from the primitive positional primitive structure in order to recode the letters in new geometrical and arbitrary signs. The first page thus operates as a key for all the other variations. (Campos 1966)

Wlademir is a cybernetic poet. His work *A ave* presented new informational-aesthetic possibilities for poetic creation, and *Solida* is organised according to probabilistic logic. The poem 'automatically allows for the employment of graphics since the positions occupied by its signs are a statistic of their use: a bar code-statistic-version' (Dias-Pino 1972). Wlademir's body of research, which called for the need to build machines to make the reading of certain poems possible, would become more accessible after the publication of a retrospective of his work by the Language Department of the Federal University of Mato Grosso do Sul (Dias-Pino 1982).

In 1964, while Pignatari was talking about poems with lexical keys, Augusto de Campos produced the poem *Olho por olho* [An eye for an eye] (1979), which represented another step towards the autonomy of purely visual language. This poem – nicknamed *'Baboeil'* by Haroldo de Campos – was the result of a collage of eyes and mouths in an unexpected inter-relationship, through which iconic signs were symbolically contextualised. In 1963, against all expectations concerning concrete poets' aversion to verbose writing, Haroldo de Campos begins to write *Galáxias* [Galaxies], a work in-between poetry and prose that he would only finish ten years later. Following Mallarmé's motto that 'fiction will bloom and then vanish, swiftly, keeping pace with the mobility of the written word', Haroldo produced a book centred around its own textuality, a semantic expansion that didn't take long to leave behind the initial traces of its own self-referentiality....

During the late 1950s and the early 1960s, with the emergence of a new and fertile pull in concrete poetry towards visuality and the appearance of neo-concrete poetry which introduced the interactive kinesthesis of non-objects, the poet Mário Chamic began to develop the theory of *Poesia Práxis* [Praxis Poetry] and to nurture the individual development of many poets who followed his thinking. In 1961, Chamic published a didactic manifesto for *Poesia Práxis*, outlining its foundations: '*poema praxis* is the poem that aesthetically organises and assembles a situated reality according to three conditions for action: a) the compositional act; b) the survey area of the composition; c) the act of consuming' (Chamic 1961, 21).

For Chamic, the 'black space', the 'intercommunicating mobility of the words' and 'the internal support of meaning' were crucial. The poet's theory explains these elements of the poem's composition. The black space should be understood in opposition to Mallarmé's symbolic white space, which was adopted and defended by the concrete poets. Chamic wanted to focus on the words themselves, as a set that physiognomically formed the poem: 'the block that resulted from the juxtaposition, superposition and connections between these words and lines constitutes the external and visual structure of the praxis poem' (Chamic 1963, 14). The intercommunicating mobility implies the impossibility of autonomous words within the poem. Each word must maintain a plural and continuous relationship with each other to make possible their unfolding into other words as well as the emergence of new semantic relations derived from their internal dynamic. The internal support of meaning, in turn, refers to the act of identifying 'decisive vectors' within the poem, that is, words that, due to their pivotal importance in the making of the poem, appear by means of their 'pronounced phonetic features', thus mobilising both semantic and structural fields....

Poetry and politics have always walked hand in hand. The work of poet José Paulo Paes is exemplary of a poetic production marked by explicit political concerns, grounded in the investigation and pursuit of his own authentic language under the confessed influence of Oswald de Andrade upon his epigrammatic production. Paes' short, precise and clarifying commentary on Brazilian politics is worth listening to: 'It's worth noting that it was Concrete Poetry that first showed interest in a formal revolution of political Brazilian poetry. In its conciseness, it found a more efficient kind of slogan, one compatible with billboards. If we were to write one of those fat baroque poems from [the anthologies of political poems] *Violão de Rua* [Street Guitar] on the street, we would need a wall as big and large as the Dutra highway' (Paes 1977).

Emerging from the core political discussions about poetic creation, based on some of the proposals and achievements of Wlademir Dias-Pino's work, the *process/poem* movement spread nationwide in 1967. New poets, among them Álvaro de Sá and Moacy Cirne, gathered around the theories and results achieved by Dias-Pino. Wlademir used to say that we must 'startle others through radicality itself', and so emerged process/poem, which radicalised what Dias-Pino had accomplished with *A ave* and *Solida*. Process/poem was a planned movement with a programmed lifespan, existing only from 1967 until 1972, when a 'tactical halt' took place.

Wlademir, in fact, had ventured across the most fertile terrains of the avant-garde. As he wrote: 'Process/Poem; awareness of the new languages by creating and manipulating them in a dynamic way, thus founding new creative probabilities. By utterly emphasising the reading of the poem's arrangement (instead of an alphabetic reading), one can deploy words in a methodical way in order to achieve a universal language – notwithstanding its Brazilian origins – without any kind of regionalism, aspiring to universality not in a strictly humanistic sense but rather in a functional one' (Dias-Pino 1971, 6). Against Mallarmé's motto that poetry is made with words instead of ideas, Wlademir stated that poems were made with processes instead of words. However, his wasn't a thorough rejection of the word. He tried, on the contrary, to avoid already codified uses of the vocabulary and thus attempted to explore new possibilities, including graphic-visual ones.

The process/poem movement wanted, therefore, to launch new theoretical proposals: it opposed poetry to the poem by principle, so that there was no process/poetry but rather a process/*poem*. Rooted in its functionality, the poem should be understood as a product to be consumed. Poetry would take place in the realm of language, meaning that poetry would be committed to the word, while the poem could still emerge in the form of a project, able to evoke different versions/readings in the audience/reader. This notion of a version, which would also be largely used in mail art, was adopted by the process/poem poets in opposition to the idea of translation, which implied recreating poems conceived in a language other than the one into which the poem would be translated. They also understood that, in poetry, there would be room for style, understood as a predictable range of probable options that followed each poets' paradigmatic choices. In the process/poem, meanwhile, poets were free from this 'ghost' thanks to the notion of a 'counter-style:' that is, the singular unfolding of the materiality intrinsic to each poem, to each problem-situation faced by the poet.

... Regarding the creation of new languages, some of the most interesting process/poems were the ones created collectively as *happenings*. In 1968, process/poem poets organised a symbolic protest ritual, a collective poem in which they tore apart books written by discursive poets, thus expressing not only a radical action against discourse in its ideological-aesthetic implications, but also a protest against the audience's silence and stupefaction regarding the young movement. Two years later, in the city of Olinda, the poets produced a two-metre-long poem-bread in all its semiological implications; the poem-bread was literally swallowed collectively and in public, on the streets (Dias-Pino 1971). One should also note the positive influence of comic books on the process/poem: not only on the pioneering *9x12*, by Álvaro de Sá, but also on the entirety of the process/poem production that was permeated by compositional elements taken from this powerful mass cultural language, such as the subdivision into frames and the exploration of onomatopoeia and of the speech bubble, among other verbal-visual means. In a time ruled by censorship, when the liberatory power of the word was being repressed, the process/poem emerged as an extra-literary poetic frontier capable of advancing experimental art without the need for words.

In 1967, as the process/poem was emerging, the 3rd Brazilian Popular Music Festival aired on *TV Record*, in São Paulo, presenting songs such as Caetano Veloso's *'Alegria, alegria'* [*Joy, joy*] and Gilberto Gil's *'Domingo no parque'* [*Sunday in the park*], thus paving the way for what later would be largely recognised as the Tropicália or Tropicalism movement. Both songs were ranked mildly in the festival but generated enormous controversy due to their strange combination of lyrics driven by chaotic numbering principles and cinematographic montage with disconcerting musical arrangements, not to mention the unexpected use of electric guitars. The audience, consisting mostly of so-called leftist college students, habitually demanded that composers should convey political-ideological 'messages' in their lyrics and disregarded the importance of melodies. One of Tropicalism's most important ruptures, alluding to a practice familiar to medieval troubadours, was the precise harmonisation between words and melody, producing a hybrid unity in which neither could be regarded in isolation, but only in their mutual relation.

In one of his most famous interviews, Caetano Veloso defined with precision the context that produced Tropicalism: 'Gil and I were busting with new ideas. We had spent a fair amount of time trying to learn the grammar of this new language we would use, and we wanted to test our ideas with the audience. We worked whole nights together with Torquato Neto, Gal [Costa], Rogério Duprat and others. At the same time, we kept in touch with artists from other areas such as Glauber Rocha, José Celso Martinez, Hélio Oiticica and Rubens Gerchman. From this mixture Tropicalism was born, as an attempt to overcome our underdevelopment as a country by using precisely what our culture regarded as "bad taste", mixing it with cutting-edge industrial elements such as electric guitars and plastic clothing. I can't deny what I have read, nor can I forget where I live' (Favaretto 1979, 12-13).

Tropicalism, therefore, was born from the profound contradiction that is Brazilian modernity, torn between technological advancement and increasing underdevelopment. Translating this into a generalising allegory: Tropicalism brought out a carnivalising vision of the world that had to do with the technical mastery of language, both verbal and musical, something akin to Oswald de Andrade's 'technicised barbarian', whose appearance would represent one of the main pillars of the movement's foundations (even though Caetano composed his song 'Tropicália' before watching the play *O rei da vela* [The king of the candle], which was his first encounter with Oswald de Andrade's writings). Even though Oswald was certainly the one who most influenced Tropicalism due to the humanistic scope of his anthropophagic ideas, it should be noted that film montage and chaotic enumeration techniques were already present among our modernists in [the Modern Art Week of] 1922 through the pioneering writings of Luis Aranha....

By diluting the national-populist ideology of its time, Tropicália inaugurated Brazilian counterculture, even though many of its members had industrial ties with mass-consumption, represented European and North American influences and were well informed about sexual freedom, drugs, *rock n' roll*, going crazy, lack of ideological compromise, psychoanalysis and other important aspects of the new sensibility. With the arrest of Caetano and Gil in 1968, the AI-5 coup and their London exile in the following year, Tropicalism came to an end as a programmatic movement (although this end had already occurred as satire in a performance where its members symbolically buried the movement). Even still, the pull of these *baianos* [people from the state of Bahia] towards the Oswaldian motto 'to see with free eyes' had a profound impact on Brazilian culture and reverberated in many social spheres, especially in the attitude of that entire generation....

Chapter 9

Two Lines of Contribution: Concretists in São Paulo / Neo-Concretists in Rio (1977)

Aracy Amaral

It's important to note that Rio de Janeiro's concrete artists, although always in contact with one another, dedicated themselves to an intuitive artistic investigation, while the artists from São Paulo, right from the start, were inclined to a more dogmatic attitude, which culminated in a kind of schematisation of expressive processes and values. During the *I National Exhibition of Concrete Art* (1956-1957), the difference between those two groups proved to be flagrant. The exhibition displayed the first experiments made by the concrete poets who, in turn, also represented two different views of creative work: the trio of Augusto de Campos, Haroldo de Campos and Décio Pignatari, from São Paulo, occupied the same rationalist, objectivist position as the painters led by Waldemar Cordeiro. Later, a manifesto signed by Reynaldo Jardim, Oliveira Bastos and myself, published in the *Jornal do Brasil* Sunday pages (23-6-1957), made explicit the distinction between the concrete poets from São Paulo and those from Rio de Janeiro. The latter represented, in opposition to São Paulo's dogmatism, a non-dogmatic position, recentring intuition as the focus of poetic labour.

– *Ferreira Gullar, 1959*

The enriching revelation of Ferreira Gullar's study was without the shadow of a doubt the possibility of clearly distinguishing the difference in attitude between the concrete groups from São Paulo and Rio de Janeiro. This made it possible to acknowledge their valuable contributions to the development of arts and visual communication in the country. It's hard to write about the concrete/neo-concrete schism without repeating what has already been said, perceived and analysed by an exceptional personality such as Gullar, an important theoretician of the constructive tendencies in Brazil and a disciple of critic Mário Pedrosa, who during the 1950s was the biggest promoter of constructivism among us.

Effectively, since Max Bill's exhibition at the São Paulo Art Museum, artists from São Paulo such as [Waldemar] Cordeiro and [Luiz] Sacilotto abandoned Mondrian and the neoplasticism that had inspired their first steps in geometrical abstraction around 1949 (very bad steps, by the way). They were moving on to other kinds of artistic speculation, on infinite space, formal innovation, serial works, modulated works and, in the case of Sacilotto as well as in the first years of [Alexandre] Wollner, on both virtual and real forms, on figure-ground ambiguity, etc. This took place right before the São Paulo group 'discovered' the geometric-abstract works by Swiss artists, which were about to be shown at the I São Paulo Art Biennial. The impact left by the Swiss delegation was such that almost immediately everyone abandoned oil painting and, inspired by the Swiss, started painting over *eucatex* fibre boards, resorting to enamel and gradually switching the brush for the spray gun, thus avoiding not only materials associated with artisanal work but also their manipulation in favour of a more industrial process.

In truth, it seems to me that the obvious difference between the São Paulo and the Rio groups would be better situated within the realism versus idealism debate.

Ortega y Gasset's famous words, 'I am myself and my circumstances', are clearly expressed in the São Paulo group's ties to industry, technology and the application of the artist's work in practical, everyday life ('art as product', as stated in the manifesto written by Cordeiro in 1956).

Unsurprisingly, the São Paulo group published their manifesto in a magazine called *Arquitetura e Decoração* [Architecture and Interior Design]. They had access both to the visual design and the local architecture and advertising sectors. If we were to list the artists who participated in the São Paulo movement, we could easily see the ties of every single one of them (with the exception of Judith Lauand and [Lothar] Charoux) with the city's business roles: industrial chemist, technical draughtsman, advertiser, architect, landscape designer, graphic designer, illustrator, textile industrial designer, poster designer, photographer, colour etcher, news designer, shop window dresser, industrial designer. Those are the professional occupations in which they made a living and which they continued to practise during the hot years of the concrete art debate as well as after the concrete wave. Even the two artists from São Paulo who would later join Rio's neoconcrete movement, Willys de Castro and [Hércules] Barsotti, had similar ties to the industrial world: they made artworks in parallel to their occupation in graphic design, branding and the textile industry. Frequently, as in the case of Waldemar Cordeiro, paintings from the São Paulo group illustrated their ideas and hypotheses. The one exception was Sacilotto, who expressed himself fundamentally through painting but with the noticeable rigour of a technical illustrator.

In fact, the whole São Paulo group came from the middle and lower-middle classes. Some (such as [Hermelindo] Fiaminghi and Sacilotto) received their education in technical schools, while others (like Wollner, Maluf, Maurício Nogueira Lima and Geraldo de Barros) took the new courses available at the then young São Paulo Art Museum. Cordeiro, already in his 1956 manifesto, refers to art not as 'expression' but rather as 'product', the 'object of an expression'. He also mentions that 'art distinguishes itself from pure thought by being material, and from everyday things by being pure thought', connecting reason to materiality in the making of the artistic object. That, however, didn't prevent him from expressing his notion of art as 'objects that have historical value to the social life of people'. Ultimately, Cordeiro's manifesto displays a clear realist tendency ('the idea of productive art is a deathblow to idealism') and seeks to integrate the artist into social development, since the new art 'emancipates art from the inferior and dependent condition to which it had been relegated' (Cordeiro 1956).

We must not forget that this was a politicised generation, which emerged from the atmosphere preceding both World War II and Brazil's institutional liberation. The country went through euphoric development after the war, with coffee prices rising globally, an influx of capital investments, new communication media, the new automobile industry and new labour markets. This euphoria would culminate in the construction of Brasília. This created favourable circumstances for the participation of artists in the emerging society. The artist passes from environmental decorator to a potential 'builder of a new world'. To some degree, the atmosphere was comparable to that enjoyed by the Russian constructivists.

In Rio, on the other hand, there was no dogmatism (which in São Paulo had resulted from Cordeiro's leadership). Additionally, as noted by Gullar, there was a certain respect for individual autonomy, for working in isolation, for the pure investigation detached from the kind of utilitarianism that characterised the research pursued by the São Paulo group. Unlike those in São Paulo, the artists from Rio – or their neo-concrete allies – had no occupational ties with the industry (apart from Amilcar de Castro, designer at *Jornal do Brasil*, and [Abraham] Palatnik, who was neither concrete nor neo-concrete, despite his solidarity with the latter group, and with their new experiments). They came from middle and upper-middle classes and were never absorbed by the professional market. Working individually, the artists from Rio, such as Lygia Clark, [Hélio] Oiticica, Lygia Pape, and even Amilcar de Castro, [Franz] Weissmann or [Manoel] Serpa, never aspired, like those from São Paulo, to become part of a new, 'revolutionary' social agenda. They did not expect the artist to fulfil a new role either. They made art and experimented. As Ferreira Gullar reminds us, the contribution of the Rio de Janeiro group was to foster a relationship with the environment, anticipating the opening to the 'pop' object that would take place in the 1960s (1969), by breaking the artwork out from its traditional space[35] and embedding it organically into real space by means of the artwork's mobility. This was especially true for Lygia Clark, whose work moved through total formal freedom, towards the rupture of the picture frame and its subsequent integration into real space. This breakthrough liberated her work from the virtual plane, to which the São Paulo group remained tethered despite the 'scientism' with which they dressed up their production.

While São Paulo sculptors made sculptures, its painters remained stuck in the two dimensions of the picture frame. In Rio, in turn, there were artistic explorations such as Lygia Clark's, who went from painting to reliefs, from reliefs to non-objects, from non-objects to *trepantes* and, from there, through *corpotacto* [bodytouch] experiences, to non-art, self-expression and the total coupling between artist and the enveloping reality. The same trajectory could describe Oiticica's or Lygia Pape's work some years later: an opening up to the surrounding environment, going from object to body and then to the relationship with the other and to film (Pape), or to the labyrinths, the spoken word, writings and recordings (Oiticica); just as Ferreira Gullar went from poem to word, then to 'buried poem', to book-poem, to revisions and to the participating life-poem, until his exile.

Amílcar de Castro, who worked in isolation, would achieve the 'minimal' before this concept even existed. In 1959, working with primary structures, he produced fashionable pieces that would only be exhibited in New York in 1966. That's a common affliction in Latin America: it also happened to [Mathias] Goeritz, in Mexico, who, like Amílcar, produced minimal pieces in 1957, before the North American art market was aware of the style. Only in the 1960s Goeritz's work began to be featured in North American anthologies (from which Amílcar's work is still absent). The same also happened to Fiaminghi, who since 1959 explored reticules, before or at the same time as Lichtenstein, but was only able to bring his work to life in 1962, through lithographic processes, whereas [Alain] Jacquet, coming from France, would only bring this experience to the São Paulo Biennial in 1966...

The possibility of new experiments came more naturally to the artists from Rio, as an evolution of their work. In São Paulo, this possibility was not so much related to the artists' processes as to the knowledge that came from abroad, especially through biennials. That was the case with works by Waldemar Cordeiro, Geraldo de Barros and Mauricio Nogueira Lima. Others, such as Charoux, Judite Lauand and Fejer, were less responsive to the new trends, not to mention Sacilotto, who would never return to the figurative work he abandoned in 1949.

In Rio, however, all through the 1950s, there was no interest in 'production processes'. In São Paulo, as keenly noted by Ana Maria Belluzo, this interest certainly stemmed from the artists' professional experience and was applied to art by keeping elements to a minimum, by the organisation of space and by how colour was used: 'art is therefore not an expression but a product', as Cordeiro says.

This systematisation of work allows us to understand, to some extent, why the São Paulo group accepted the dogmatic and theoretical leadership of Cordeiro, even though Fiaminghi would cut all ties to him in an open letter from June 1959, when the dissolution of the group began.

If the general contribution made by the neo-concretists from Rio seems denser with creativity and possibilities for experimentation – as seen in the work of Lygia Clark, Amílcar de Castro and Weissmann – that doesn't mean we should disregard the achievements of the concretists from São Paulo, who were impacted by Max Bill and by the ideas of the Ulm School of Design, which were more akin to São Paulo's industrial atmosphere. In fact, [Almir da Silva] Mavignier and Mary Vieira, two among the 14 artists who came from Rio in 1950s to see Max Bill's exhibition at the São Paulo Art Museum, went off to Europe right afterwards, and would only return to Brazil as tourists, having had no participation in the country's constructive movement. São Paulo's contribution is clearly noticeable in industrial furniture design as well as in the creation of the Design Department of the School of Architecture and Urban Planning of the University of São Paulo, in the production of posters, in advertising, in brand logos that the group would produce later in the decade, in landscape design and even in textile printing.

In Rio, oddly, no neo-concrete artist was absorbed professionally or proceeded to work in the areas of design, graphic arts, landscape or industrial design, save for the already mentioned exceptions. Quite the contrary: the Design School of the Rio de Janeiro State University (ESDI/UERJ) was built in 1962 based on a project conceived by Maldonado, a concrete artist from Argentina who moved to Ulm and, by 1958, was already running the school founded by Max Bill. ESDI's inaugural teaching body included, among others, Décio Pignatari and [Karl Heinz] Bergmiller. The former was part of the concrete poetry movement from São Paulo and the latter an industrial designer from Ulm who came here encouraged by Wollner (who at this point was already reintegrated in São Paulo as a graphic designer, after four years of studying at the Superior School of Form).

Another thing that confirms the diversity and recognition of the contributions from the artists from Rio, such as Weissmann, Amílcar and Lygia Clark, is the prestige their work has enjoyed in the art market, featuring in private collections even in São Paulo. Artists from São Paulo from the same generation did not receive the same prestige. Their work is still, for the most part, kept in their authors' homes. It may be strange to highlight this difference since, as the Brazilian art market is so small, one cannot attribute it to an overdedication of the art dealers from Rio. The most active dealers operate simultaneously in both cities.[36]

Uninterested in changing an all-too-complex reality, the group from Rio would travel the path of purely aesthetic speculation, while the group from São Paulo – and Mary Vieira – wanted to adapt Brazilian reality to Swiss standards, standards that could never survive in Brazil due to the precariousness of its industrialisation and the instability of its satellite economy. Though they yearned for rigour, the concrete works of the São Paulo group could not achieve Swiss precision either in concept or in it realisation. The group's perfectionist aspirations can be noted, however, in their attempt to come closer to industrial processes. But even Geraldo de Barros would state, in an interview about industrial design, that the Brazilian expectations in that area border on the unrealistic: 'It's useless to produce something the audience doesn't want to buy. They want plastic trinkets, period. What can I do? Shut down my factory? Make Italian glass of fine design? Nobody wants it!'. Then he adds: 'Décio Pignatari also said it: "if the market wants glasses with little flowers, it's useless to make glasses with little squares, since it's a market phenomenon"'. Additionally, Geraldo de Barros stated:

> I don't believe in industrial design in countries such as Brazil, because I think that industrial design comes from the evolution of the people, from culture. Thus, you can find popular industrial design in socialist countries: Sweden, Denmark, Norway, England, Germany. These countries have already reached a high level of socialisation. There's no industrial design in Russia or in the USA. In the USA, you can't find it because of the damned 'marketing', so there's no way they can have industrial design. There are exceptions, of course, but they are not the rule. The American car was a symbol of 'styling', of 'marketing'. But in comparison to a European car, such as the Mercedes, it has a much poorer design'. (Barros 1976)

In a very bitter article from 1961, Décio Pignatari would document the twofold artistic practice of the São Paulo group, noting that their 'professional occupation' was characterised by the same lycanthropian hybridism as any other production technique in an underdeveloped country: half-artisanal, half-industrial. The same applies to their art. 'That certainly doesn't invalidate the quality of their work', he adds, '[which is] generally of a good standard – whether in one area or another'. However, while they were performing their 'professional duties, most artists kept producing paintings, sculptures and drawings. For them, there is an intermittent museum, one that gives them the illusion of being active and relevant: the Biennial'. Yet, Décio Pignatari acknowledges that even the 'creative aptitude of the concrete artists, hesitating between an insufficient pragmatism that dares not say its name and a diligent and interesting yet scarce theoretical basis, elaborated and *à la diable*, could not take advantage of the right information at the right time, and got therefore carried away by the tachist torrent'.[37]

In summary, the pragmatism of the *paulistas* ran the show in São Paulo, just as the sensorial appeal of the *carioca* freedom led to more intense forms of self-expression in Rio. The exciting moment of 'internationalist information/development euphoria' that attracted the artists in São Paulo could perhaps be interpreted through Mario de Andrade's statement about Anita Malfatti's exhibition from 1917, which clearly describes the difference between the two cities: 'in the mischievous Rio, an exhibition such as Anita's could generate spontaneous publicity, but nobody really gave in to it. In São Paulo, a city devoid of malice, it produced a new religion'. This is also what seems to have happened regarding the contact with the Argentinians,[38] Max Bill's individual exhibition at MASP and the impactful Swiss participation in the 1st Biennial and to the constitution of the São Paulo group under the intellectual leadership of Waldemar Cordeiro, in opposition to the expressiveness of the movement in Rio.

Chapter 10

The New Possibilities (1977)

Walter Zanini

Many artists have answered the call from the Museum of Contemporary Art of the University of São Paulo (MAC-USP) to take part in this exhibition, which aims to represent a new opportunity of encounter for those who work in international multimedia circles. Meaningful support continues to arrive from all the world, from Latin America, Eastern Europe, North America and Western Europe, and its presence is as meaningful as the presence of invited Brazilian artists. Only a few people, interpreting the *Poéticas* [poetics] in the title of this exhibition in the strict aesthetic sense of the word, or mistaking it for questions particular to Visual Poetry, have abstained from contributing. The dialogue between MAC-USP and the artists working in the field of alternative communications in its broadest sense has grown steadily over recent years, turning the present exhibition into a one-of-a-kind experience in the whole hemisphere that shows continued trust in this university museum.

Seeking to survey the activity of artists and art organisations that communicate chiefly across inter-individual circuits or whose work – with some exceptions – may have difficulty overcoming their limited environments, the exhibition *Poéticas Visuais* [Visual Poetics] focuses, therefore, on the many media that, interchangeably or simultaneously, employ both images and words. The exhibition presents a vast sample of the technical resources currently used by artists, educates us on the range of explorations taking place in the field of intersemiotics, reveals new structural investigations into the word and the image, and confronts the creativity of a practice/theorisation not yet subjected to the circumstances of traditional art. Among the many media here represented, there is a decisive presence of publications, including dense anthologies. The 'artist's book' figures prominently. Together with some of the most relevant individuals in international art, the show also features unknown artists, some who were brought along by the invited artists. Signs of a perhaps too scattered set of participants should not prevent us from observing the existence of many diversified coordinates of artistic inquiry. Though a certain dispersion indeed exists, it should be regarded as important and inevitable evidence of the emerging phenomenon that characterises our decade and points decidedly towards the future.

The *Poéticas Visuais* exhibition will have an odd look and feel. The audience will be able to acquire a photocopy of almost all documents presented here, thus transforming this exhibition into a portable one as well.

Chapter II
International Multimedia (1979)

Walter Zanini

Many artists whose outputs represent the most poignant aspects of today's cultural phenomenology have left a deep mark on the 1970s by highlighting the semantic aspects of their work. Overcoming the old discussion about aesthetic subjectivity in art, the contribution made by such activism took place by means of unlimited ways of approaching reality and taking advantage of present-day technological society's ample operational resources. The domain of multimedia has become an advanced field of language; its results never cease to surprise us, to stimulate our imagination and to make us believe in new and revealing developments. Multimedia's inherent critical nature and their participative qualities constitute two essential values of the universalistic process they embody, through an awareness of their methods and freedom. Thus, a conflicting situation was automatically generated when multimedia's transformative presence confronted traditional art models.

By exploring interdisciplinary structures, the context of new media has expanded and associated its signs with the tense flow of everyday life. It's an attitude of commitment that provoked in various countries the emergence of authentic communities of artists, creators of their own artistic circuits, displaying a *modus operandi* inseparable from the content of their messages. Such organising forces, closely tied to historical precedents, are always searching for the most conclusive contemporaneity. A partial though ample glance at this cultural movement was precisely the goal of this exhibition at the School of Communication and Art of the University of São Paulo, planned and produced thanks to the intelligent and hard work of students from various departments (Radio and TV, Visual Arts, Journalism and Film).

After the many national and international exhibitions promoted by the University's Museum of Contemporary Art at the end of this decade, and by merging with other struggling endeavours all around the country, especially in the city of Recife, it was possible to achieve an exemplary mobilisation of more than 200 artists from all over the world. Our goals are not restricted to the creation of this isolated event, but also encompass the creation of an indispensable centre for multimedia activities. Such an initiative was the work of our young generation, a fact deeply significant in and of itself.

II

Social Communication Systems

Chapter 12

Social Communication Systems

Gabriel Menotti and German Alfonso Nunez

Brazil's late modernisation process would soon be hijacked by a bloody military-civil dictatorship, which ruled the country from 1964 to 1985. At the time, at the height of the Cold War, many countries in South and Central America were controlled by similar authoritarian governments backed by the United States. It was a dark period, characterised by the curtailing of civil liberties, institutional rigging, widespread censorship and state violence. In the hands of the military, the country acquired a taste for social conservatism and anti-communist paranoia. In a push for a unified country, electronic media such as radio and TV took centre stage, with nationwide broadcasting being subject to mass censorship and employed as the chief vehicle for official propaganda and the promotion of a more compliant mass culture.

The first computer art exhibition of Latin America opened in São Paulo in 1969, amidst the worst days of the Brazilian dictatorship – our *anos de chumbo*, or 'years of lead'. Entitled *Computer Plotter Art*, the show had been put together by the American Consulate of São Paulo and the United States Information Agency (USIA) as a way to promote US computing industries in the country. One could go as far as to say that it was organised more like a technical showroom than an art exhibition. The majority of the participants were US engineers, whose work involved plotted drawings of mathematical visualisations typical of early computer art. The most conventional artist in the event was also the only Brazilian: Waldemar Cordeiro, who used to be a figurehead amongst concretist painters of São Paulo in the 1950s. Cordeiro was a last-minute addition, though. The artist himself seized the opportunity to show his computer artworks by offering them to the exhibition organisers (Nunez 2020).

Although minor both in its size and conceptual scope, *Computer Plotter Art* had some interesting repercussions in the Brazilian art world, mostly because it had Cordeiro's name attached to it. In the following months, the show would travel to the Museum of Modern of Rio de Janeiro, where it was accompanied by a seminar led by Cordeiro. This created some popular interest in computer art, which resulted in a couple of articles in the local press. But that wasn't all. The momentum generated by *Computer Plotter Art* would lead to another exhibition, spearheaded by Cordeiro in 1971: *Arteônica*. Held at the Brazilian Art Museum of FAAP, a private elite university in São Paulo, *Arteônica* presented the first artworks made with computers in the country. It would also have featured an international seminar with leading pioneers in the area from the US, UK and Germany, but it was apparently cancelled due to a lack of resources. The show materialised concretists' interest in cybernetics, systems theory and algorithmic composition with a cosmopolitan, international outlook. It could also be seen as the crowning of Cordeiro's bold vision for electronic art. In the catalogue text, Cordeiro framed the crisis of contemporary arts in terms of their restricted informational capacity. While denouncing the 'hedonistic' tendency of computer art towards technical virtuosity, he praised its unparalleled ability to attend to the global scale and complexity of communication in modern society (Cordeiro 1972). In sum, *Arteônica* was international in scope, programmatic and exalting a whole new kind of generative art with Brazil at the centre. Unfortunately, that was as far as Brazilian computer art would go for a while. The tragic passing of Cordeiro at the age of 48 and the continuing lack of access to computers in the country would deter the development of similar experiments for almost two decades.[39]

Meanwhile, Brazilian counterculture flourished. For many artists, the sheer celebration of modernity was no longer enough. The new political reality called for a revision of old positions and the invention of more socially engaged practices. This led to a reaction against the use of new technologies in the arts. Following similar movements elsewhere in the West (Goodyear 2008; Taylor 2014), technology came to be seen as a proxy of the military-industrial complex: alienating and dehumanising. Concretism was framed as dogmatic or, even worse, reactionary (Brito 1999). Many concretists abandoned the largely abstract, cool formalism of the past in favour of some more nuanced forms of rationality. Emerging artists, such as Hélio Oiticica (Rio de Janeiro, 1937-1980), advocated for a poetics based on the body, gestures and subjectivity, which had been taboo for the previous generation.

The second section of *Barbarian Currents* delves into this era to explore the rise of multiple media arts practices, against the backdrop of a renaissance in neoexpressionist painting, powered by the growing art market (Canongia 2010). In the previous decades, most Brazilian artists who flirted with new technologies evoked the esotericism of computers as a means towards a more rational poetics. Now, in the military years, artists began to experiment with a much broader range of tools, exploring their uses as social systems and interactive platforms. The avant-garde aesthetics of concretism would even find its way into rock'n'roll, thanks to the synthesis between modern art and the cultural industries elicited by the booming Tropicália music scene.

Many art forms emerging in the 1970s and 1980s highlight dialogical aspects of communication technologies as well as their formal ones. They subverted both existing and new media to create channels for forms of expression that would challenge the authorities. One common approach, championed by Paulo Bruscky (Recife, 1949), involved repurposing ordinary and corporate systems, such as mail, fax and photocopy machines. These initiatives, coupled with interventions in public spaces and distribution systems, like those performed by the 3NÓS3 collective and Cildo Meireles, laid the foundation for more capillary-like artist networks. On the more high-tech side, the development of multimedia poetry would lead to pioneering experiments with holography and teletext. These works were only possible due to the private sponsorship of companies interested in the promotion of their new technologies or services, as was the case with computer art abroad.[40]

Institutions had to rethink themselves in relation to this emerging production. Gallery exhibitions were not made to accommodate these newly created processual works. 'Manifestation' was the term used for shows that attempted to move beyond traditional art and exhibition formats, incorporating (found) objects, actions and other communication media. It was a change not only in name, but also in modes of operation. As if in response to the blurring of boundaries caused by participatory art, Frederico Morais would argue for an art criticism that actively engaged in exhibition-making. Artists had become proponents of 'dematerialised' concepts and interactions. Curating, in turn, was to grow into a materially bound, creative practice. Along those lines, Morais organised projects that involved special commissions, occupied unconventional spaces and deployed bold installation design to respond to the artworks on their own terms.

Morais' exhibitions and writings provide a compelling example of how Brazilian arts of the time displayed a shrewd *media* consciousness, even when they refused the cold logic represented by computers and new technologies. Artists sought to intervene in the environment and affect how their work was communicated and contextualised. Even the ones who were not necessarily deploying electronic systems and dynamic displays were concerned with how information circulated and connected to various audiences. Perhaps that was inevitable, given the continuing state control over the media. Beyond any conceptual interest in the 'dematerialisation' of the artwork, there was an urgent need to build forms of togetherness that bypassed censorship and repression. As evidenced by Meireles' famous use of empty Coca-Cola bottles and banknotes as vehicles for 'subversive' messages,[41] anything could become a breach in which exchange and encounter took place. This sort of *systemic awareness* pervades most of the pieces discussed in this section. At the time, the enthusiasm for networks was also a deep yearning for democracy.

Chapter 13

Art in Hard Times (1964-c. 1980) (2004)

Aracy Amaral

...

The 1950s were a decade of great euphoria for Brazil: the rise of our commodities' prices (such as coffee); the implementation of the automobile industry; President Juscelino Kubitschek's policy, which set as one of his leading goals the ever-delayed construction of the new capital of Brasília, launched in 1960 on the country's central plateau. These were all reasons for a promising environment around the developmental aspirations of all Brazilians.

After Jânio Quadros' disastrous 1961 presidential term – which lasted only seven months and ended in his resignation – social and economic instabilities erupted in João Goulart's populist government (1961-1964). Goulart, allied with the left wing, was deposed by a military coup in March 1964, which ousted the sitting president and replaced him with a junta. A military regime was then installed in the country that would last until the mid-1980s, when the nationwide clamour for direct elections became impossible to ignore.

During the military period, the arts had to adapt to the censorship and restrictions imposed by the regime. The most targeted arts – obviously – were the ones that attracted greater audiences, such as popular music and theatre as well as daily or weekly journalism. Repression, arrests, torture, the disappearance of members of the resistance forces and violent military police actions became part of everyday life in the large Brazilian cities. As we know, it is in these hubs that artistic creativity is centralised, particularly when it comes to the visual arts.

At that moment, American pop art had a strong influence in Brazilian artistic proposals, mainly within urban environments. Disposable and plastic materials, as well as alternative techniques such as photography, comics, performative actions and happenings, began to appear in Brazilian art, becoming popular for their expressive possibilities.

The critic Ferreira Gullar, author of the Neo-Concrete Manifesto of 1960 who was responsible for books that were important to subsequent generations, such as *Cultura Posta em Questão* [Culture in Question] (1963) and *Vanguarda e subdesenvolvimento* [Avant-Garde and Underdevelopment] (1969), withdrew from the Neo-Concrete movement to integrate a nationwide movement of activist and popular culture.

It was a time when artists – like intellectuals and academics – began to actively participate in political events. The reality of censorship, the restriction of basic freedoms, exiles and even the surveillance of attitudes of artistic and intellectual personalities started to affect artistic creation.

From the younger generation, Cildo Meireles mentions how the beginning of the military regime affected him: 'In my early drawings, which were very free, there was great social charge, but also a kind of poetic delirium, a kind of attempt.... At some point, however, social and political events overwhelmed us, not only me but the whole Brazilian society. I had a personal project. It's curious... there's a drawing I made in 1968, after four years of methodical, obsessive work with drawings. It started with masks, with faces. Later, this turned into a dialogue between two characters and later still it turned into action. It was the last drawing I made at that time. (I wouldn't draw again until 1973). It was a street intersection, the place of action' (Enguita 1995, 25).

Like Ferreira Gullar, who went into exile for many years, Mário Pedrosa, the former director of the Museum of Modern Art in São Paulo (MAM-SP), an art critic and a thinker who encouraged constructivist movements in Brazil in the 1950s, took shelter abroad at the end of the 1960s. While in Chile, Pedrosa directed the Salvador Allende Solidarity Museum. He later lived for several years in Paris. Those exiles led to the loss of their precious presences in Brazil during the 'years of lead' of the military regime.

Popular music played a fundamental and mobilising role during this harsh period for its capacity to gather large audiences into auditoriums, audiences of a scale that the medium of visual arts never experienced. Geraldo Vandré, Chico Buarque, Maria Bethânia and Tom Zé, among many others, became prominent figures of a movement that left behind the *bossa nova* of the 1950s, a time closely associated with the optimism of the Juscelino Kubitschek era.

The 1960s stand out as a decade of intense vibration in the avant-garde and the controversial theatrical milieu. In reaction to the 1964 coup, a group of visual artists formed the *Opinião* company, which in 1965 had a hugely successful show in Rio de Janeiro and São Paulo, followed by an exhibition of the same name. This exhibition, which included European and Brazilian artists, would be a milestone. But not, as Ferreira Gullar emphasises, in the sense of effecting 'a historical change in painting' but in the sense that the artists 'also discovered that, on the other side, in everyday life, there was a lot, not to say everything'. This was the highlight of the show: an 'interest in the things of the world, in the problems of the people, of the society where they live. And hence the possibility of a whole new art that defines itself as humanistic' (Ferreira Gullar 1965).

Mário Pedrosa would stress that 'the social communicative warmth of the exhibition, especially of the young Brazilian team, was really compelling. It was the live result of serious events that had moved all of us Brazilian cultural consumers, both artists and non-artists. Social characters, for example, were promoted to mythical categories, such as the General, the Miss, etc., not to mention the presence of pure collective expressions of urban communities, such as samba and carnival' (Pedrosa 1975).

For Pedrosa, *the Opinião* company also had the merit of being an outlet for the citizens feeling asphyxiated by the climate of terror and cultural oppression that prevailed after 1964. In this context, he quotes: 'a formidable revolutionary and symbolic creation emerged, which was [the song] *Carcará* by João do Vale'. Sung by Maria Bethânia, *Carcará* became a resounding success after it was performed in Rio and São Paulo. It embodied, in a piercing cry, the possibility of artistic expression at a sombre moment in our political life (Amaral 2003).

Other significant theatrical events during those years included: *Liberdade, Liberdade* [Freedom, Freedom] (1965), by Millôr Fernandes and Flávio Rangel; *Arena conta Zumbi* [Arena narrates Zumbi] (1965), by Gianfrancesco Guarnieri and Augusto Boal; *Se correr o bicho pega, se ficar o bicho come* [If you run, you get caught; if you stay, you get eaten] (1966), by Ferreira Gullar and Oduvaldo Viana Filho; *Morte e vida Severina* [Severine Death and Life] (1966), by João Cabral de Melo Neto; *O rei da vela* [The king of the candle] (1967), by Oswald de Andrade; *Arena conta Tiradentes* [Arena narrates Tiradentes] (1967), directed by Augusto Boal; *Roda viva* [Living wheel] (1968), by Chico Buarque; and *Cemitério de automóveis* [Car graveyard] (1968), by Fernando Arrabal. These shows elevated a young and enthusiastic audience that projected onto them their desired political resistance. Plays by the *Teatro de Arena* company such as *Arena conta Zumbi* and *Arena conta Tiradentes* were connected to political theatre, increasing 'interest in class struggles'. Meanwhile, those of *Teatro Oficina* (*O rei da vela*, among others), by José Celso Martinez Corrêa, were grounded in what Roberto Schwarz describes as the 'inner experience of bourgeois disintegration in 1964. On the stage, this disintegration is ritually repeated as an offense. Their shows made history, scandal and enormous success in São Paulo and Rio' (Schwarz 1978).

Also of paramount importance during this time were the achievements of Brazilian cinema under the direction of the charismatic and visionary Glauber Rocha, with his films *Black God, White Devil* (1965), *Land Entranced* (1967) and *Antonio das Mortes* (1968) leading a new crop of young filmmakers and being awarded prizes at the Cannes Film Festival.

In the plastic arts milieu of 1965, the young artist Antônio Dias introduced a series of powerful pieces with his work *Nota Sobre a Morte Imprevista* [Note on the Unforeseen Death]: a single composition made of an image sequence ending close to the floor, like a violent comic strip, using predominantly the colours black, white and red. At the top of the composition, three frames in a diamond shape contained smaller comics with the morbid presence of skulls and symbols, such as gas clouds referencing death. In the lower part, Dias used bright upholstered fabric and plastic materials. The work thus acquired real volume, projecting itself out of the canvas with a three-dimensional effect. The series would change after Dias' move to Europe, when his work would gradually become more antiseptic, reducing its compositional elements, until it began to manifest itself conceptually in ways more connected to his political concerns.

After 1966-1967, performances and happenings also emerged in the arts scene, especially in Rio de Janeiro and São Paulo. All these events took on a public, rebellious and mobilising character in response to the coercive situation at the time. Hence the importance of an exhibition such as 'A

Month of Public Art' (1968), curated by Frederico Morais in Rio de Janeiro, as well as the release of the *Tropicália* record in the same year.

In 1968, the National Congress was dissolved, and popular resistances began to organise themselves in direct action groups. There was a surge in urban guerrillas, especially in São Paulo, leading to an increasing repression of anti-military sentiments. Inspired by the conflicts, artists began to address militarism, the theme of the moment; this could be seen in the engravings of Ana Maria Maiolino (such as the woodcut *O Herói* [The Hero] (1966)) and in the work of Antônio Henrique Amaral (whose 'generals' series was withdrawn from the 1967 Biennial of Bahia).

Even more glaring events would take place during the IV Salon of Brasília. In 1967, the year of the dramatic death of the revolutionary Che Guevara in Bolivia, Cláudio Tozzi exhibited a large triptych called *Guevara, vivo ou morto* [Guevara, dead or alive], a work that was attacked and stolen, to be returned mutilated to the artist only six months later. Besides Tozzi, other artists had their works withdrawn: Rubens Gerchman, who also approached Che's theme in *Um bilhão de dólares* [A Billion of Dollars] and *Só* [Alone], as well as *Ele* [He], by José Roberto Aguilar.[42]

In order to test their power to communicate through art or just to provoke the military regime, artists exhibited silkscreen flags in the Nossa Senhora da Paz square, in Ipanema, Rio de Janeiro (1968), and on Brasil Avenue, São Paulo. Works such as Tozzi's, with the face of a dead Guevara, or Samuel Spiegel's, depicting a fictional governor-general of Brazil from the colonial period with the electoral appeal to 'Vote' (when there were no elections in the country due to the military dictatorship), were public provocations. Similarly, the street exhibition on Brasil Avenue included a silkscreen by Hélio Oiticica, based on a drawing sent by the artist and printed in São Paulo by Tozzi and Marcelo Nitsche, with the words '*seja marginal, seja herói*' [be a criminal, be a hero], in reference to a young offender killed by the police in Rio de Janeiro. In other words, artists made provocations and made their works seen.

The provocations would, however, cease for, after 1969, the political situation got worse. Events such as armed conflicts in the two main cities (Rio de Janeiro and São Paulo), the kidnapping of the US ambassador Charles Elbrick by left-wing activists (aimed at prompting the release of their imprisoned comrades) and the death of leftist leader Carlos Marighella led to increasing cultural censorship and a crisis in the universities in Brasília and São Paulo. As a result, the regime promoted the Institutional Act No. 5, severely curtailing artistic activity. Thus, when Antônio Manuel, during his participation in the Youth Biennial in Paris, denounces police violence, the sending of a Brazilian delegation to the event was cancelled by the government. On the other hand, after a ban on the exhibition of artists selected for the VI Paris Biennial, the ABCA – the Brazilian Association of Art Critics – staged an energetic protest at the Museum of Modern Art in Rio de Janeiro (MAM-RJ).

After that, artists became more careful in their creative projects, employing metaphors or conceptual language to express their thoughts and positions.

An international event such as the 10th São Paulo Biennial (1969) would also provoke a rally against censorship and the repression experienced by both Brazilian and foreign visual artists in the country. A boycott of the Biennial was in place: many Brazilian and foreign artists refused to participate in the event in São Paulo. Gradually, these political incidents began to cross borders. The Brazilian Ministry of Foreign Affairs, for instance, would refuse to welcome critic Jacques Lassaigne, president of the Paris' *Biennale*, as the French delegate to the São Paulo Biennial because he had signed a note against the arrest of Mrs. Niomar Muniz Sodré, president of Rio's Museum of Modern Art. In France, at a meeting at the *Musée d'Art Moderne* on June 16, 1969, 321 artists and intellectuals would sign the manifesto *Non à la Biennale*, based on witness statements and documentation about the censorship in Brazil (Amaral 1970).

From the mid-1960s onwards, Rubens Gerchman focused his work on the theme of the 'disappeared' (i.e., arrested activists, whose fate was unknown, who had been tortured or were dead, their identities hidden by the military during the dictatorship). Gerchman also favoured themes of the city, its crowds and the housing problem, as shown in the series *Caixas de Morar* [Housing Boxes] (1966). With simple language, he used copies of images combined with freehand drawings and assembled with photos published in newspapers and magazines to portray the reality in which we used to live.

Pedro Escosteguy, a veteran artist working alongside the youngsters of that time, came from poetry and displayed words as if they were aggressively pitched proposal ideas. He showcased his talent as a poet and visual artist by using solid colours to simulate a conflict by combining words, paintings, geometric shapes and objects – a ladder, two legs and a cogwheel, in the work *Linha de força(ação)* [Line of force(action)], from 1965.

At the beginning of the 1970s, Cildo Meireles was the most sensitive and intelligent agent of a new type of engaged art positioned against the regime, simultaneously experimental and attentive to its time. For the event *Do Corpo à Terra* [From the Body to the Ground] (1970), curated by Frederico Morais and held in Belo Horizonte on the day celebrating Tiradentes (the martyr of Brazilian independence), Meireles created a Tiradentes-totem: a monument to the political prisoner. On this occasion, he set chickens on fire in a bizarre ritual, alluding to the waves of repression and torture. The action took place precisely when the military were planning to rehabilitate the figure of Tiradentes – Joaquim José da Silva Xavier

– as a national hero. Still, the audience did not react so well to Cildo's performance.

Cildo Meireles' commitment to reality was evident in other works from the same period. It was the case, for instance, with the series entitled *Inserções em circuitos antropológicos* [Insertions in Anthropological Circuits] (1971), which provided the public with instructions for how to produce their own payphone tokens, thus circumventing the system, as well as with the interferences he made by stamping money bills with provocative statements, later releasing the bills back into circulation.[43] As part of the same series, he also printed *Zero Dollar* bills with images of Indigenous Brazilians or Uncle Sam.

Cildo's *Inserções em circuitos ideológicos: projeto Coca-Cola* [Insertions in Ideological Circuits: Coca-Cola Project] (1970) was a series of Coke bottles onto which he applied stickers with statements referring to the current political moment of the country before returning them to commercial circulation. For Cildo, this series addressed questions of authorship: being a conceptual work, it could be made by anyone. Its meaning, according to him, was 'individual practice against hegemonic power. I wanted to create a mechanism of expression for the subject against society. Of course, one of the things I had to decide was which objects to use ... how to store them'. Cildo concluded that 'the best place for a work of art is memory. It doesn't matter how you get there. *Inserções* ... dealt with this question, it entailed individual practice on an industrial scale'.

His installation *Sermão da Montanha: Fiat Lux* [Sermon on the Mount: Fiat Lux] (1973/79), in turn, made the audience uneasy because of the very situation it created, which reflected this political moment of persecution, repression and fear. The core of the work was a perfect cube made of matchboxes, like a potentially explosive situation. Surrounded by people disguised as bodyguards and secret police agents, mirrors and powerful lights, the cube created a peculiarly tense atmosphere in the exhibition space. It was, perhaps, Cildo's most substantial and direct work about Brazil's situation during the dictatorship.[44]

Metaphors appeared in many artworks, such as Marcelo Nitsche's *Bolhas infláveis* [Inflatable Bubbles] series, particularly the *Bolha amarela* [Yellow Bubble] (1968), which may have seemed like a playful work at first glance but then expanded, taking over the entire gallery space and pushing the visitors against the walls, triggering reflections about the repression experienced by artists under the regime. In a similarly allusive way, sculptor Ivens Machado showed the dramatic *Camisas-de-força* [Straitjackets] during the 1973 São Paulo Biennial, evoking the vigorous censorship in operation at the time. A few years later, in 1979, Machado would return to the theme of national violence (contradicting historian Sérgio Buarque de Holanda's thesis about Brazil as the country of 'cordiality') with the work *Mapa mudo* [Dumb map], a gigantic map of Brazil made of concrete, covered in pointed shards of glass.

Paintings would also frequently employ metaphors. In the mid-1970s Antônio Henrique Amaral, for example, created a whole series that used anthropomorphised bananas to convey instances of torture.[45] Ambiguity would also drive the search for tortuous forms of expression, such as the series of 100 lithographs and ten gigantic and powerful paintings by João Câmara Filho that engaged with the political trajectory and the rule of [president] Getúlio Vargas.

Mail art was another resource available during those times of censorship and economic crisis. It allowed artists to share their subversive or underground messages either by mail or in person, using texts and photocopied reproductions in limited editions. Several artists participated in these actions, particularly Paulo Bruscky in Recife and Mario Ishikawa in São Paulo. In one of his Xerox multiples,

Ishikawa presented the text of the Universal Declaration of Human Rights gradually dissolving through graphic interferences, in clear allusion to the aggressions suffered by the Brazilian population.

One cannot downplay the brilliant contribution of the multiple personalities of Ana Bella Geiger's work. By using photography and combining sensibility with an acute mastery of graphic reproduction techniques, Geiger made pieces in alternative formats such as postcards, which provoked the spectator's gaze by using metaphors and symbols that referred to the challenging times in which we lived.

Artur Barrio was perhaps one of the artists who created the most scandalous 'situations' for his works, directly reflecting the fearful atmosphere of resistance against the military regime. In 1969, he left several bundles made of bloody clothes on the beaches and in various other places in downtown Rio de Janeiro, as a denunciation of, or a warning about, the murder and torture that were taking place within the system of police violence.

These examples demonstrate how the practice of artists working during the Brazilian dictatorship was based not only on the direct desire to shock, but also on visual intelligence and sensibility. Even though artists did not have the same political success as musical concerts and the theatre, both of which greatly mobilised students in the big cities, they attempted to convey their 'messages' with personality and openness to artistic avant-gardes; each one in their own way, in galleries and, whenever possible, in Biennials....

Chapter 13

General Outline of the New Objectivity (1967)

Hélio Oiticica

New Objectivity is a formulation of the state of the current Brazilian artistic avant-garde, whose main characteristics are: 1: general constructive will; 2: a tendency towards the object that refuses and overcomes easel painting; 3: spectator interaction (corporal, tactile, visual, semantic, etc.); 4: political awareness and ethical concerns; 5: focus on collective proposals and the subsequent abolition of the '-isms' characteristic of the first half of the century (a tendency described in Mário Pedrosa's concept of 'postmodern art'); 6: the resurgence and new formulation of the concept of anti-art.

As it defines a typical state of Brazilian art today, the New Objectivity also characterises it internationally, differentiating it from the two great currents of our time, Pop and Op, and those connected to them, *Nouveau Réalisme* and Primary Structures (Hard Edge).

The New Objectivity, being a state, is not, therefore, a dogmatic aestheticist movement (like Cubism and other '-isms' constituted as 'unities of thought'), but rather a 'destination' constituted by multiple tendencies, where the 'lack of a unity of thought' is an important characteristic. The conceptual unity of the 'new objectivity' is a general confirmation of the multiple tendencies it assembles. A similarity, if we will, can be found in Dadá, acknowledging the distance and differences.

Item 1: General Constructive Will

In Brazil, visionary movements generally present their unique characteristics in a specific way: as a remarkable constructive will. This can be verified even in the [modernist] Movement of 1922, which is, in our opinion, what led Oswald de Andrade to the famous conclusion that our anthropophagic culture would entail an immediate reduction of all external influences to national models. This would not be possible without something distinctive in us, something special or latent in the way we apprehend such influences: general constructive will. From this constructive will was born our architecture and, more recently, the so-called Concrete and Neo-Concrete movements – which, in a certain way, solidified such creative behaviour. Additionally, we want to believe that the prevailing social conditions of the country, still under development, have further crystallised this tendency: we are a people in search of a cultural character, and that fact distinguishes us from Europeans, with their millennia-long cultural weight, and from North Americans, with their super-productive demands. Both Europeans and North Americans compulsively export their cultures for the weight of these cultures makes them overflow. But here, social underdevelopment implies a quest for the character of national culture, which is translated specifically through our first premise: constructive will. This may as well occur to other underdeveloped nations, but it is a particular case in Brazil. Anthropophagy would be our defence against external domination, and constructive will – our primary creative weapon. This has not prevented all kinds of cultural colonialism, which we now want to abolish, from absolving it definitively into a super-anthropophagy. In response to this there emerge the primary needs of the New

Objectivity: to look for characteristics of our own, both latent and under development; to crystallise a general creative state one could call Brazilian avant-garde, solidifying our culture (even if we might use anticultural methods for that); to objectify and gather the main elements of individual creative efforts in an attempt to assemble them culturally. The constructive will emerges from this task as the main element, its spiritual mover.

Item 2: Tendency Towards the Object by Refusing or Overcoming Easel Painting

The phenomenon of the demolition of the frame, or the refusal of easel painting, has unleashed a chain of transformations in Brazilian art from 1954 onwards, with the successive creation of reliefs and anti-paintings leading to spatial or environmental structures and the formulation (or rather arrival) of the object. This phenomenon took place in many different ways until the current outbreak. In 1954 (the concrete art era), Lygia Clark began her long and painful experience of disintegrating the traditional frame, the plane, the pictorial space, etc. Within the Neo-Concrete movement, this experience led to the proposal for object-poems (Gullar, Jardim, Pape) and culminated in Ferreira Gullar's 'Non-Object' Theory. Chronologically, the problem of the object was continuously being reformulated in response to the fundamental needs of artistic production. After Clark's *démarche*, the process came to rely on many different handicaps; thus the transformation that, with Clark, took place slowly, addressing the primary structures of the artwork (such as space, time, etc.), would occur in the work of other artists in a faster and more explosive way. In my own work (from 1959 on), the problem appeared immediately, but still within a purely structural approach and dissolution. Later, in the work of Antônio Dias and Rubens Gerchman, we see it happen in a more violent and dramatic way, involving several simultaneous processes, no longer in a purely structural dimension, but also by involving a dialectical dynamic that Mário Schemberg described as realist. In the artists one would call 'structural', this dialectical dynamic takes place more slowly. Dias and Gerchman confront structural and dialectical needs in a single shot. It is worth noting that Schemberg's 'realist' dynamic had already been expressed in poetry, when Gullar broke away from the premise of transcendental order to theorise the broader problem of how to create a participatory culture that would be able to face emerging national issues. This resulted in his monograph, *Cultura posta em questão* [Culture in Question]. The realism expressed by Dias and Gerchman's proposals, as well as by Pedro Escosteguy (whose objects always carry some sort of social message), was a consequence of the new premises introduced by Gullar and his group, and by the *Cinema Novo* movement, then at its peak. I consider the decisive turning point of these transformations in the pictorial-plastic-structural field to be Antônio Dias' work *Nota Sobre a Morte Imprevista* [Note on the Unforeseen Death]. Dias conveys at once profound issues of ethico-social and pictorial-structural natures, gesturing at a new approach to the problem of the object. In fact, I consider this work to be an anti-painting, provoking a revolution in the concept of the frame and ushering a 'transition' from painting to object. Thenceforth arises in Brazil a series of 'transitions' towards the object and towards dialectical-pictorial proposals, which we are not able to analyse here in its full extent. There is no other reason for Dias' tremendous influence on most of the artists who came after him. I plan on doing a detailed analysis of his work elsewhere. Still, I want to note in this outline that his work was decisive for the formulation of the very concept of 'new objectivity' that I would later materialise. The depth and seriousness of his *démarches* have not yet exhausted their consequences: they are only just budding.

Gerchman's experiences emerge in parallel to Dias'. Departing from his expressionist roots, he at once materialises issues of social nature and builds a stage for a dramatic confrontation between plane and object in a remarkable series of proposals. It is also too much and impossible to analyse it here. Still, I want to believe that his experience was likewise decisive in the dialectical transformation of the frame and in the creation of Schemberg's concept of 'realism'. Gerchman's work combines social content (almost always associated with observation or protest) with the search for new structural orders of utter and radical expression (as I do, too, in a certain way): the lunch box, the elevator, the altar where the spectator kneels are specific structural manifestations as well as elements that affirm dialectical concepts, as their author wishes. This approach inspired the creation of the social *Parangolé* (works in which I attempted to provide social meaning to my discovery of the *Parangolé*, even though that social meaning was already latent since the beginning, having been created by Gerchman and I in 1966). His experience also became highly influential in this short period.

The third decisive expression of Schemberg's notion of 'realism' is the experience of Pedro Escosteguy, a long-time poet who revealed himself to be a great visual artist through works of surprising clarity and creative spontaneity. Pedro engages with the object from the outset: the semantic object, where the laws of the word rule, the keyword, the protest slogan, words whose poetic dimension also conveys a social message, which may or may not be full of naivety. The ludic aspect of his proposals enables him to develop with versatility certain projects of the neo-concrete era, such as the object-poems by Gullar and Jardim, and Lygia Pape's *Livro da criação* [Book of Creation], where poetry and play come together. Pedro, a staunch dialectician, wants his expressions of protest to take place in a playful and even naïve tone, as if in an amusement park (for which he has a project). The positive aspect of his proposals makes him a good angel of the 'new objectivity'. In the annotations it contains, in the unrestricted use of the word, of the 'message' and of the constructed object, Pedro's experience repositions the problem of anti-art in his own terms. This problem also occurs in the work of other artists: Clark's *Caminhando* [Walking], made at that time, which we'll analyse below; Dias' proposals of ethical-social nature; Gerchman's sematic structures; my own *Parangolés*.

In São Paulo at the same time (1964-65), Waldemar Cordeiro introduces the *Popcreto*, a proposal that merges the structural aspect (the object) with a semantic one. For Waldemar, the disintegration of the physical object was likewise a semantic disintegration, through which a new meaning was built. His experience was not a fusion of Pop with Concrete art, as many would have it, but a decisive transformation from purely structural proposals into semantic-structural ones, which were also participatory. In Cordeiro, different from what happened in the works of the Rio de Janeiro group, this transformation had a universalist character, aware of industrial civilisation, etc. According to him, to aspire to objectivity was a way to keep oneself away from intimist elaborations and inconsequential naturalisms. With *Popcreto*, Cordeiro foresaw the emergence of the concept of 'appropriation' that I would formulate two years later (1966), when I proposed a return to the 'thing', to the ordinary object appropriated as artwork.

In the period between 1964-65, the introduction of the realist dialectic and the participatory approach would finally overcome purely structural concepts (as complex as they might have been, as they encompassed elements of various nature and already proposed an opposition between the tactile-sensorial field and the purely visual one, e.g. in the glasses and boxes of my *Bólides* from 1963). This took place not only in São Paulo with Cordeiro, but also in Rio with Clark and I. In Clark's work, the most critical *démarche* was her discovery of an immanent creative process in opposition to the old one, based on transcendence. That's where *Caminhando* [Walking] comes from. This fundamental discovery would inform the artist's creative process, culminating in a 'discovery of the body', a 'reconstitution of the body' through supra and infra-sensorial structures and in collective acts of participation. This *démarche* is impregnated by the new concept of anti-art, leading to a powerful ethico-individual structuring. We can't describe here at length the whole dialectical development of Clark's work; we can only indicate the moment of its dialectical turn, which was extremely important for Brazilian art. Frederico Morais intensified this process by formulating his theory of an 'art of the senses', fully aware of the metaphysical threats underpinning it.

Finally, I want to mention my own awareness of the crisis of pure structures, which was a surprise to many, with the discovery of the *Parangolé* in 1964 and the theoretical formulation that resulted from it (see writings from 1965). The main point of interest to us is the sense of participation that was born with the *Parangolé*: collective participation (wearing capes and dancing), dialectic-social and poetic participation (poetic and social protest *Parangolé*, with Gerchman), playful participation (games, environments, appropriations) and their main driver: the proposal to 'return to the myth'. I won't describe this process here either (see the publication *Teoria do Parangolé* [Parangolé Theory])....

Item 5: Tendency Towards Collective Art

There are two ways to create collective art: the first would be to put individual proposals in contact with the public on the streets (works that are intended for this purpose, of course, not conventional ones); the second, to propose creative activities to this public, for instance, the very creation of the work. This tendency towards collective art is what really concerns the avant-garde artists in Brazil. There is something of a programmatic fatality about it. Its origin is closely connected to the problem of spectators' participation, already considered a program to be followed even in the most complex structures. Today, after sparse experiences and attempts from the Neo-Concrete group (my projects and *Parangolés*, Clark's *Caminhando*, happenings by Dias, Gerchman and Vergara, the project for an amusement park by Escosteguy), there is an urgent demand for open works and proposals. This is indicated by the current concern around the 'serialisation of works' (Vergara and Glauco Rodrigues), the planning of 'experimental art fairs' by another group of artists and all kinds of proposals of collective nature.

These programs are still waiting to be made, however, since their proposals are only becoming possible now. In my opinion, the request for collective art has been intensified with the discovery of organised popular manifestations (*samba* schools, *ranchos*, *frevos*, parties of all kinds, football matches, market fairs) as well as spontaneous or 'accidental' ones ('street art' or anti-art created by chance). Ferreira Gullar once highlighted the sense of total art expressed by a samba school, where dance, rhythm and music are inextricably tied to the visual exuberance of colour, clothing, etc. Taking this into account, it's not strange for artists to go looking for collective solutions for their proposals in the autonomous unity of popular manifestations, of which Brazil has an enormous archive of unparalleled expressive wealth. Happenings such as the one organised by Frederico Morais at the University of Minas Gerais, where Dias, Gerchman and Vergara attempted to 'create' works of my authorship, 'finding' in the urban landscape elements that corresponded to such works, introduces the naïve spectator to the creative phenomenology of art not as something closed and apart from them, but as a proposal open to their full participation.

Item 6: The Resurgence of the Anti-Art Problem

Finally, we must address and outline the reason for the reappearance of the problem of anti-art today. In our view, this problem takes on a more important and, above all, new role. It is the reason why Mário Pedrosa felt the need to isolate today's experiences under the notion of 'postmodern art', for they represent a change in the artist's creative attitude towards ethico-individual and general social demands. In Brazil, one could ask: can we explain and justify the appearance of an avant-garde in an underdeveloped country not as a symptom of alienation, but rather as a decisive factor in the country's collective progress? How can we situate the artist's activity therein? The problem could be approached with another question: for whom does the artist create their work? It is evident that this artist feels a need greater than to simply create; they need to communicate something that is fundamental to them. However, this communication must take place on a large scale, beyond the small circles of experts, and even against this elite, by means of unfinished and 'open' works. This is the fundamental aspect of the new notion of anti-art: not only to clash against past art and old concepts (an attitude still rooted in transcendental aspirations), but to create new experimental conditions, where the artist becomes a 'proponent', an 'entrepreneur' or even an 'educator'. The old problem of 'making art anew' or overthrowing hegemonic cultures must be formulated in a different way. Nowadays, we must ask which proposals, means of promotion and measures should be adopted to amplify popular participation within the creative realm occupied by artists. On this rests the survival of art and, in that sense, of the people as well....

Chapter 14

Mail Art: Art in Synchrony (1981)

Julio Plaza

Art today can't be thought of in diachronic terms, since the speed of change ended up changing even the means of production. What we see now is no longer a succession of '-isms', schools or trends as in the near past, but a synchronic intervention of artistic and unartistic events that explode precisely the linear idea of time as understood both by tradition and the avant-gardes. Contemporary art can be thought of as a formidable synchronous bricolage of history (distant past, recent past and present) in non-antagonistic contradiction.

In parallel and as an alternative to the official cultural systems, the 'unartistic action' of Mail Art or Postal Art appears as a phenomenon critical to the propriety status in art and to culture as an economic practice. Instead, it proposes artistic information to be a process and not an accretion. Mail Artists organise themselves spontaneously in affinity groups to exchange ideas and information. The movement is international in scope (though not in the same way as multinational art companies or official state culture), unartistic and paratactical, individualistic and Dada-inspired, as it stresses that 'the arts have no nationality; what they have is style' (Octavio Paz).

Displacing artistic production from the great international centres, Mail Art owes its power in great part to reproductive media, which facilitates the transmission of back and forth messages. If traditional art transformed itself into an 'imaginary museum' (Malraux) by quadrichromatic reproduction, Mail Art works directly with these reproductive media (as foreseen by Walter Benjamin) by introducing multimedia and intermedia elements into the context of art, while deploying operative techniques that are not sequential anymore, but simultaneous and synchronous.

Mail Art: Media Art, Art and Postal Craft

Mail Art is among the multiple media conceived as extensions of art and artists. It is a complex time-space structure that absorbs and transmits any type of information or object, that penetrates and dilutes things in its communicational flux, generating confusion about its own definition. However, it is not in our interest to define what is and what isn't Mail Art, since this type of art is suffused with the spirit of mixture, of media and of languages. The game is precisely to invade other time-spaces.

Mail Art (which is also a pleasurable craft) is essentially an art of media and interpersonal communication, made for microgroups at most. Within it, all is content: media inside media. In at sense, Mail Art consists in any material or information that gets into its flux and whose predominant function is communicative. Hence the tendency not to consider works of purely 'aesthetic' character or even those created by traditional means as forms of Mail Art.

This new means of production emphasise the importance of the material substrate of signs: graphical reproduction, books, records, videotape, photocopy, film and photography, among other information media. The Mail Artist has at their disposal the world of information, interacting within it, creating and recreating, translating and manipulating information through those media.

The Mail Artist (as a cultural strategist) is more interested in the world of signs and languages as a form of interacting in the world than in the manipulation of objects, since the passage from the world of things to the world of signs offers greater operationality at a minimum cost. This operation is a 'dematerialisation of art'. The use of various languages leads the artist to relinquish the poetic or aesthetic function of language as predominant, emphasising other functions such as the referential, the documental, the expressive and also the impressive (related to propaganda), fostering in the work a rhetoric that can convey its artistic ideology.

Mobilising these elements, Mail Art creates a circuit inside the system of art, expanding it, but not without contradictions. One of these contradictions involves its penetration and appropriation by other circuits, even institutional ones. It's not in the nature of Mail Art to be exhibited to the public at large; when this occurs, Mail Art becomes saturated. The experience of fragmentary information within microgroups becomes an experience of simultaneity.

Mail Art: Indexical Art, Art of the Here and Now

As a means of expression, Mail Art has above all a phatic function, which accentuates and tests the channel. It is associated with the expressive function of language, which gives emphasis to the 'medium as a message' as well as to the sender. The 'I am here' and the 'I'm an artist' is what is communicated to others. Engaging in Mail Art as an artist implies engaging in the production of an aesthetic of reception, in consuming Mail Art, and, above all, in maintaining a dialogue with its artistic community. The Mail Artist knows that the artistic information produced and conveyed today is consumed in an ephemeral and diluted way, through various communication media. For them, more important than the production of *quality* is the sheer presence of information, that is, the act of receiving it. Mail Art doesn't manifest art for the future, but makes it for the present, and almost always for the trash bin of history.

Mail Art: Art in the Rhythm of Bricolage or Artistic Communism

Amidst the prevalence of *quantity*, the Mail Artist finds the world of information within their reach. The mail arts and craft operate as the collage and mixture of information, turning *informationism* into a rhythm of rhetorical and semantic *bricolage*. As a potent consumer of the graphic industries that demonstrates our immersion in the culture of printing, what Mail Art offers us is a parody. At planetary and international scale, this culture of bricolage within the artistic community materialises Andy Warhol's idea: 'Everyone will be known universally for fifteen minutes'.

To engage in Mail Art is to become a 'Brother in Mail', since Mail Art's structure is not hierarchical. The objective seems to be the constant and continuous inclusion of new sender-receivers in the community. Mail Art democratises the practice of art, but it has not been able to overcome the dialectical impasse between quality and quantity. The thing is that art has nothing to do with democracy (as Marcel Duchamp has shown).

Mail Art: carnivalisation and parody of the dominant culture

Mail Art: a suicide sign, since the excess of signification destroys significance and sense

Chapter 15

Mail Art and the Great Network: Art, Today, is this Statement (1977)

Paulo Bruscky

...

In Mail Art, art renews its main functions: information, protest and denunciation. It is a movement without nationality in which the underground explodes simultaneously all across the world.

Artists theorise the Mail Art movement and create spaces that replace galleries and museums. Envelopes, postcards, telegrams, stamps, faxes and letters are executed with collages, drawings, ideas, texts, xerox, proposals, logos, visual music and sound poetry, which all are sent to the receivers. An example is the *Postal Móvel* [Mobile Postcard] and the *Envelope de Circulação* [Circulation Envelope], which, after passing through the hands of several people and through many countries, eventually returns to the sender, becoming a boomerang work. Part of Paulo Bruscky's actions also involves repurposing and re-circulating commercial envelopes, plane tickets and advertisement leaflets with interferences, a practice he has called *Arte Porte Pago* [Postage Paid Art]. Mail is used as a vehicle, as a means and an end, both part of the work and also the work itself. It was the only means of communication uncontrolled by censorship since the process of handling correspondence was manual. The artists who paid to make mail art broke through bureaucracy and put into question its archaic regulations. Sending a sculpture by mail is not Mail Art:

> When a sculpture is sent by mail, the creator limits themself to using a determined means of transport to translate an elaborate work. In the new artistic language [of Mail Art], on the contrary, the fact that the work must travel a certain distance is part of its structure. It is the work itself. The piece was created to be sent by mail and this fact conditions its creation (dimensions, postage, weight, nature of the message, etc.)

This excerpt from the article *Arte Correio: uma Nova Forma de Expressão* [Mail Art: A New Form of Expression], by the Argentinian artists Horácio Zabala and Edgardo Antonio Vigo, defines the use/circulation of mail as art exceptionally well.

The First International Exhibition of Mail Art in Brazil was held in Recife in 1975, organised by Paulo Bruscky and Ypiranga Filho. Besides the problems caused by the outdated bureaucracy of the Post Office, there were difficulties with censorship across Latin America. The Second International Exhibition of Mail Art, held on August 27, 1976, in the Hall of the Post Office building in Recife (Brazil), which sponsored the showcase, was closed minutes after its opening by the Federal Police and the SNI (National Service of Intelligence). The exhibition, which saw the participation of 21 countries and three thousand works, could ultimately only be attended by a few. At the occasion, the Brazilian mail-artists Paulo Bruscky and Daniel Santiago, organisers of the event, were dragged to jail by the police and cut off from communication. The artworks were only released after a month. Aside from being damaged, several pieces by Brazilian and foreign artists were retained and are attached to the police file to this date. Another absurd consequence caused by 'cultural repressions' in Latin America was the imprisonment, by the Uruguayan government, of the mail-artists Clemente Padin and Jorge Caraballo from 1977 to 1979. In April 1981, El Salvador's dictatorial military force kidnapped the Mail Artist Jesus Caldamez Escobar, who only survived because he managed to flee into exile in Mexico. It is always like this. Those who pretend to be 'owners of culture' always try to impose their 'methods'. In the Mail Art movement, especially in Latin America, artists were unafraid to face censorship....

Artistic Xerography: Art without an Original (from the Invention of the Machine to the Xero/graphic Process) (1985)

Paulo Bruscky

...
Art is the Copy Art is the Copy

Among contemporary media, the medium that best embodies German philosopher Walter Benjamin's 1925 essay *The Work of Art in the Age of its Technical Reproducibility* is the artistic Xero/graphy. The reasons vary: from the direct multiplication of works, most of them without matrices, to the low cost of production and circulation, mainly through the Mail Art circuit.

This new artistic expression came not only to stimulate but also to disseminate the practice of Xeroxart through a simultaneous exchange of works/exhibitions/surveys, etc., in which xerographs are interfered with and sent to other receivers/transmitters, becoming, in some cases, a boomerang that returns to the initial sender after traveling through several countries. Within the practice of Mail Art, Xeroxart is also used to make postcards, stamps, envelopes, publications (artists' books and collective magazines), etc. One can also proliferate the practice of Xerography through courses in which some students make their first work as a copy. The student, when starting a Xerox course, is like any learner getting into a car and beginning to drive for the first time. They have to synchronise everything: thought, action, unforeseen elements, practice, research/action, relationship and infinity. Sonia Sheridan conducted the first research course in Copy Art at the School of the Art Institute of Chicago in 1970. In Brazil, the First Course on Art Research in Xerox – Xeroxart was taught by Paulo Bruscky at the Catholic University of Pernambuco in January 1980. In June of the same year, Hudinilson Jr. held a Xeroxart course, as did Bené Fonteles at the University of Caxias do Sul.

It is worth pointing out that, while we were breaking machines and heads experimenting/inventing/creating, the 'art market' as a whole repelled, as it still does today, any artistic initiative that comes to question the value/significance of the unique work of art due to the bourgeois prejudice towards the ownership or possession of any object, be it art or not. We can take the example of photography, which to this day is perceived by most as a minor art.

In large part, xerographic work is also distinct from other media because it doesn't prescind from a pre-established matrix. Due to the multitude of things that can be used as a matrix in each copy, as well as the re/use of the copy that adds another infinity of matrices, we have infinite copies: copy, copy, copy, copy, copy, copy…

In addition to the multiplication of artworks, xero/graphy allows for an infinity of investigations/effects, which include: 1. flattening/stretching/curving/rotating/amplifying/ reducing, etc. one or several images; 2. copying three-dimensional objects; 3. image superpositions/halftones, including colour copies merged with black and white/slides/photographic negatives/bi- and three-dimensional objects/transparencies. The latter material is mainly used for projectable pieces, as is the case of Paulo Bruscky's book *Transparence – Um Livro que Também Pode Ser Projetado* [Transparency – A Book that Can Also Be Projected], which was exhibited/projected with an overhead projector at the *Xeroxarte* show in the Museum of the State of Pernambuco (1980), and at the International Biennial of São Paulo, Mail Art section (1981), which donated a copy of the work to the Office of Postal Art of the São Paulo Cultural Centre. In addition to transparencies, artists can use many other kinds of paper or media for their experiments, which becomes a creative concern. Plastic, fabric (woven) or other similar materials, for instance, may result in a perfect image, which only needs to be fixed with a fixing spray.

Another effect that can be achieved with the machine is the use of light against light, deploying mirrors to short-circuit the device and record its confused vision, which on several occasions generates significant visual depth in the explored images. Another variation is to copy a copy of the same image, achieving the total deformation/transformation/destruction of the initial one. Using a paper roll in xerography, the artist can create a kilometre-long piece or use it to make large panels. Other alternatives are exemplified by Paulo Bruscky's most recent research: negative Xerox, through which a black image comes out white and vice versa, using ordinary paper with normal matrices; and Xeroperformance, which we have been developing since January 1980, as a record of the artist's relationship with the machine through a series of more than a thousand copies that are later transformed into a Super 8 film.

One can make Xerofilms from images fixed by a copying machine. With simultaneous recording, the production of movement on the screen of a copying machine produces a series of still images, which, once filmed, recompose the original movement in a specific rhythm determined by the artist. The Xerofilms thus produced are disconnected from the formal narrative structure of conventional filmography and meant to sharpen our visual perception concerning form, colour and movement. *Pure. In themselves.*

As a secondary outcome, this exploration may lead to the development of a new animation technique that is both extremely simple and accessible to a large audience. Additionally, the field of experimental cinema has a lot to gain from a unique process that combines the production of images with the reproduction of movement. This research was awarded the Visual Arts Award from the Guggenheim Foundation in New York, USA, in 1981, and was put into practice with a colour photocopy machine in 1982. The Xero/graphic works result from the participation/co-authorship of the device. The most important thing is not to use the machine as another means of re/production but to interfere through distortions, superpositions and other effects. In short, to experiment with chance and risk, beyond using one's own body, also using water/fire/animals/vegetables and many other objects and things (in 1980, I made a xerofilm in which I set fire to several items on top of the Xerox machine). Xeroxart is above all everything you cannot do in print, offset, photography or mimeograph, among other means of reproducing the unique work. It is the record of the mo(ve)ment. I always thank the machine for its creative partnership as I finish each piece.

Due to the challenges of putting some projects into practice, we elaborated, in 1980, a photocopy machine made specifically for artistic work/research. It would be a reflex model with a swivel stool attached, among other features, such as storage space for different materials used in our studies.

It is the artist once again mindfully modifying the machine's destiny/action and the possibilities of xerography as an artistic procedure, which have only been depleted for the people who approached it as a trend (as happened within the Mail Art movement).

... In 1970 in Brazil, Paulo Bruscky began his research in Copyart and exhibited the results the following year in the solo showcase *Xilogravura e Xerogravura* [Xylography and Xerography], held at the gallery of the Pernambuco Tourism Company (Empetur) in Recife, as reported in the *Jornal do Commercio*'s Cultural Supplement of December 5, 1971. In the same year, Uruguayan Henry Katzer showed his xerographic works in Rio de Janeiro. In 1972, Aloisio Magalhães created his xerographic artist books, *Viva I* and *Viva II*. In 1973, William Gray Harris started a colour xerographic self-portrait in the United States. Since 1974, some of the most engaged Brazilian artists to use the machine's possibilities have included: Hudinilson Jr, J. Medeiros, Daniel Santiago, Unhandeijara Lisboa, Bené Fonteles, Roberto Keppler, Gabriel Borba, Mário Ishikawa, Bernardo Krasniansky, Alex Flemming, Rafael França, Maurício Silva, Mário Ramiro, Lourenço Neto, Ypiranga Filho, Anna Bella Geiger, Carmela Gross, Milton Kurtz and Wesley Duke Lee.

Among more recent collective proposals, it is worth mentioning a project by Paulo Bruscky, together with Roberto Sandoval, which is the *Fac-Similarte*, held at Fundação Armando Álvares Penteado (FAAP) in 1985. This proposal involves exchanging works/exhibitions/ information across the country using facsimile machines (Telecopier)....

Chapter 17

Conversation with the Reader (1986)

Júlio Plaza

I

Invented over a decade ago and recently introduced in Brazil, Videotext is the newest language vehicle. Its contemporary nature and lack of historical tradition make it hard to understand. Its effects on communication in the social field and influence on other disciplines and mass media have not yet been evaluated. At this moment, Videotext is an unknown entity, an 'image enigma' that only the future can define. One thing is for sure: it is here to stay.

Videotext is an object of use, experimentation and also investigation. This research is born in a context of doubts and uncertainties, at the level of both hardware and software, as well as in the communication field. I came into contact with Videotext in 1982 in the course 'Videotext: Electronic Publishing' (the first postgraduate course on the medium in Brazil, held at the Communication and Arts School of the University of São Paulo – ECA-USP) taught by Prof. Fredric Michael Litto. From this class emerged several project proposals on my part, among them a workbook in which I explored Videotext from the perspective of visual and pictorial language organisation. This workbook became the source of this volume.

The new medium was introduced into Brazilian art by another one of these creative proposals, materialised in the exhibition *Arte pelo Telefone: Videotexto* [Art by Telephone: Videotext] (curated by myself in December 1982 at the Museum of Image and Sound in the city of São Paulo – MIS-SP). This exhibition was contemporary with the first Videotext exhibition held in New York City, organised by Martim Niesenhold under the auspices of New York University.

Arte pelo Telefone: Videotexto gathered artistic, visual and poetic works by artists and poets connected with the alternative visual poetry magazines edited in the 1970s. Afterwards, other exhibitions were held, such as *Arte e Videotexto*, during the XVII São Paulo International Art Biennial (1983) – then extended to the capital cities of Curitiba and Porto Alegre (1985).

Interventions into the new medium aimed at extracting from it the maximum expression in terms of visual, written, chromatic and kinetic language. It was a quest for the possibilities of Videotext poetics.

From another angle, I worked for hours on end at the editing keyboard to develop messages for the exhibition (Videotext was, at the time, in its first implementation phase).

I had not yet finished the course at ECA-USP when I found myself teaching the first class on visual language for Videotext with the help of the workbook I had prepared. This course has been offered many times since, reformulated each time as my experience with the medium increased.

The attraction, curiosity and enchantment with Videotext led me to formulate the following questions: what can be done with this medium? How does it work? How is its language produced and transmitted? What are its function, performance and capacity? What are its historical antecedents?

The volume you are reading is the product and result of such experiences and one of the answers to those questions that emerged at that first moment, so full of curiosity and enchantment.

II

Videotext (VDT) is the latest vehicle for language production and information distribution. What differentiates VDT from other mass media is the fact that the latter firmly centralise information while VDT is interactive, since it is born from an interpersonal medium: the telephone. VDT, a product of Telematics (an adaptation of informatics to telecommunication systems), has operated regularly since December 15, 1982, in the city of São Paulo under the care of Telesp [São Paulo public telephone company]. Through this association between a telephone, a TV set and a computer (the centre of the system), with a couple of keypresses (similar to a phone call), the user can have access to the most diverse types of visual and written information.

Whatever our first contact with the medium might be, VDT makes it clear that it does not substitute for previous media, but actually feeds off them. It is a strongly hybrid and inclusive medium that integrates other media. Its production process is born from the complex agglutination of a heterogeneous network of aspects from those other media. It is a vehicle that is by its nature intermedial, at the same time that it absorbs different representation systems.

The tendency of the contemporary world with regard to the quality and complexity of media and technologies (multimedia) is to synthesise and create interpenetrating relations between those media (intermedia), thus achieving other hybrid media and technologies, a qualitative product of the association of several media.

The invention of Videotext took place in several countries simultaneously, but Sam Fedida in England managed to deploy the first VDT system worldwide. 'Operating for the public for about three years, under the control of the British

Post Office and Telegraph (BPO), this service was initially named Viewdata, but is known today as Prestel'.

Videotext development began more than ten years ago and has since spread to several countries as it's adapted to various transmission technologies. Currently, the Videotext systems have adopted four leading technologies: Prestel itself, Télétel (from France), Telidon (from Canada) and Captains (from Japan).

Brazil, through Telebrás [Brazilian public telecommunications company], bought the French system (Télétel) 'due to its advantages in quality and cost' and entrusted Telesp with the initial testing phase in the country.

From now on, every mention of Videotext in this book will be referring to the system derived from Télétel, imported and transformed by Brazilian electronic technology. References to other systems will be clearly identified by their respective names.

The operational process of Videotext comprises three operative groups: the system operator or company that controls and looks after the service as a whole, which in this case is Telesp; the service supplier, which are the firms and institutions that transmit the information through the equipment supplied by the system operator; and the user or consumer who uses the system. The latter must have a telephone, a TV and a visual-acoustic signal decoder or adapter with a remote-controlled keyboard through which they can access the service.

Although this study does not address Videotext within the panorama of communication, it is worth mentioning one of its most striking qualities. Videotext is an innovative communication system, for it can interfere with and remodel the performance of other existing contemporary media, disarticulating instituted environments. VDT, with its 'interactive' character, breaks the unidirectionality of the messages within the world of communication, which seems to mean the beginning of the end for mass society (which here implies the mediation by unidirectional communication systems), to the extent that the user can interfere and create information, becoming a potential editor. The tendency of the contemporary world, within the universe of electro-electronic systems, is none other than this increasing democratisation of the emission and reception of information.

This study aims to outline the possibilities of Videotext from the point of view of videographic language, that is, the use of graphic-electronic language in visual communication.

Videography in Videotext focuses mainly on the following aspects:

1 Electronic Videography, as a recent recovery of (prehistoric) pictographic signs, displaces the optical-photographic emphasis of television to the more schematic and Eastern projective-mental image. The retinal visual is therefore displaced by the ideographic visual. Hence, Videotext is an eminently translating and rationalising medium of imagistic and pictographic languages inherited from history; languages that, coupled with verbal language, force us to develop a mode of thinking that oscillates between the iconic-concrete and the abstract-schematic.

2 Videotext's hybridity announces its strong synthetic characteristic, which is also manifested in how the systems affects the languages it absorbs, as it forces these languages to be translated for display in the concrete space of the medium. Thus, Videotext creates an interface with the reader, compelling them to a reductive-schematic thinking and fast and spontaneous perception. Therefore, one should study the maximum conditions of the simplicity and potency of language in order to facilitate a good interface between the mental retina and the medium.

3 Research that analyses both the medium's possibilities and the synthesis of videographic configurations, thus reflecting on the physical generation of the message as well as its potential for perception. Applied knowledge should guide the formation of visual languages and their syntax in the new electronic medium. This is necessary to grasp the possibilities of Videotext, its dimensions and reach, and to understand how it incorporates other media and the information that we feed into it.

Finally, I hope this volume (which doesn't provide any readymade recipes) will be helpful to those who are concerned with the problems and challenges created by the new, ever-changing relationships between language and the recent technologies in the contemporary world.

Chapter 18

By Way of Conclusion (1986)

Júlio Plaza

Videotext is a sight for sore eyes.

Technologies are juxtaposed with other technologies. So, in order to make considerations about Videotext, the newest media of them all, one must also consider its relationship with its counterparts in the mass cultural industry – adopting, of course, the point of view of videography in Videotext.

The combination of audiovisual media, telecommunications and information technologies configures new possibilities for expression. Technological evolution is much faster than our capacity to assimilate and use the new media.

Initially created to edit and convey information, Videotext is configured as an intermedia system capable of interfering with and remodelling the performance of other existing media by disarticulating the instituted environment, for Videotext is an anti-environment. Videotext tends to radically transform the traditional distribution of information by the written, spoken and televised press, placing this same information with even greater efficiency and instantaneity on home video terminals.

Editing in electronic media such as Videotext, intended for large and differentiated audiences, transforms and confounds the reception and production of information.

Thanks to movable types and high printing speeds, the press ensures an excellent distribution of knowledge. After all, printed information reaches increasingly diversified strata of the population. The old dream of universal wisdom and knowledge industries, exemplified by the great encyclopaedias distributed all over the planet, seems to come true with the instantaneous access to information allowed by telematics. The intrusion of electronics, the replacement of paper culture by video screens and the substitution of mechanical printing processes pose questions related to all the components in Videotext's electronic system as well as to those that are outside of it.

The prolonged exposure to video screens, the rapid assimilation of information and the speed of the eye-brain connection developed by human beings, the influence on professional and personal life: such changes in perception and behaviour are brought about by the new technology of Videotext. It also changes our language because the *interface* of electronic media with the user is a decisive link in this chain. Rejection or acceptance of the new medium will largely depend on how messages are finally perceived during this connection.

In laying out the necessary conclusions from this work, it is almost impossible not to refer to the McLuhanian ideas regarding media in the electronic age. These ideas are so internalised in our culture that any similarity to what has been exposed here should not be considered mere coincidence.

Although we have focused our research on aspects of Videotext's electronic videographic languages, we should not fail to acknowledge other elements that, in our view, constitute truly new qualities of this medium.

Intermedia synthesis produces unusual data. We will conclude our work by addressing two aspects that characterise Videotext in relation to its users. Even though the first one has not yet been treated with due importance, most future research should focus on it, with the benefit of a distance and perspective we don't yet have.

These two aspects are:

- Videotext is the first dialogic vehicle since it establishes a democratic relation in the system: user-editor and user-user, presided over by dialogue. Electronic Videography, as a recent recovery of (prehistoric) pictographic signs, displaces the optic-projective-photographic emphasis to the schematic projective mental image. The retinal visual is therefore displaced by the ideographic visual.

- Videotext's hybridity announces its strong defining characteristic, which is manifested in how the systems conforms to the languages it absorbs, as it forces these languages to be translated for display in the concrete space of the medium. Thus, Videotext creates an *interface* with the reader, compelling them to a reductive-schematic thinking and to fast and spontaneous perception.

Videotext, unlike all mass communication media, is interactive because it is born from an interpersonal medium: the telephone. Other kinds of media strongly centralise information. With its interactivity, Videotext can be characterised as a dialogic vehicle since it breaks off the unidirectionality of the messages within the world of communication, which seems to indicate the beginning of the end for mass society (which here implies mediation by unidirectional communication systems), to the extent that the user can interfere and create information, becoming a potential editor.

Videotext is hence characterised as a democratic vehicle since its bidirectionality allows for the expression and return of information, departing from the principles of causality, unidirectionality and authoritarianism characteristic of mass media. With Videotext, it's not possible to 'raise the political consciousness' of the masses.

Videotext offers the possibility of individual participation in social and communitarian life, marking a step forward in the democratisation of information.

This tendency has been taking shape since the 1960s. The socialisation of the means of production and reproduction, through the popularisation of reprographic systems (such as offset or photocopying, among others), already enabled the possibility of copying whole volumes, putting into question notions of authorship and, above all, copyright. At the same time, these processes enabled the production of thousands of limited 'author editions' and alternative magazines in the 1970s.

This democratisation and socialisation of the means of production and reproduction provides us with the necessary tools for the creation of low-cost electronic publishing houses (compared to newspapers, for example), of small groups or user-based editing enterprises based on the principle of spontaneous and informational affinity. At the same time, it calls for the user's consciousness when choosing and interacting with information.

This establishes an economic principle where no one is forced to pay what they did not ask for. The users' consciousness grows in proportion to their engagement with the medium's interactivity. Videotext could thus be characterised not as a mass medium but as a medium for publics and communities of individuals that are conscious of the information they are after.

Based on the premise that Videotext accepts any kind of information, various possible uses and purposes could be achieved, such as the organisation of courses, electronic magazines, newspapers, plebiscites etc., which would allow for the creation of inner circuits and even closed user groups with appropriate access codes. Cultural mobilisation and the consequent decentralisation of information are thus possible.

Videotext's application in pedagogy seems to be one of its strongest features, as it offers conditions (not only by illustrating verbal lessons or offering 'audiovisual aids', but as a result of its interactivity) for the deverbalisation of classes, making them more participatory and interesting, not to mention the possibilities it allows for the immediate (*online*) recovery of any programmable information.

Since it is not tied to any objects, 'information', says Prof. Nora, 'is a unique and revolutionary economic and cultural good'. It is not destroyed when it is consumed, but rather qualitatively transforms people and their living standards. The poet Stephane Mallarmé believed that 'the world exists to end in a book'. 'Nowadays, we are in a position to go beyond that, transferring the whole spectacle to a computer's memory'. Currently, the Dow Jones (in the United States) is working on transcribing the 21 volumes of the Academic American Encyclopaedia into Videotext.

At the same time as it reorganises all the previous tools (hardware) into a system, Videotext also reorganises information and the ways of manipulating, perceiving and storing it, whether in the form of objects (books, newspapers, etc.) or their spatial and energetic relations. Today it is possible to organise, produce and transmit information in a decentralised way from any location, that is, from a home office, thus getting rid of additional energy costs (entailed by the movement of people and things, the storage and archiving of information-objects) typical of industrial activities, thus rationalising and saving energy and space.

Now, with Videotext, any user can have an entire newspaper stand or even a library in their office without taking up space, with the comfort of having the information they want appear on their television set.

A 'cold' medium that it is, Videotext compels the user's participation and establishes a balanced compromise between traditional newspaper and book; for if the book expresses an 'individual perspective', the newspaper, with its mosaic-like juxtaposition of events, tends to be communitarian and social. As a dialogic vehicle, that is, a product of the increased speed of information that engages the audience and decentralises decision-making processes, Videotext creates participatory consciousness. McLuhan had already observed that faster information processes create a political disposition apart from the delegation and representation of power. In comparison, slower information processes tend to call for more representation and delegation. And for Norbert Wiener, 'information is more a matter of process than of accumulation'.

The funny thing is that History (and prehistory) seem to self-reproduce through Videotext because the new contexts absorb and define the previous ones as content, *artifying* them. Signs think.

The VDT operator faces the same challenges as the Neolithic people when they were trying to adapt and translate the analogue design of an organic form into the geometric thread of a basket, adapting a 'vitalistic' drawing into an abstract scheme, thus foreshadowing the ornament and the source of future writing.

While Videotext incorporates history, it also makes a selection from it and gives it meaning. The medium breaks into the world of communication where photographic-verisimilar signs predominate, substituting the world of photography-thing-of-things with a pictographic language that appeals to analogue codification. Videotext exchanges the visual-optical perceptual world for ideographic-mental perception. By displacing our interest from the 'retinal-optic image' to analogue mental images, Videotext displaces the world of things into the world of abstract and schematic signs.

While photography 'turns people into things' and turns relations into objects, electronic videography evokes pictographic and ideographic writings 'that represent an extension of the visual senses able to store and facilitate access to human experience'. Its effect is integrative and encompassing rather than being disaggregating as phonetic translation is. As the two kinds of signs – the verbal-written and the visual – intertwine in Videotext, their effect becomes complementary.

Videotext confirms that writing and drawing have the same graphic substance. The Videotext space is not a projection space in the guise of cinema but a space that projects the Eastern mental sign, an area that is not neutral but radiant with energy. In this space, each light-point is a sun, a see-through light (as in the multi-dimensional space of medieval stained glass) that converges to synthesise the history of Eastern painting and ideography into intensely organised and condensed cultures and creations.

The new system imposes a different sensibility while simultaneously socialising an ideographic visuality instead of a photographic one. In the silence of the screen, images, words and colours flow with absolute calm and serenity, demanding the necessary concentration from the user who holds the electronic book.

Writing and image absorb and iconise each other, creating their own silent space-time rhythms; simultaneously, the repetition of the point-light pattern creates the synesthetic effect of groping, walking and feeling: time and space as if they slipped through our fingers. Videotext is visual-ideographic, essentially tactile. It leans towards the visual to the extent that it forsakes the phonetic-digital and establishes an ideogrammatic-gestalt inclusive visual – for the ideogram, in McLuhan's words, is a gestalt that does not analytically dissociate the senses as phonetic writing does. The graphic-electronic artist can only lend tactile values to retinal impressions, reaffirming their commitment to the visual-sensorial culture, 'for tactility embraces all the senses just as white incorporates all the colours'.

To make graphic messages with Videotext is to extend consciousness, to create a context of awareness as it inserts an anti-environment within previously established ones, thus deautomating perception. Videotext has nothing to do with TV, comics and other media; it has its own specificity.

To program Videotext is a conversation in an 'intervisual', 'intertextual' and 'inter-sensorial' rhythm with various codes of information. In the gaps between these codes, one establishes a fluid border between information and ideographic pictoriality: a margin of creation. In these gaps, the medium acquires its actual dimension and qualities, as each message (like each technology) cannibalistically swallows the previous ones, since they are all formed by the same energy.

The medium confirms and conforms the message, makes it part of its truth, and creates a new interface between man and artifice, a simultaneous and analogic connection between the optical channel (eye) and the technical channel (terminal). It also creates the conditions for the immediate perception of the received languages. It stimulates a kind of schematic abstract thinking, spontaneous and concrete-qualitative.

While blending written and visual languages, Videotext also forces them to adapt to new videographic possibilities. By means of translating operations, it transforms these languages and adapts them to schematic and abstract messages, where epigraphic concision, maximum simplicity with minimal tension, short telegraphic style and humour prevail over the discursive drowning of signs in gratuitous graphics, for the brain reconstructs these messages at electronic speed.

The conformation (formatting) of language to Videotext, just as the automation of syntax it proposes, allows for the mechanisation of all universal writing systems and places. For this very reason, many of the avant-garde projects of the beginning of the 20th century become relevant once again, as they advocate for universal rather than particular (i.e., individual) expression by means of aesthetic programs, programs which are harmonious with the industry (constructivism, neoplasticism, the dadaist ready-made and concretism, among others). Through the schematism of languages, videotext similarly advocates for the collective and universal character of those very same languages. If there is no place for 'universal expression', as Mondrian would say, it 'can only be created by a true equation of the universal and the individual'.

Productive conditions no longer belong to primary craft nor to secondary industrial activities, but rather to electro-electronic activities that are all-encompassing and instantaneous. Electronic technology, superimposed over the landscape like a form of Eastern writing, creates within us an inner landscape, or inscape, that also irradiates light-energy, generating its own rhythm-spaces and changing our perception. Light, as information without content, illuminates and recreates us, integrating inscape and landscape (the subjective interior and the ambient exterior), for the electrical circuit is the extension of our central nervous system and brain.

In the end, with the help of a scrutinising sensibility and the 'antennae' that allow us to see the probing forms of new languages under the present conditions, the electronic-Neolithic people will intertwine their amazing informational basket and dress, using their 'cursor' as an 'electronic brush' as they interface their central nervous system with Videotext.

Chapter 19

Holopoetry and Perceptual Syntax (1986)

Eduardo Kac

The holopoetry project creates a new poetic language through the improbable possibilities of immaterial textual volumes produced through the holographic process. The main problem in poetic expression today is not one of compositional unit (whether letter to sentence), but one of syntax, which is no longer organised in a line ('unidimensional flow of signs' – Max Bense) or structured on a flat surface ('a textual surface' – Bense). With holopoetry, syntax is organised in discontinuous space.

Instead of reducing rhythm to the limitations of a flat surface, holopoetry makes it possible to create a poetic language in which it does not matter whether one is using phrasal, vocabular, syllabic or literal structures. Expression is similar to the enigmatic states of consciousness while spatiotemporality operates at an extreme, pluri-dimensional level of complexity.

This new holistic perception, the source of the fruition of real immaterial objects (volumes without mass), requires a response in the structure of language: the possibility to transform the instrument of intellectualisation – the word – into a sign as fluid and elastic as thought. By taking over an optic or (better yet) an optronic system of production, distributing the elements of the composition in the surrounding space and registering this information on a flat device, holopoetry enables a perceptual syntax, relativising the cognitive process according to the different points of observation in space.

Quantum theory (Heisenberg's 'uncertainty', Bohr's 'ambiguity') teaches us that two properties associated with atomic and nuclear objects cannot always be measured at the same time, and that the possible values of these 'observable quantities', or quantised physical magnitudes, can be discontinuous. Holopoetry is coded according to this principle, to take on quantified verbal configurations whose reading is done in leaps, irregularly, discontinuously, according to each point of view. The way one looks at it modifies the holopoem. The act of looking in itself implies a specific spatial position of observation, in which one must consider the distance between the two eyes (approximately 6.5cm) which are situated in different points in space. Looking at a holopoem, therefore, is more than receiving the wavefront of a verbal light code; it is reading it according to a changing order. To read a holopoem is to impose upon it a grammar without defined outlines, discovering its meanings in space itself.

Perhaps holopoetry is contributing towards a new and vital human experiment. Restructuring the dimensional field of language can be an adventure as rich as scientific revelations in physical and mathematical fields. Holopoetry demands an urgent reformulation in the methods of conceiving, producing and enjoying poetic states, for in the holomatic era the artist intermediates their creation through techno-systems, increasing the quantity of information in shorter periods of time and, consequently, intensifying the sensorial experience of the spectator.

In these three years of work with [Eugênio] Catta-Preta, I have created four works: *Holo/Olho* (Holo/Eye), which uses orthoscopic/pseudoscopic bipolarisation; *Abracadabra*, analogically constructed in relation to orbital systems, with rhythmic chromatic control; *Oco* (Hollow), in which an image of conflict between desire and idleness is created; and *Zyx*, which uses the old Cartesian coordinates of tridimensionality, reorganising syntactic space in dimensional leaps.

The development of holopoetry as a hybrid poetic language is an interdisciplinary project, for it deals with a hybridisation of genres (visual and verbal) and of structure (syntax and pictorial space) that coordinates the infinite possibilities of the word-image, written with the revolutionary spatial focalisation of holography. It would not be worthwhile to try to find, in the pages of literary publications or even in any couple of verses, the radical poetic rupture that will reflect the deep alterations in knowledge and perception resulting from new developments in the techno-sciences. It will not be found there, simply because it was not invented to live in books – at least not in those we know today, printed in two dimensions.

Two monumental exhibitions that took place in 1985, the Tsukuba Fair in Japan and *The Immaterials* at the Beaubourg in France, are the best proof that in the next millennium, perception and sensibility are bound to undergo a deep transformation, a metamorphosis that we cannot even imagine. But at least one thing can be affirmed beyond a shadow of a doubt: in the future, new art forms will emerge. In time, however, these new art forms will become as classic as the enigmatic smile of Leonardo da Vinci's Mona Lisa or the provocative goatee of Duchamp's *Gioconda*.

Chapter 20

Pretext for an Intervention (1984)

Annateresa Fabris

At first glance, the artistic and critical operation of 3NÓS3 seems to tackle two distinct and almost contradictory domains: the art circuit and the city. Three interventions from 1979 – the bagging of statues, the *X-Galeria* operation [X-Gallery] and the *Tríptico* [Triptych] – primarily address the former. The subsequent group *interversions*, in contrast, leave behind any polemic or dialogue with the arts milieu and turn explicitly to the urban space, no longer treating it as a passive container for preexisting structures and objects nor the reference point for an exhibition, but rather as a true site of artistic action. The group's actions, in the latter case, acknowledge the essential relation between space and the materials that give shape to the temporary physiognomy of an artwork.

In both cases, however, the 3NÓS3 method of operation has remained consistent (namely, to interfere with a given space), as has the environment in which their actions unfold (the street). This consistency imbues the seemingly contradictory domains of the art circuit and the city with the same logic and understanding with regard to what it means to make art. The city is similarly used as a 'drawing sheet' in the interventions and in the *interversions*, drawing out new possibilities for visualising habitual spaces that have become 'neutral' in our perceptions due to distracted consumption.

Since its first actions in 1979, what 3NÓS3 calls into question is the relationship between art and the city. They want the artistic object to exist *a priori*, and they want the artist to intervene in the urban space to add information to it, creating zones of colour within the indistinct grey of overpasses and avenues. Whether the group's operations might be a parody or not, their concern is always artistic. This idea is conveyed through the metaphor of the 'drawing sheet' and the group's deliberate distancing from an the apparently similar practice of sociological art.

While 3NÓS3's work briefly assimilates art into the city and turns the urban space into the stage for their actions, the inherent ambiguity of this approach cannot be ignored. Art and city, in fact, never fully merge. The covered statues, the exposed canvases on the sidewalk and the interference on large road structures with cellophane and plastic do not represent a desacralisation of art, but rather become works and create spaces for aesthetic appreciation in themselves. Despite the use of poor and precarious materials (garbage bags, masking tape, cellophane, plastic), the group's actions are able to make the statue more of a statue, the canvas more of a canvas, the overpass or the avenue a substitute for the museum and the gallery. Though they might be temporary, their interventions suspend time and evoke values that uphold the fixity of art, running against the flow of life.

In that sense, 3NÓS3's most blatant action has been *X-Galeria*, serving not only as a testament to the closed circuit of the art market but also creating a potential tautological short circuit by eliciting the expected reactions from art critics and those affected by its 'boomerang effect'. Gallery owners referred to the intervention as 'jinx', 'discontentment', 'terrorism', 'joke', 'childish play', with very few showing any appreciation for it. The system's self-defence mechanisms: art criticism's immediate reaction was to uphold a long-established curriculum of disciplines that young artists must master before 'daring' to create; galleries were advised to only showcase works 'of merit', a concept incompatible with the anonymity of nocturnal 'guerrillas'. No one attempted, however, to delve into the reasons behind the group's interdicting gesture or to understand the artwork proposed within it. Rejecting the act altogether proved more comfortable and easier, transforming it into a mere provocative and inconsequential outburst, eliciting predictable paternalistic advice that confirmed a widely known dogma: the sacredness of art as merchandise is undisputable.

Press activity around *X-Galeria* (like that around the bagging of statues, on a smaller scale) directly served the group's objectives. Their actions required mass media to be broadcast, to be recorded and exist in a dimension beyond the few spectators that witnessed them as they unfolded as ephemeral events. From the art supplement to the local news, 3NÓS3's trajectory across newspaper pages highlights two distinct attitudes from the press. Firstly, the estrangement of art critics since the '*X-Galeria* scandal', which has resulted in rare and often pejorative references to their work, implying lack of originality, derivative proposals and the like. Secondly, the documentation of events by city reporters who, oblivious to any artistic question, framed interventions as one fact among others and put their aesthetic intentions in quotation marks, as they did not recognise these intentions, since they were not part of the repertoire of the common person that the news addressed.

Even though this public relations approach may have amplified the reach of 3NÓS3's work among readers, it may also have undermined the group's overarching intentions. While 3NÓS3's early interventions targeted consecrated targets, favouring sociological interpretations, their later *interversions* experimented with visual elements such as 'contrasts', 'groupings' and 'relationships with form, space and colour',[46] demanding a response from art criticism. Thanks to the group's elusive provocations, however, art critics became no longer interested in their work precisely when 3NÓS3's proposals most needed to be discussed in proper aesthetic terms.

Although 3NÓS3's association with urban space remains ambiguous, since it can only be squared through the framework of art, their activity demonstrates an acute awareness of the new status of cities in contemporary society. Cities are no longer conveyors of values but rather of news; they are no longer historical constructions but rather information systems (Argan quoted in Migliorini 1975, 135). This is evident in 3NÓS3's relationship with the press, both as newsworthy material and as a producer of news (in actions such as *A Categoria Básica de Comunicação* [The Basic Category of Communication] and *3NÓS3/ Interversão Urbana* [3NÓS3/ Urban Interversion 1981], for example).

These interactions with mass communication media bring the actions proposed by Mario Ramiro, Rafael França and Hudinilson Jr. closer to one of the fundamental principles of sociological art: the creation of a 'surprise event' which invites critical discourse and produces a liveable event aimed at a larger public through the mediation of newspapers and television. While 3NÓS3's operational procedure 'fixes' itself in the moment when it comes to life, it does so as a communication system rather than as a crystallised 'work of art'. Their work is the creation of 'surprise events' as social manifestations rather than projects. There is substantial research work underlying those 'colour spots' that bring new tonalities to the monotonous urban landscape. This research unfolds as a drawing on paper before being transported to the immeasurably larger sheet that is the city.

X-Galeria's sibylline message, 'What's inside stays / What's outside expands', summarises 3NÓS3's whole work philosophy. 'To work on the outside' means to take a critical position vis-à-vis the established art circuit, rather than putting oneself on the sidelines. This approach insists on the existence of art outside the frame, even if it requires the creation of some new, rapidly perishable frames. But this dialectical movement, common to all interventions that focus on the city, is one that 3NÓS3 could not resolve in its brief lifespan.

Chapter 21

Museums and New Communication Media (1976)

Walter Zanini

To give up on aesthetic elements saturated of meanings; to develop critical investigations within the framework of new media, which render fields of knowledge more interdisciplinary; to engage with behaviour in its broader sense; to look for a wider audience – such are the strongest characteristics of the current artistic language. Artists who increasingly use technological media show their interest in broader participation in social reality. They have realised that the art immediately associated with everyday life was being marginalised and worn-out. By escaping both the label of idealism and formal stylistic singularities, by making use of the vehicles of transmission proper to today's society and by being aware of the critical application of their sensibilities, these artists are seeking to establish effective relationships with the public in their daily lives. This is the same as making objective values denser; in other words, to manifest a new and closer interconnection between the plane of abstract creativity and the concrete territory of existence.

The major consequence of this state of affairs is a deprivatisation of communication exchanges. The substitution of visual expression systems by flexible mechanisms of presentation dissipates the mystique of the unique artwork and its implications for aesthetic and economic values. The traditional limitations of the usual circuit of access to art (museum, gallery, private collector) tend to be broken by the work's ubiquitous irradiation. Obviously, this phenomenon has been more directly stimulated by conceptual currents, and it is more than an assumption that makes us believe that this broad dialogic disposition of art, an acute characteristic of the 1970s, is going to be further consolidated in the future.

While observing these crucial transformations from the art museum's perspective, one must consider the need for the revision of its institutional functions and its adaptation to the new demands of communication, starting from the very space in which the museum is situated. It is a fact that a decisive part of artistic production today is not restricted to space but extends into the dimension of time, which means that we must foresee changes to the architectural conception governing the spirit of the museum building. The operational techniques of art forms that require electronic equipment, in turn, introduce modifications to a museum space whose goal has almost always been the exhibition of static objects.

Although recent works have dematerialised into forms of communication, thus allowing for a much more flexible diffusion, we believe that the museum's chambers should persist in being nuclei for evaluating, confronting and developing different production processes. Several museums in the world today are restructuring their spaces and installations to formulate the program for this new cultural reality.

One of the museum's functions is to build collections of media such as audiovisuals, a field that has greatly expanded recently, as well as of the multiple vehicles for the communication of ideas by means of text, image or the body. The promotion of exhibitions and transmissions of various media modalities is an obvious concern. Still, the museum cannot be restricted to its traditional and univocal form as a receptacle of objects, that is, to situate itself *a posteriori* in a passive hierarchy of the creation of the work. The museum must also become active as an operating centre; it must become a privileged space of experimentation, favouring and assembling creative dispositions within several research fields.

Therefore, the scholarly field of the museum should not be confined to the current limits of museology, art history and criticism, or other specialties that merely encompass established domains, such as industrial design and cinema. In a situation increasingly addressed towards interdisciplinary development, the museum cannot prescind contributions from the anthropologist, the sociologist, the psychologist and other scientists.

Another way for museums to accomplish their cultural and educational missions is to spread out beyond the walls of their headquarters, establishing links of true community outreach by using current communication resources, especially TV systems, through which they can greatly reduce their distance from the public. This strategy, which could force future museums to have their own transmission networks, would not only imply a diffusion or a general democratisation of the museum, but also an empowerment of specific formulations of creativity. Museum activity will thus include both centralising and decentralising activities as components of a broad combined program.

Chapter 22

Introduction to the 17th São Paulo Biennial (1983)

Walter Zanini

The 17th Biennial seeks to consolidate the objectives outlined in the previous edition. The exhibition is once again divided into articulated nuclei: the first one, structured by languages, strives at capturing relevant aspects of the current artistic production in its multiple technical and expressive conditions; the second includes exhibits of artists and movements that introduced new creative processes in the 20th century. This change was fundamental in the making of the previous edition, which also saw the end of the national sections and opened a decisive instance for the comparative reading of art being developed in different cultural areas.

Two years ago, the preparation of the Biennial was performed in too short a period of time to allow for the necessary dialogue with the leaders of the many foreign delegations. This time, under explicit guidelines, more particular recommendations were given by the curatorial team, taking into account the quality and organic logic of the exhibition in its nuclei I and II. This critical engagement, which encompassed a direct invitation to artists, did not fail to bring results. It is evident that this process is still in its initial phase and that it will require a great deal of creativity and efforts from future curators.

The first nucleus of the Biennial attempted to look past aesthetic restrictions towards technique, while also rejecting organisational solutions based on other problems, such as the adoption of arbitrary themes. Divided into two vectors, the nucleus was opened to the energies of modernity where they could be found most easily. In this sense, the Biennial differs entirely from the latest versions of its European counterparts.

The exhibition's purpose is to outline the artistic emergence that followed the historical avant-gardes, be it in connection with the technologies of mass culture or within handicraft traditions. The selection of works implies responsibilities at various stages; the public, final addressee of our messages, can evaluate the results of this process and meditate on the great changes taking place at this historical time, when possibilities of creating and interpreting art proliferate.

Amidst the many traditional art forms going through a vigorous renaissance, painting stands in a privileged position, being represented in this exhibition by a larger number of works than any other media. Painting, which seemed to be a species on the way to extinction, has resumed its quest for new artistic investigations and ideas. In the last few years, an emblematic imaginary has taken over, representing a return to the world of shapes and colours, with iconography and style that draw from both recent and ancient art history and the new mythologies of mass media. Works by masters of free figuration, eminently subjective and aggressive, are exhibited around the Ibirapuera Park. Once again, a movement seems to grow so much that it seems to overshadow its supposed creators, as Heidegger would have it. This is ultimately the result of the interaction between collective and individual energies.

Sculpture, in turn, has exploded into new conditions of existence of its own: some sculptors are reinterpreting anthropomorphic images using either new or old materials, others are conveying singular visions of the consumer society using its everyday residues. Many of them are participating in this exhibition. It is also important to mention photography, a field under continuous transformation, with a strong presence in the show.

We have redoubled our efforts to include in the exhibition the most valid productions exploring the languages of new media, which even the most conservative critique has begun to acknowledge. The saga of the information currents driving our world is of utmost significance to the fate of art. The field of videoart has always known how to incorporate new intuitions through its dual visual-verbal affordances. Art in videotext began its journey around 1982 and would soon demonstrate its importance as an electronic system that allows for the interaction between emitter and receiver. For the first time, there is a medium that makes visible every successive step of a linguistic process, whether graphic or verbal. In addition to videotext works, the exhibition features art made with satellites, cable TV and new computer applications that expand the connections between art and technology.

The second nucleus has a special function in an international exhibition taking place in Brazil, a country where the largest part of the audience is young and lacking contact with art from other nations. This section has the task of situating elements in consistency with the consolidated perspectives of contemporary art. The presence of Manzoni and the Fluxus group, of Flávio de Carvalho and Bram van Velde, certainly opens the path for the great work that the Biennial will accomplish in the future, connecting the living past with a history in development.

Chapter 23

For a Creative Criticism / Curating Exhibitions as Creation (1989)

Frederico Morais

I

1. Criticism and Critics

The theme of an Art Critics' Meeting held in Ontario, Canada, in 1961, was 'Crisis of Criticism: Are Critics Liberators or Oppressors?'. In other words: is criticism creation or judgment? To create is to liberate; to judge is to oppress. The criticism that multiplies the meanings of an artwork is creative. The one that seeks to enforce a single and final meaning closes the work and oppresses the artist. As judgment, criticism is science; as creation, it is art.

In the concluding report of the 9th Meeting of Art Critics in Bratislava ... in 1969, Giulio Carlo Argan calls attention to the antithesis between creation and judgment: in all religions, the history of the world begins with creation and ends with judgment. Judgment destroys creation. It corrects creation's fatal error. But despite this theological origin, criticism has fought against every form of discretionary power.

For Mário Pedrosa, 'the critic must keep their head above the current. At each moment, they must accompany the artist in their investigations, in their creative restlessness, but they must also strive to know not only how to capture these investigations but also how to place them in a given situation'. That is, the critic cannot assume as their own 'the artist's unilateral perspective, because to explain, defend, situate and hierarchise, they must also see things from other angles'. In that sense, the first function of criticism is to place itself against every discretionary form of power and authoritarianism, including the tyranny of the artist or of hegemony.

2. Criticism and the Artist

The critic can only grow morally and intellectually if they find in artists the necessary stimulus for their reflection. Conversely, artists must respond with their works to the originality and depth of critical thought.

It is, therefore, a true *potlach*, an exchange of gifts. The critic, in their activity, appropriates the work of art as a matter of reflection, just as the artist appropriates elements from nature, or objective or subjective reality, to elaborate their work. With their reflection, the critic adds value to the piece, and the artist, receiving their work revivified by critics, responds with new pieces that already include those previously mentioned values. The more vitalist the artist's founding gesture, the more motivated the critic feels to add to the work's imaginary and intelligible dimensions. Thus, the artist, the critic and the work grow together. And the audience does too.

3. Criticism and Literature

At the Congress of Art Critics held in 1961 in São Paulo on the theme 'Functions and Phases of Art Criticism in Brazil', Mário Pedrosa pejoratively called the first Brazilian critics 'literati', stating that they 'knew art only through reproductions and hearsay, making criticism on a literary basis'. Professional criticism, Pedrosa said, came only with the São Paulo Biennial, as it was only since then that critics had began 'to address artworks as elements that could be analysed in themselves, to be later coordinated in a set'. Pedrosa's position is understandable in its concern to define the critic's space of action and their criteria for engaging with the work of art. And his activity, like that of other critics, was crucial in defining a specific vocabulary for criticism. However, some critics from the literary tradition have exercised their craft with the most outstanding competence. I'm thinking of Mário de Andrade, Sérgio Milliet, Murilo Mendes, Ferreira Gullar and João Cabral de Melo Neto.

Cabral, for instance, the author of an essentially plastic poetry, has been exercising criticism through his poems. Calling himself 'incapable of being vague', João Cabral has shown interest, above all, in the visual art of evident rigour. Among the constructive artists, he prefers Mondrian, whose work he has analysed in more than one poem. Besides his monograph on Joan Miró, he has studied Juan Gris, Rego Monteiro, Weissmann, Mary Vieira, Max Bense, Brasília, etc.

But as with art history's rapid succession of '-isms', criticism, having defined its specificity, soon became a literary quasi-genre, or what Roland Barthes has dubbed *Écriture*. In this new situation of the 'general crisis of commentary', Barthes says, 'the critic becomes, in their turn, a writer'.

4. Criticism and Anthropology

Pedrosa's criticism of the literati could be extended to professionals of other fields when they make incursions into the visual arts. In presenting the exhibition *Universo do Carnaval* [Carnival's Universe] (1981), the anthropologist Roberto da Matta states that 'the paintings are no longer a contemplative and neutral space, but an area of reflection where the artist and their art join us in search of hidden meanings of the Brazilian world, seen through its most vast showcase: carnival'. It's worth saying that Da Matta analyses paintings from his perspective of carnival, usually choosing less visually attractive works to illustrate his anthropological theories. These theories are better applied to pieces of discursive or descriptive nature. But they fail to account for plastic aspects such as colour, form, time, space, etc.

5. Criticism and Psychoanalysis

But since we are all human, no art critic is exempt from projecting their desires onto the artist's work and career. In order to allow the artwork to live out its own structure and express its formal values, the artist represses within it the subjective motivations that led to its excellence. Often, to live, a work must destroy the artist's biography. In trying to decipher and decode the work's mystery, the critic, in turn, ends up revealing that which had been veiled by the artist. But as they add their values, the critic once again veils the work, transforming their interpretation.

The history of a work of art is thus an endless game of veiling and unveiling, of partial revelations. The artist veils while desiring to unveil. And often the critic, in order to analyse an artwork, must reconstruct within it the veiled biography of the artist (a simulacrum). The critic is an amorous voyeur with their eyes fixed on the artwork. They want to go ever further, to discover what is hidden and veiled in the piece. In this process, they are very similar to the psychoanalyst – or the police officer.

6. Phenomenological Criticism

Art criticism rarely takes into account the artist's creative processes: how they work, whether they paint like this or like that, by day or night, with music or without music, with their wife by their side, with their dog, etc. It rarely considers whether, as Ad Reinhardt recommended in his 'Twelve Rules for a New Academy', artists try to avoid all domestic contamination. Critics also don't consider how facts external to the work, to the studio and to the artist's career influence creation. My criticism, for example (journalistic criticism, to be precise), has been more acidic or lyrical, milder or angrier, depending on my own mood, on the greyness or brightness of the day, on the failure of the government's economic plan, on the campaign for direct elections, on the last movie I saw, on the last book I read, on the phone call that interrupted my writing, on the tooth that broke, on the fluctuations of the dollar or on the new '-isms' in the to-and-fro of artistic trends. As a critic, I have not been averse to or estranged from the styles, pressures, affections, passions, dislikes and prejudices that exist, for I have been alive, fucking, suffering, liking and hating.

One of my fantasies is to write an affective history of art one day. To discuss the affectivity of form, situating the passionate relationship of the critic with the work as the most advisable way to penetrate the meaning of artistic creation. I want to show how affective relationships between art producers or creators and their private worlds sometimes have a decisive impact on artistic creation. In their analyses, art critics and historians tend to hide this affective side, thus denying the artist's subjectivity and, deep down, their own. And often, due to theoretical excesses, the critic becomes a bouncer of the work, deflecting all affective contamination. Many advancements and retreats in the history of art or certain phases or eras of an artist have resulted from friendships, enmities, romances; carnal or platonic exchanges; betrayals, withdrawals, frustrations, etc.

Lionello Venturi has already touched upon this subject in his History of Art Criticism: 'When we talk about the artist's personality, we want to talk about the moment in which they create. At that moment, they are the representative of the eternal in art. It is generally considered, however, that in the work of art the individual character is ephemeral and contingent, and one builds "the laws of art", whose observation would lead to the eternal value of the artwork. But the study of art and the history of criticism show that these laws of art are actually ephemeral and contingent, valid only for a certain period or school, never for all times and all places'. In sum, for Venturi, artistic personality must be considered a law of its own.

7. In Conclusion

I support criticism as creation. I consider the eye to be more important than knowledge and intuition to be more revealing than intelligence. Artistic sensibility is a vital source of critical intuition. What is fundamental to the critic is not to be trained in philosophy or anthropology but rather to be sensitive to the work of art and, before anything else, to meaning and life. Poetic apprehension is more effective than theoretical apparatus.

I believe in a loving, engaging and involved form of criticism. Like Susan Sontag, I propose to replace hermeneutics with an erotics of criticism, the dull and pedantic discourse with a loving discourse. Baudelaire, one of the founders of modern criticism, wrote about the 1846 Salon: 'I sincerely believe that the best criticism is that which is amusing and poetic, not the cold one that, under the pretext of explaining everything, has neither hatred nor rancour and that voluntarily divests itself of all temperament'. And he goes further: 'To be fair, that is, to have its *raison d'être*, criticism must be partial, passionate and poetic, that is, made with an exclusive point of view, a point of view that opens horizons'.

II

1. The Critic and the New Means of Expression

Each day, art critics encounter fresh challenges, demanding increasing resilience and a breadth of knowledge that enables them to address an ever-expanding universe of projects with their comments. In addition to painting, sculpture, graphic arts and photography, the critic must deal with the Object, installations, performance, architecture, design, video and cinema, the various manifestations of high-tech art, etc. These new means of expression, while demanding from the critic a multidisciplinary vision, are imposing a process of specialisation within criticism.

But the exercise of art criticism is not restricted to the journalistic text produced in the heat of the moment, nor to the slow theoretical elaboration of the essay or the book. Art criticism also takes place in poetry, audiovisual, art film, video, exhibition and performance, when it ceases to be merely a judging activity to become a poetic and creative exercise.

2. Curatorship

Curating exhibitions is part of critical activity. It is part of creative, not academic criticism. Exhibition curatorship is a task for the art critic and not for collectors, art dealers, artists, etc.

The curator must have the same qualities as the critic-creator: knowledge of art history, capacity for analysis, sensibility and boldness. Curating involves several professionals, but only one is responsible for the meaningful totality of the exhibition-work. The result of good curatorship is, above all, the creation of a climate or atmosphere that involves the visitor emotionally but also stimulates reflection. It is also a recreation, a simulacrum, which authorises bold gestures, confrontations, etc. Therefore, one should avoid encyclopaedic exhibitions, which overwhelm the visitor with too much information. Much like a work of art, a show must welcome the visitor poetically.

Chapter 24

From the Body to the Ground (2001)

Frederico Morais

In the history of Brazilian Art, we talk only about *Do Corpo à Terra* [From the Body to the Ground]. But, in reality, *Do Corpo à Terra* was two simultaneous and integrated events: the exhibition *Objeto e Participação* [Object and Participation], which opened at the Belo Horizonte Art Palace on 17th April 1970, and the manifestation *Do Corpo à Terra*, which took place at the Belo Horizonte City Park between 17th and 21st April of the same year, promoted by Hidrominas – the Minas Gerais State tourism company. The events were initiated by Mari'Stella Tristão, director of exhibitions at the recently created Art Palace and creator of the Ouro Preto Salon, an event dedicated to a different medium every year. Under that rotation system, in 1970 it would be sculpture's turn. Mari'Stella invited me to curate that year's show, which would be exceptionally held at the Art Palace, and I proposed to change the category from 'sculpture' to 'object' while occupying the surrounding City Park with artists' performances.

In the second half of the 1960s, the 'object' was the order of the day. Already in the *Vanguarda Brasileira* [Brazilian Avant-Garde] exhibition, which I organised at the Rectory of the Federal University of Minas Gerais in 1966, I had defined the object 'as a new situation, which configures or is the most adequate vehicle to express the new realities proposed by postmodem art'. The following year, a movement started in Rio de Janeiro in protest against a 'contest for box-shaped artworks', resulting in the *Nova Objetividade Brasileira* [New Brazilian Objectivity] showcase at the Modern Art Museum of Rio de Janeiro in April 1967. As the curator of the 4th Modern Art Salon of the Federal District (December 1967, in Brasília), I included for the first time the object as a category within the guidelines of a Brazilian art salon. It was a contradiction I openly embraced as, in a new text published that same year, I reaffirmed my perspective that 'the object cannot be labelled as any particular medium of expression. It corresponds to a new existential situation of humankind, to a new humanism'. My intention was to widen the debate around the topic. Yet, Hélio Oiticica radicalised the concept in both text and work. In 'Instances of the Object Problem', he states: 'the Object is seen as action in the environment, within which objects exist as signs and not simply as "artworks". It is a new stage of pure vital exercise, within which the artist is a proponent of creative activities. The Object is the discovery of the world at every instant; it is the creation of whatever we want it to be. A sound, a scream can be an Object'. And it was this broad notion of the object that grounded the two events in Belo Horizonte.

Moreover, I had already developed the idea of utilising outdoor areas as an extension of museums and galleries on at least two occasions: during the event *Arte no Aterro – Um Mostra de Arte Pública* [Art on the Embankment – A Public Art Exhibition] in 1968, and in my correspondence with Luciano Gusmão about the installation *Territórios* [Territories], which he developed in the outdoor area of the Pampulha Museum of Art, together with Dilton Araújo and Lotus Lobo. In the first case, the Flamengo Embankment was considered an extension of the Museum of Modern Art in Rio de Janeiro. In the second, a rope tied to a rock inside the museum extended into the garden, thus functioning as a kind of umbilical cord, which I considered 'a beautiful finding' in my letter to

Luciano from 4th February 1970. And I added: 'Today, only the art entirely situated outside museums and galleries has any vitality. Better than the Art Palace is the City Park around it. Better than the Rectory's exhibition hall is that empty space all around it. Better than the Pampulha Museum is the mountain nearby'.

There were several innovative aspects in both events: 1) for the first time in Brazil, artists were invited not to exhibit already completed works but to create their pieces directly on site. For this, they received airfare and lodging (when they were not from the state of Minas Gerais) and a stipend; 2) although there was a scheduled time for the opening in the Palace, the works in the Park took place at different times and places, which meant that no one, including the artists and the curator, could witness all individual manifestations; 3) the works in the Park remained there until their destruction, emphasising the ephemeral character of the pieces; 4) the event was promoted through the distribution of flyers in the streets and avenues of Belo Horizonte, as well as in movie theatres, theatres and football stadiums (as we had done before for *Arte no Aterro*). Also, for the first time, an art critic worked simultaneously as a curator and artist. Since creating the showcase *Vanguarda Brasileira*, I have already been questioning the exclusively judgmental character of art criticism by giving it a creative dimension. Curatorship is an extension of critical activity and the critic is an artist.

There was no catalogue. By way of a combined presentation of the two events, I wrote a text that was mimeographed and circulated among the artists and the public. This text was also reproduced, entirely or in part, by the presses of Minas Gerais and Rio de Janeiro. A little earlier, in February 1970, I had published in the *Vozes* magazine the essay *Contra a arte afluente: o corpo é o motor da obra* [Against Affluent Art: the Body is the Engine of the Work], which analysed the recent Brazilian art production based on the notion of 'artistic guerrilla'. Despite its poetic tone, as it practically defined the critical text as a new literary genre, the presentation of the two events clarified some of these concepts and ideas. I must admit, however, that the text often slipped into dogmatic rhetoric, reminiscent of the language of other manifestos of historical avant-gardes. Regardless, I believe that was entirely justifiable, given the radical proposals of the artists involved in the project.

It is impossible to transcribe the entire 'manifesto' that was available at the exhibition. Here I highlight this quote as an example: 'From art to anti-art, from modern to post-modern, from avant-garde art to counter-art, an opening is always something *major*. The horizon of art today is open and imprecise. Situations, events, rituals, or celebrations – art is no longer clearly distinguished from life and the everyday. ... The life that beats in your body – there is art. Your environment – there is art. The psychophysical rhythms – there is art. Intrauterine life – there is art. Supra-sensoriality – there is art. To imagine – there is art. The pneuma – there is art. The appropriation of objects and areas – there is art. The pure appropriative gesture of human situations or poetic experiences – there is art'.

In the interview I gave to Francisco Bittencourt for the article he published in *Jornal do Brasil* ('A geração tranca-ruas', 9 May 1970), I took these words even further. Answering his question about whether the events in Belo Horizonte were a new *Semana de Arte Moderna* [Modern Art Week], I replied: 'Mário de Andrade, in a conference celebrating the 20th anniversary of the *Semana de 22*, said: 'We were the last children of a civilisation that is over'. We are more pretentious: if our civilisation is rotten, let's go back to barbarism. We are the barbarians of a new race. Let the emperors of the ancient order take care of themselves. ... We work with fire, blood, bones, mud, earth or garbage. What we do are celebrations, rites and sacrificial rituals. Our instrument is the body itself

– against the computers. We use the head – against the heart. And the viscera, if necessary. Our problem is ethical – against aesthetic onanism'. And I added: 'Avant-garde is not to update materials; it is not technological art. It is a behaviour, a way of looking at things, people and materials; it is an attitude that defines itself against the world. It is precarity as the norm, the struggle as a life process. We are not interested in conclusions, in providing examples, in making history "-isms"'.

In April 1970, Institutional Act 5 was still in force. Issued by the military dictatorship on 13 December 1968, it had put the National Congress in recess, established media censorship, suspended individual rights and 'made torture official'. This led to the cancellation of legislative mandates; the compulsory retirement of artists, professors and intellectuals; the imprisonment, torture and death of student leaders and political activists; the invasion of universities; the censorship of works of art; the exodus and exile of artists. The reaction to these measures of exception came in the form of bank robberies, the kidnapping of ambassadors and the national and international boycott of the São Paulo Biennial. The artists' response was an 'artistic guerrilla', jamming the predominant art system.

All the artists who participated in *Do Corpo à Terra* received a letter signed by the president of the Hidrominas company authorising them to perform their works in the City Park. The official support would further stimulate the radicalism of their pieces, which was a supreme irony. After all, as Luiz Alphonsus remembered, 'it was this letter that allowed the artists to transgress the rules'. As expected, this attitude generated several conflicts with the police and the Park's employees.

The 'bloody bundles' that Barrio threw into the Arrudas river, drawing the attention of a large audience, created unbearable tension, eventually leading to the intervention of firefighters and then the police. The ritual burning of live chickens performed by Cildo Meireles was criticised by deputies in inflammatory speeches at a lunch preceding the award of the Inconfidence medals in Ouro Preto, during which, by coincidence, chicken in bloody gravy was served. Pressured by the police from a patrol car, Lotus Lobo had to interrupt his corn planting performance. The seeds did not germinate. On one side of the park, Luciano Gusmão and Dilton Araújo surrounded an area with cordons, while on the other, employees were undoing their work. And in a work executed by Lee Jaffe based on an idea of Hélio Oiticica, before the ants could begin to devour the sugar thrown on a trail atop the red soil of the Curral Hill, the piece was destroyed by a mining company's tractor.

Metaphors and political messages were featured in several other creations, such as in Thereza Simões' stamps containing inscriptions such as *Dirty, Verbotten, Fragile* and *Act silently* (a statement by Malcolm X), which were applied to the walls, panels and windows of the Art Palace. Her stamps established a parallel with the words *(Ver)melha* and *(Grama)tica*,[47] written on the grass and the sidewalks of the Park by José Ronaldo Lima, including next to them newspapers with headlines about China's Cultural Revolution and the Vietnam War. The painted wooden crates by Alfredo José Fontes, resembling animal traps, were defined by the artist as metaphors for political behaviour: left, right, reverse. No less political was Luciano Gusmão and Dilton Araújo's proposal to restrict areas of the Park and redefine them as spaces of repression or of freedom, alienation or contemplation.

Undoubtably, this 'critical field' predominated in most artworks made at the City Park. But artists also provoked reactions with the use of unorthodox materials and formal structures, such as explosive smoke grenades. Even though those grenades have now been made banal by football fans, in those 'years of lead' they were exclusive to the army. These elements radically subverted the language of visual arts. Misunderstandings on the one hand, and the enduring authoritarianism of the country on the other added political content to the works. Luiz Alphonsus said that his objective in setting fire to a 15-meter-long plastic strip stretched across the grass was 'to mark the ground, to leave a trail of art on the planet'. Lotus Lobo, more modestly, just wanted to 'see the corn growing and blooming in an unusual place'. Hard times those were.

But, besides this political dimension, another aspect became evident in several works, anticipating one of the current strands of art – cartography. Artists scrutinised the enormous extension of City Park, demarcating territories, delimiting borders, appropriating locations, places or areas; seeking new functions and meanings for each of those spaces; trying to apprehend them poetically, imaginatively and conceptually, or following socio-urbanistic and anthropological parameters. Without any previous arrangement between the artists, these works got into a dialogue with one another, thus establishing new connections of meaning. Luciano Gusmão and Dilton Araújo's 'geography' prompted a conversation with the photographic appropriations of my *Quinze lições sobre arte e história da arte – Apropriações: homenagens e equações* [Fifteen lessons on art and art history – appropriations: homages and equations]. The first of these appropriations reverberated in the work of Dileny Campos, which, as Marília Andrés Ribeiro observed, 'pointed out the deconstructive aspects of the city, leading passersby to see another landscape within the landscape – the landscape of urban archaeology'.

A third line of work stood out alongside the political and cartographic strands. It was almost a trend, anarchic and desacralising, that was once adjacent to the Dadaists' and 'fluxists'' nihilism and to the concept of generalised creativity, questioning art's myths and postulates. A certain number of works recuperated the question of the spectator's participation, which simultaneously affirms and denies the work of art. At the Art Palace entrance, George Helt extended a strip of paper with his footprints printed in lithographic ink and then asked visitors to walk over it. Terezinha Soares requested visitors to lie down on her work: three beds with mattresses in the colours of football teams, cut-out shapes depicting players and coaches, and a playful title: *Ela me deu a bola* [She passed me the ball / she is flirting with me]. Eduardo Angelo spread old newspapers on the grass to stimulate the free creativity of the Park's visitors, and José Ronaldo Lima made tactile-olfactory works at the Art Palace.

But Umberto Costa Barros and Dilton Araújo were the two artists who best expressed this 'anti-artistic' attitude. Most of the time, the public isn't even aware of Umberto's works, or initially perceives them as something wrong, untidy or out of place. During the 2nd Summer Salon, in 1970, he intervened in the very exhibition system by disarranging the exhibition panels, and at the National Modern Art Salon later in the same year, he gave a new arrangement to the window shutters of the Modern Art Museum of Rio de Janeiro. In Belo Horizonte, he chose a room in the basement of the Art Palace, still under construction, where he precariously stacked and balanced bricks, remains of panels and pedestals, ladders, clay and other construction materials that were collected from the site itself, creating a very subtle installation in which the structures oscillated between chance and order, between the undone and the remade.

As discreet and elusive as his colleague from Rio de Janeiro, Dilton Araújo, working together with Luciano Gusmão, also left his mark in situations and actions he improvised during those days, e.g., throwing lime stones around or sneakily placing a matchbox in the room where the *Objeto e Participação* exhibition was taking place, next to which he wrote 'A possibility!'. The text of his provocative proposal, sent to me before the exhibition, includes an intelligent theorisation about the pamphlet as a 'work of art' and statements such as: 'To make art or kick an old tin can down the street. Not that I despise art, but I give more importance to kicking an old tin can down the street'.

Finally, it is worth mentioning that in the wide range of options offered by Belo Horizonte's simultaneous and integrated events, there was room for the participation of artists from different generations, whose works engaged with various trends in contemporary art. Carlos Vergara cut figures out of corrugated cardboard as if they were clones of mass-produced human beings. Meanwhile, Manoel Serpa and Manfredo Souzaneto, working together, monumentalised two clothes pegs, pulling them out of their everyday banality. While residues of American Pop Art persisted in the works by these three artists, Ione Saldanha and Franz Weissmann renewed the constructive tradition, the former through a sensitive use of colour, with the support of strips and bamboos, and the latter by building a linear labyrinth – the apex of his concept of sculpture as a drawing in space, but also the consecration of another of Weissmann's ideas: a habitable sculpture.

It is true that those were difficult times – of truncated freedom, censorship and repression. But that did not mean that Brazilian artists stopped creating, thinking, questioning and defending their creative freedom against everything and everyone – freedom that, as Mário de Andrade stated when closing the aforementioned conference about the *Semana de 22*, 'is not a prize, it is a sanction. That is meant to come'.

III

Moving Images

Chapter 25

Moving Images

Gabriel Menotti and German Alfonso Nunez

During the military dictatorship, the growing relevance of audiovisual media in Brazil would make it a particularly fertile and contested field. In the late 1960s, the popularisation of cheaper film formats such as Super 8 and 16mm, along with the use of slide projectors, gave artists yet another means to break away from aesthetic conventions and work across media. A prominent example is Hélio Oiticica, one of the main figures behind the neo-concrete movement, who famously collaborated with marginal filmmakers and developed his own feverish, expanded cinema practice while in exile in London and New York. But a similar transversal interest would characterise the work of filmmakers such as Glauber Rocha, forefather of the Brazilian *cinema novo* [new cinema], who wrote avant-garde manifestos and later contributed to TV shows on the Tupi TV channel.

Audiovisual art forms arrived in Brazil during the most brutal period of the military dictatorship, following the AI-5 [Institutional Act 5], a 1968 decree that virtually suspended all civil rights in the country. The country's tense situation gave its new media decidedly political undertones. Even works that did not intentionally stand against the homogenising force of TV as an official state apparatus played the role of alternative communication spaces. The third section of our book highlights the particularities of that era, as we move along the country's slow redemocratisation and the rise of more consistent support, both public and private, for new technological art forms.

One particular kind of audiovisual media that enjoyed unexpected popularity in Brazil was the use of slide-projection synchronised to recorded audio, dubbed simply 'audiovisuals'. In addition to being largely experimented with by artists, likely due to their accessibility and ease of use, audiovisuals were also deployed by critic-curator Frederico Morais to enable an early mode of media-based critical discourse. In 1973, audiovisuals would be highlighted at the survey exhibition *Expoprojeção 1973*, curated by Aracy Amaral, alongside other forms of emerging Brazilian production that made use of projected images.

At that same year, videoart was featured at the XII São Paulo Biennial as part of a section on Communication Arts coordinated by researcher Vilém Flusser (Prague, 1920-1991). Despite several technical problems, this 'video-makers' biennial' would be considered an influential landmark. In the following years, the work of curator Walter Zanini also proved essential for the promotion of the medium in Brazil. Zanini spearheaded video commissions from established Brazilian artists to be shown in exhibitions abroad and was responsible for the creation of a video production core at the Museum of Contemporary Art of the University of São Paulo (MAC-USP), which purchased one of the first portapak cameras in the country and made this very expensive equipment available for artists. Without this degree of institutional support, it is unlikely that video could have prospered in Brazil in the ways it did.[48]

In his essay 'Videoart: The Brazilian Adventure', critic and historian Arlindo Machado states that, since the late 1960s, 'video has stood out as one of Brazil's most important and lasting cultural phenomena' (Machado 1996, 225). It is fitting that many local artists got involved with audiovisual media first and foremost because Brazil was a 'television-centred country'. Televisual broadcast played a central role in the country's burgeoning postwar cultural industry, catering to both the masses and intellectual elites wary of 'Americanised' cultural goods (Napolitano 1964). In time, cheaper film formats and eventually video formats enabled local artists to experiment with new media technologies. By contrast, more complex forms of electronic technology were virtually inaccessible to them. Apart from the few examples dealing with videotext (as seen in the previous section) and the individual efforts of well-connected artists (like Waldemar Cordeiro and Décio Pignatari), computers were an expensive piece of equipment whose use was restricted to industries and universities. Compared to computers, audiovisual media offered 'the best options in terms of production costs' within Brazil's economic and industrial conditions, making it 'possible for independent authors and non-profit groups to explore autonomous cultural projects' (Machado 1996).

This situation would not change for a while. Even in the late 1970s and early 1980s, when personal computers were becoming more readily available in the Global North, Brazilians would have little access to them. This was partly due to the way computing technology was framed by the military junta as a strategic sector. In order to protect the development of a national industry, the government deployed an industrialisation policy based on import substitution, which barred the entrance of foreign technology into the country. However, despite its initial good results, import substitution didn't do enough to kickstart a strong Brazilian computer industry. What it effectively did was prevent national access to the latest PC technologies, keeping them out of the hands of the vast majority of the country's population (including artists) until the mid-1990s, when the Brazilian market would finally reopen to foreign goods.[49]

The 1980s, considered to be a 'lost decade' for the Brazilian economy, constituted an important period of socio-cultural transition. As the grip of the military regime started to loosen and the country moved towards neoliberal economic policies, the artistic field became more professionalised and began incorporating new and powerful patrons. Commercial TV channels, no longer under strict governmental control, enlisted young artists to deploy new image technologies for the development of aesthetics that embodied the spirit of individual expression. The rise of cultural marketing would foster various exhibitions, institutions and, eventually, new media activities. Corporate-sponsored events such as the Videobrasil festival, first held at São Paulo's Museum of Image and Sound in 1983, promoted artists' bold, futuristic visions as the country left the 'years of lead' behind. Two years later, the dictatorship would finally be over.

Chapter 26

Poets, Artists, Anarcho-Super8 -Filmmakers (2001)

Rubens Machado Jr.

decrease and
appear
— *Cacaso, 1975*

At each step, the irony that
goes from the part to the whole, from
fragment to unity, from
men to man casts
questions. Asking,
he doubts; doubting, he searches for
an answer that is given
by a cyclical irony
endless because
constantly renewing.
— *Jomard Muniz de Britto, 1964*

Would it be an exaggeration to say that half or two-thirds of Brazilian experimental films were made in the Super 8 format? Few people could agree or disagree, given the elasticity of the concept of experimental cinema worldwide, which is even more significant in the Brazilian case. In the tenuous but resilient American and European circuit of museums and specialised movie theatres, there is a renewed tradition that converges the genres of 'artist's film' and 'experimental film'. Here in Brazil, however, this has rarely been the case, even though visual artists have worked very closely with the research of our experimental filmmakers and vice-versa. Moreover, it is impossible to discuss an experimental panorama of the country due to its large production in smaller gauges (the regular 8mm, as well as the first video formats), whose 'technical irreproducibility' often makes the memory of its elusive and auratic first screenings the only way to access the works. That is to say, these works have hardly been watched or rewatched by any audience, not even by researchers, since the 1970s, which was the era of their wider production and diffusion.

The multiplicity and diversity of aesthetic proposals is one of the distinctive marks of audiovisual production in the 1970s, imposed, in part, by the fragmentation of experiences enacted by the authoritarian political regime. Alongside the vigorous expansion of TV and the relative success of [the state-owned film company] Embrafilme, an unprecedented proliferation of experimentalism took place, most often segmented and localised, involving communitarian microspheres such as intermittent festivals, artistic exhibitions and myriad small events. In looking for the most interesting commonalities between these events, we will undoubtedly find in Super 8 some of the most representative material. However, there have been no studies or panoramic surveys of the Brazilian Super 8 production, except for half a dozen books and theses on regional scenes, generally of little critical ambition and leaving aside the larger centres such as São Paulo and Rio. Even the most renowned films produced in Super 8 have been the object of only very few short lines of critical character.

In the survey we have been conducting since 2000, which first resulted in the Marginalia 70 exhibition,[50] we addressed *experimental* Super 8 (which, like *animation*, is a genre less present in film festivals when compared to the more prolific genres of *documentary and fiction*) in an attempt to cover the many implications of this concept. For the selection of the exhibition, however, we have been more judicious within each definition, aiming on the one hand to keep a somewhat representative picture of the plurality of experimental proposals while also provoking a greater understanding of some of Super 8's most successful and popular approaches. Thus, we have privileged works more radically oriented towards research, not only in terms of language but also in what specifically concerns the Super 8 gauge (from conception to exhibition), associating the most important artistic traditions with the new aesthetic, behavioural and political attitudes of their time. We decided to curate a broad spectrum of styles, even though our timeframe forced us to leave out some relevant aspects of experimentalism that were linked to the conventions of fiction, documentary and animation. Even more so because radical anti-conventionalism is at the core of the more rigorous notions of experimental cinema. The latter attempts to explore cinematic possibilities that aren't so common within current social practices.

This historical review will give us a glimpse of a formidable and rarely-before-seen *corpus* of the Brazilian audiovisual universe. The aspect of *terra incognita*, which has sometimes given Brazilian production an aura of something fabulous and unfathomable, can now be duly analysed, unveiled and demystified. Beyond their proximity to visual artists, the experimentalism of Super 8 filmmakers finds another relevant parallel in the new poetic productions of the 1970s as well as so-called mimeograph literature. For instance, they all share the same localist trace, which reveals itself in an explosively strange telluric verve, less romantic than realistic or concrete (or neo-concrete). The turmoil of the here-and-now is taken to the edge of the physical consciousness of bodies, of the world and of the specific medium of expression through various forms of self-reflexivity. With this in mind, this exhibition seeks to create the greatest possible dialogue between those three parties: poets, visual artists and the provocative restlessness of the young filmmakers. This triple confluence may help us explain the budding filmmaker, who equates the lines in their films with the best marginal poetry; the artist, who decoupages and animates their tapes with rhythm better than many career filmmakers; and the poet, who has become a good practitioner of cinematography.

For our screening program, instead of separating themes or styles, we tried to keep alive a hybrid spirit that would be faithful to the attitude of coexistence that characterised the largest festivals of the period, such as *Jornada* in Salvador and *Grife* in São Paulo. These were spaces of democratic possibility, multiple forms of expression, political protest and a more or less veiled scorn of the status quo. The grace and joviality of the most spontaneous expressions tempered the artistic formality and conservatism that persisted even within those festivals. Under a flagrant authoritarian regime, the aggravated isolation of creative processes prepared the ground for the sudden confrontation of conflicting mentalities.

A closer look will highlight, beyond their impact on cultural behaviours, a wealth of foreign aesthetic proposals that could be right at home within this set of films in both concept and attitude. Without evoking any particular terms, one could speak of this cinema as structural, abstract, independent, radical, marginal, inventive, interventionist, different, unaligned, negationist, anti-cinema, found-footage, oneiric, conceptual, minimalist, materialist, prop-art, constructive, pop, nocturnal, *odara*, pure, absolute, free, beat, visionary, underground, parametric, concrete, neo-concrete and so on. Though these generic terms are no doubt relevant for future analyses of the chosen films, it would be more interesting to try to find more singular concepts within the films themselves. In their rich proposals, the filmmakers already gave us several possible clues: the rudimentary cinema, the living cinema, the almost-cinema, the experiential, the primitivist, the erotic anthropophagy, the *terrir* [terror-laughter], egg cinema, scoundrel, the academic avant-garde, the megalomaniac neonewestcinema, the salon cinema, the anarcho-Super 8-filmmaking...

Despite the tropicalist and post-tropicalist tendency to quote from, dialogue on and incorporate various media discourses, an ingrained characteristic of general Super 8 production that distinguishes it from cinema made in other formats (even the so-called Marginal Cinema), is its clear opposition to anything that has to do with TV, its utmost antipode at the time. Another curious type of Super 8 filmmaking interacted with the precariousness of the medium, adhering studiously to its grain, to its texture, to the 'aberrations' of its easy manipulation, mobility and automatic exposure; and to the contingent yet purposive de-ritualisation of the entire production process. This was undoubtedly a contribution from visual artists who frequently participated in film festivals. Super 8's immediate connection to daily life was a twin sister of what the young mimeograph poets were doing. This kind of media awareness, which acknowledges the medium's precariousness, constitutes the strongest reverberation of Glauber Rocha's *Aesthetics of Hunger*, written in 1965, a text perhaps more prophetic than his author would have intended. The growing ruthlessness of national politics made Rocha's motto 'a camera in the hand and an idea in the head' even more meaningful and phallic. The transformation undergone by the phallic *motif*, related to the psychoanalytic order and fatherly presence, is figured in an ambiguously invasive reality curdled in ironic symbols and monumentalisations. Due to its intrinsic characteristics as both an artistic and social medium, experimental Super 8 filmmaking practices stood in sharp contrast to the country's circumstances in the 1970s. An aesthetic denial with a civic dimension, it represented a stand against not only a cultural and political status quo, but also a behavioural one, leading to its stigmatisation as reckless debauchery in spite of its numerous countercultural impacts.

Chapter 27

Some Ideas around Expo-Projection 73 (1973)

Aracy Amaral

At this very moment, Brazilian artists seem to be caught between formalism (materials, conceptual proposals, systems), the radicalisation of an esoteric avant-garde, and surreal and magical currents that seek to liberate the unconscious. However, none of these tendencies offers a glimpse of daily life in their production processes, a fact that could be a taken as a rejection of the environment (something present even in the São Paulo depicted by Gregorio [Gruber], whose work crystallises the metropolis' oppressive and gloomy atmosphere). Nevertheless, at this very moment, experiments with film, audio-visuals and sound explode everywhere, here as well as in other Western countries. Artists are seeking to use such unconventional means to express themselves through the selective ordering or recording of reality 'as notes of situations that impress [them] very strongly' (Miguel Rio Branco). [Arthur] Barrio is another case in point, as he uses similar [audiovisual] notes to convey information about his work as it develops through intermediary stages, since 'photos can never capture the totality of research'. The camera and/or recorder is therefore a device for documenting – or creating – the environment of one's own work as a cinematic sequence with or without sound; a recreated reality, neither composed in alignment with a pre-Cubist perspective of the represented object nor a post-Cubist one, which is multiple while contained in a single fixed image.

The artists at this manifestation employ cameras; one can tell through their projections who does it with total freedom and who still betrays a certain clumsiness in relation to the machine. I cannot speak for all the works that will be shown, as there are many that will arrive only on the eve of the opening. But it will be possible to notice a wide range of approaches towards the medium, as Antonio Dias has very lucidly observed: 'there are different attitudes concerning the use of film. Ivan Cardoso, for example, is more interested in film itself, while others attempt to see film as just another medium, an extension of the work they already did in painting. For me, it's unbearable to feel the camera moving through the scene and choosing angles from the voracious perspective of *media*. The camera must be fixed; it must accept my work organisation. That's why it has been very difficult for me to collaborate with other people'. Then he mentions a different approach, favoured by Yole [de Freitas], his wife: 'she is interested in the space of the film, in the movement, in the optical effect; she manages to make an inquiry into the subject of film in such a particular, detailed and animated way that it would be difficult to accomplish it in a medium different than Super 8. ... This means that, for now, there are films that enter a larger cinematic circuit, while others prefer to operate in small venues, with an audience dedicated to the study of new communication systems'.

The latter is considered by Lygia Pape as the greatest draw of working in Super 8 as opposed to conventional cinema. She situates experimental film among the most valid expressions [of art] she sees nowadays: 'Super 8 really is a new language ... especially when it is free from a more commercial involvement with the system. It is the only source of [innovative aesthetic] research, the touchstone of invention today'.

For years, she adds, 'I followed the day-to-day of Brazilian cinema, watched hours of screenings of rough cuts at Lider's laboratories. I saw the most incredible things – open structures – full of creativity. Then the castration process began: editing. The cleaning up of the most interesting material in the name of the commonplace, of the average taste, as demanded by the box office or by the lack of openness from the author-director. Right after that, the final cut came to reduce everything to commercial length, adding descriptive music and silly text or dialogue on top. In short, it changed film from a living, pulsating thing into a well-behaved, *cinemanovista* amorphous mass'.

Super 8 therefore represents for many the 'immediate record, free from the analytical schemes of traditional film editing'. This quality, preserved above all due to a tacit lack of commitment from those involved in the commercial circuit, has the same gestural quality as certain kinds of painting. A short while ago, while writing about [José Roberto] Aguilar's work, Jorge Mautner evoked something 'immediately frontal, instantaneous, almost television-like', a form of 'spontaneity' achieved as if through spray painting, with nerves coming to the surface of the canvas, the freshness of an immediate record. All of this was preserved with no fear of imperfection. This deliberately selective *nonchalance* and the disregard for editing by many who work with Super 8 bring to mind one of the aspects of realism (the fixation of the everyday), clearly reflecting an exaltation of what is understood as the qualities of television. At the same time, it makes us reflect upon the ideas of two figures from different periods who addressed both imperfection and the recording-as-art: The first is [John] Ruskin, an English critic of the 18th century who, during the Gothic revival that took over England during the industrial revolution, praised medieval craftsmen for moving away from elaborate and classical beauty and instead embodying imperfection in their works. As Ruskin states, 'imperfection is in a way essential to all that we know of life ...; to banish imperfection is to destroy expression, to check exertion, to paralyse vitality'. The other great theorist is Harold Rosemberg, our contemporary, whose latest work (*The De-definition of Art* 1972) states that, in this era of 'earthworks', 'information-systems art', process-art, 'electronic-phenomena art', casual art, 'data registration art' and conceptual art, 'the artist has become, as it were, too big for art. Their proper medium is working on the world'. For this reason, artists themselves are ready to demystify what they do, as Robert Morris once did by removing the word 'art' from the name of one of his works. And so have many others: 'nothing is left of art but the fiction of the artist. The artist disdains to deal in anything but essences. Instead of painting, they deal in space; instead of dance, poetry, film, they deal in movement; instead of music, they deal in sound'. According to Rosemberg, this increasingly intense rejection of aestheticisation in the most advanced artistic circles (where art can be breakfast, a frozen lake, a hole dug in the ground or a letter with the exact time when the artist will climb on a chair in his studio), this de-aestheticisation of art, implies a 'real aestheticisation of all forms and events in human life – the world itself becoming a museum'. At this point, it is good to feel the proximity of these artists to the environment, their integration, or lack of it, with the community in which they live and their clash with the pressures in which they now participate more vividly than ever.

It cannot be emphasised enough that there are diverse positions, as seen in this 'Expo-Projection', and the interest of this manifestation will be precisely to show this diversity of contrasting languages made from the same alphabet. Perhaps the clearest element coming out of it will be Super 8 itself because of its formal range, which encompasses everything from the raw material of films to plain recordings. On the other hand, despite the considerable differences between the various authors' origins, artistic and cultural maturity, etc., as well as the objectives pursued in their work, it's possible to notice features common to certain groups (which often haven't had any contact with one another): the fixed camera; nostalgia for nature or return to nature as a theme, sometimes as a quasi-pre-Raphaelite revival; the visible formalism of some artists in contrast to the completely open and uncommitted work of others; cinema without structure; the use of handheld cameras; fascination with capturing events in real time, with a minimum of planning. One should not always believe that what seems to be improvised and spontaneous has not in fact been designed right down to its smallest details precisely for that purpose. But artists are always prepared for the possibility of incorporating unpredictability to enrich their process (as in Henrique Faulhaber).

Everywhere we see the same passion for the flowing image, whether in the carefully-sequenced *The Body* by Abrão Berman, or in Claudio Tozzi's *Grama* [Grass], or in Raimundo Colares' *Broadway Boogie-Woogie*, which he considers an 'attempt to capture/redo Mondrian's masterpiece of the same name in cinematic format'. A film-work, an artwork-film, a work-in-film: in short, works stripped of the commercial aspect of gallery offerings, vital forms of expression outside of the art market. They may be rough but they are no less worthy, just as an artist's diary or notebook is sometimes as important as a conventional artwork.

At this point, the autonomous audiovisual work takes on the aspect of revealing what is there to be seen, transcending how it's usually interpreted as a narrative illustration of a given theme. It is not possible, however, to refer to any specific artist (though one cannot fail to mention works by Paulo Fogaça and João Ricardo Moderno, from Rio), since not all the pieces on show have been watched in advance. Several works are still on their way from New York (that of Hélio Oiticica), from the Belo Horizonte group and even from Rio. Frederico

Morais, writing about his work *Cantares* [Songs], distinguishes between audiovisuals and cinema: 'If cinema is apparently freer in capturing reality in motion, in the projection room it becomes a closed structure. It can be said that the reality of cinema is in the *camera* and that of the audiovisual is in the *projector*. In other words, the infinite possibilities combining its material elements (slides, sounds, light sources, feedback, *zoom*) with each other and at the moment of projection (which in turn can involve several projectors) make the audiovisual an open structure. Of course, in the Moviola the filmed reality is modified, but once the editing is completed, the possibilities of film are exhausted. Thus, the less that cinema is "moving images" – a tendency of the post-Godard modern cinema – the closer it gets to the audiovisual'.

Even though he uses slides and sound, Hélio Oiticica, in turn, prefers to call his work 'NONNARRATION', which he defines as 'NONDISCOURSE/ NON "ARTISTIC" PHOTOGRAPHY/ NON "AUDIOVISUAL": soundtrack/ is a continuity punctuated by improvised accidental interference/ in the radio's recorded structure'.

It is curious that explorations of *sound* have been few and far between, but we believe this is a matter of time, and presenting these works will surely inspire the creation of others (as happened, for example, with some of Tomoshige Kusuno's experiments in sound coupling). As I see it, both Cildo Meireles' piece (*Mebs/Caraxia*) and Antonio Dias' soundwords (*The Space Between – 1. Theory of Counting, 2. Theory of Density*) draw comparisons to their graphic and pictorial production. In my opinion, Cildo Meireles' piece, which he admits to having been an extension of his drawing experiments, emphasises linearity and questions of depth. Antonio Dias', in turn, explores current aspects of the artistic production, the concretisation of sound being a form of the objectification he has always pursued in his creations. In both sides of his record, space-time is clearly expressed: in one, organically, through the body (inspiration-expiration); in the other, through what sounds like a percussive instrument. An article by Germano Celant ('The Record as Artwork'), published in *Domus-520* in March 1973, after this catalogue went to print, revealed this instrument to be the sound of a clock, famous for its geometric precision. These are two faces whose common denominator is the fusion of antagonistic forces, which emerge clearly through Antonio Dias' intuitive personality.

In the face of the long process required to bring together these artists and these artworks, it is important to emphasise the enthusiasm of all the participants, even those from far away. Although we started from the premise of showing only works made by visual artists who are now experimenting with film, sound and photography, and who are using Super 8, audiovisuals and phonography recordings, this idea was soon abandoned. This is because, as I began to watch works from São Paulo and Rio, it seemed much more interesting to promote debate and dialogue by showing almost everything that came into our hands. The result can serve both to demystify what people say is being done 'out there' as well as for to discover pleasant surprises and mostly unknown works, made by those who do not frequent the usual circles. On this occasion, many artists will be able to see their works shown in public, particularly the four who reside abroad: Hélio Oiticica, Antonio Dias, Iole de Freitas and Raymundo Colares.

It was bound to happen that the project would inspire many other people who created new works (audiovisuals as well as Super 8), especially for the 'Expo-Projection'. This was rather satisfying, since it implies the stimulus to production and to the exploration of a new medium.

I must give special thanks to the friendly understanding of the entire team of Grife (*Grupo dos Realizadores Independentes de Filmes Experimentais* [Independent Experimental Filmmakers Association]) – represented by Malu de Alencar and Abrão

Berman – who not only provided us with their venue but also acted as collaborators from the very beginning; to *Centro de Artes Novo Mundo* [New World Art Centre], for having supported the production of the catalogue; to *Fotoptica* for their participation in the project; to Marcio Sampaio, coordinator of the Belo Horizonte group for the 'Expo-Projection;' to Antonio Dias and Hélio Oiticica for their encouragement – via Milan and New York – ever since the first steps towards this manifestation were taken in December.

The 'Expo-Projection' is a manifestation because it is a public presentation of new forms of collective artistic expression. In the current state of permanent information obstruction, many other forms of expression take place simultaneously, all of which are legitimate and alive. But I believe it is important to continually look for the most recent ones and keep a record of them. This is not for classification purposes, which would be irrelevant. Rather, it is to show that creativity, even under pressure, remains sensitive to its environmental conditions. It is also an attempt to see how the creative gesture can always bring about a diagnosis of that same reality.

Chapter 28

(Audiovisuals) (1973)

Frederico Morais

A new phenomenon that has emerged in art salons over the last three years is the *audiovisual*. This is the result of the introduction of the 'Object' into salons and the consequent liberation of artists from traditional art categories.

In fact, when I was invited to organise the IV Modern Art Salon of the Federal District in 1967, I introduced the Object into the competition's rules. Of course, the Object is not a new category of artistic mediums, alongside painting, drawing, printmaking or sculpture. It is the negation of all categories. However, by making it a regulated aspect of the competition, I wanted to draw attention to this new field of action for artists. If, as Breton said, the role of the artist is to break the routine of everyday life, the Object fulfilled the same role of disruption within the Salon. Yet even at that time I did not see the Object as an object in the traditional sense – as something three-dimensional, occupying a specific place. For me, the Object could be an event, a situation, a concept, an action or a behaviour. With the development of postmodern art, the Object received new names: conceptual art, body art, *arte povera*, land art or simply activity.

Audiovisuals closely follow the revolution of cinema (Super 8), television (VHS) and sound. In other words, they are part of the process of miniaturisation of technology in the 20th century. This miniaturisation is leading to the creation of a portable, pocket culture – a new camping tent culture. Of course, the system is gradually taking over these new proposals or media and commercialising them. Today, for example, Super 8 is part of a manager's or businessman's toolkit, and it's used to sell stocks or services. And, following a dialectic of their own, the mediums trade places with one another, with Super 8 now occupying the position previously held by audiovisuals in the last decade. For a long time, audiovisuals had been used in education, as a form of professional training, as a means of dissemination and advertising and as a business tool. However, they had always been used in an academic and not very creative way.

Only recently, by the initiative of some artists, audiovisuals came to be regarded as a form of art and poetic expression; in short, as a language.

I have personally contributed to this trend in our country. In fact, the second comment I made within the terms of the *New Criticism* project (1969) was in the form of an audiovisual. I confronted the images (slides) of works presented by São Paulo artists Resende/Baravelli/Fajardo/Nasser at the Museum of Modern Art in Rio de Janeiro with images of construction sites, drawing the viewer's attention to what I called 'an archaeology of the urban'. The landscape in the city is always precarious, volatile; it's always changing. At the same time, the images were complemented with a kind of sonic memory of the city: sounds of hydraulic hammers, workshops, bells, flowing water; images that flowed together with texts from Bachelard, Molles, Langer. In short, I resorted to audiovisual resources for my critical commentary. A month later (November 1970), I made another audiovisual commentary, now about [Arthur] Barrio, a marginal artist and one of the strongest names of our avant-garde. These two audiovisuals, along with another one, won awards at the II National Salon of Contemporary Art held at the Museum of Art in Belo

Horizonte and organised by the young critic Márcio Sampaio. For the first time, a Brazilian Salon recognised the audiovisual as a living expression of contemporary art, opening an unlimited field for artists: that of the projected image.

From that point on, the importance of audiovisuals grew and became more widely recognised. In 1971, the Eletrobras Salon (*Light and Movement*) awarded two special mentions to works in the format, including one of mine, *Cantares*. A few months later, the Belo Horizonte and the São Paulo Salons, without clearly mentioning it in their regulations, once again opened space for audiovisual montages. In the first, three works were presented: one of them, the wonderful hymn to the earth by Beatriz Dantas, won. And the São Paulo Salon awarded a new special mention to *Cantares, Memory of the Landscape* and *The Bread and the Blood of Each One*.

Audiovisual was thus definitively established as a new form of expression and this would be later confirmed in the final two Summer Salons, in the last one in Belo Horizonte and in various exhibitions, especially those of an experimental nature. Notable among those was Carlos Vergara's exhibition at the Museum of Modern Art in Rio, in which Super 8 and audiovisuals were projected daily in an makeshift auditorium. Finally, Belo Horizonte, confirming the city's pioneering role in the field, held the First Brazilian Communication & Audiovisual Salon, with the participation of several artists. The event included, among other manifestations, a contest of audiovisual montages on the theme 'Sound and Image of Minas Gerais'. About 20 works were presented, three of them awarded; *Carta de Minas* received the first prize.

Now it's São Paulo that leads the way, with the first individual exhibition solely featuring audiovisuals, and with *Expo-projeção-73*, which will take place in a few days, and which Aracy Amaral organised in collaboration with Grife, bringing together Super 8, audiovisuals and audio recordings of 40 artists from three different states.

Initially, with *Memory of the Landscape* and *The Bread and the Blood of Each One*, audiovisuals served me as a new tool for art criticism. It was a new attempt, or a continuation from the exhibition I held at Petite Galerie in 1969, to move away from textual criticism, from written commentary; in other words, to provide criticism with a creative character. This concern is still present in more recent works, such as those I made about Klee and Volpi, even though here the didactic aspect predominates: namely, the audiovisual as a kind of introduction to the exhibitions for the lay public. It proves to be an instrument that is as necessary as, or even more useful than, an exhibition catalogue, despite its precariousness.

Since *Cantares*, I have been concerned with affirming the specificities of audiovisuals as a language, as a new mode of poetic expression and as an instrument capable of capturing, in objective and subjective planes, a specifically modern sensibility. Today's world is characterised by fragmentation, dispersion and discontinuity. In the mosaic world of the 20th century, humankind is subjected to a bombardment of information and images that continuously modify their formal environment, sharpening and activating their existence.

Giulio Carlo Argan, in one of the most profound studies ever conducted on the work of Klee, says that 'everything that we know of reality (and this reality includes ourselves, the clear world of our consciousness and that murky and crepuscular world of the unconscious) comes to us through this tormented paradox. Nor is it a single and grandiose image which imposes itself on us by the logical system of its eternal values, but a hasty sequence of images, often dissociated and enigmatic, and always fragmentary throughout the full cycle of our existence. In turn, our existence is no more in its time-space reality than that self-same succession of images'. There is not a single moment of our life that is not an experience of images. In other words, the vital process consists of a continuous production of images. Reality is, therefore, the image.

The artist is essentially a producer of images. Klee produced almost 10,000 images (including paintings, drawings, watercolours, etc.). These 10,000 images constitute his life because images, according to Bachelard, they are an excess of imagination. I imagine, therefore I exist. If I exist, I produce images. Which leads us to the following equation: life = image = art.

The audiovisual as the systole and diastole of life, as a way of knowing/living reality.

The modern world only aggravates the problem by involving the human in images almost to the point of paroxysm. Visual arts (and here I refer especially to their traditional forms) have proved powerless when it comes to capturing the dynamic of this iconic reality, and cinema, by establishing the 'continuity of the image', deforms that reality.

If cinema is apparently freer in capturing reality in motion, in the projection room it becomes a closed structure. It can be said that the reality of cinema is in the *camera* and that of the audiovisual is in the *projector*. In other words, the infinite possibilities of combining its material elements (slides, sounds, light sources, feedback, *zoom*) with each other at the moment of projection (which in turn can involve several projectors) make the audiovisual an open structure. Of course, in the Moviola the filmed reality is modified, but once the editing is completed, the possibilities of film are exhausted. Thus, the less that cinema is 'moving images' – a tendency of the post-Godard modern cinema – the closer it gets to the audiovisual. Conversely, the possibility created by the *dissolver control* to establish continuity between the slides during the projection brings the audiovisual closer to cinema, in my view to the detriment of the former's own language.

There is no contradiction there. When I refer to *zoom* as one of the possibilities of the audiovisual, I want to characterise the peculiarity of its use in conjunction with the image projector. Similarly, dissolving one image into another means nothing if this dissolution is not part of the formal structure or meaning. In the first work of the *Bachelardianas* series, the images of water and stone establish a clear and crystalline continuity: 'soft water on hard stone, strikes until it bores through'.[51] That is, the images show the work of water on the stone. And for almost the entire duration of the projection, the water is present only as sound. Another use of the specific affordances of the audiovisual as a language is what I propose in *curriculum vitae*, when the sound/image rhythm of the light/dark of the slide transitions is combined with the very noise of the movement of images, creating an atmosphere of tension and surprise.

A slide constitutes in itself a unit of time and space. But, when related to other slides, it creates a new spatiotemporal rhythm. Each slide therefore contains its own time. And there is a freely structured virtual time that is accomplished by the sound and image synchroniser. In cinema, each frame presupposes its unfolding onto the next one, establishing a sequence from which meaning emerges. There is no surprise, so to speak. In the audiovisual, however, the next image is always unexpected. And it may not even exist when it's replaced by a focus of light and/or its darkening. Discontinuity is part of the structure of audiovisuals, as it is of the image of the modern world. In both cases, the state of discontinuity requires active mental participation from us.

It is in the still image, however, that much of the expressive power, fascination and poetry of the audiovisual resides. Paulo Fogaça, the author of the photographs used in several of my works and a creator of commended audiovisuals in his own right, refers to each projected image or to its set as a *diapoem*. In this sense, it can be said that the audiovisual is to poetry what cinema is to prose.

Chapter 29

Block-Experiments in Cosmococa – Program in Progress (1973)

Hélio Oiticica

COSMOCOCA was initially conceived by NEVILLE D'ALMEIDA as a new film project: he invented the name and more than a film project it became – program *in progress*: COSMOCOCA-program *in progress* should then appear in all the references made to the experiments:

emphasis on it being *program in progress-open* in an effort to show that COSMOCOCA is meant to embrace a much wider spectrum of experiments and as such should not be identified exclusively with these BLOCK-EXPERIMENTS (abbreviated CC followed by corresponding number): they are a first experimental part of COSMOCOCA-program in progress conceived by NEVILLE AND MYSELF the first 5 BLOCKS born of our liaison: alone I would never have the necessity to start: our extended raps on the limit situation proposed by NEVILLE'S MANGUE-BANGUE provided the inertia: these BLOCK-EXPERIMENTS are really a kind of *quasi-cinema:* a structural innovation within NEVILLE'S work and an unexpected field for my longing to INVENT in the light of my dissatisfaction with 'cinema language': not to be contented by the relationship (mainly the visual one) of spectator-spectacle (nurtured by cinema-disintegrated by teevee) and the widespread indifference of such notions: the prevalent blind-faith acceptance of that relationship's immutability the spectator's hypnosis and submission to the screen's visual and absolute super-definition always seemed to me too prolonged tile pictures changed but somehow remained the same: why?: not even ABEL GANCE's instructions for the role of two screens in some of his films were followed: one screen and be sure the picture has not been chopped up: something had to give: something had to happen: TV HITCHCOCK's THE BIRDS is the first great TeleVising of the natural film sequence to which we were accustomed: then G-O-D-A-R-D: how can anyone muse over the 'art of cinema' yet ignore GODARD's meta-linguistic questioning of the very quintessence of filmmaking?: as with MONDRIAN in PAINTING there came to be a *before* and *after* GODARD: in ten years he took to the limit consequences which had never even occurred to other filmmakers: meanwhile within the plastic arts things were much slower (to the point of no interest even): CAGE continued to open the windows of music to the fresh air of INVENTION: GODARD dissected cinema-language with a checking and multi-evaluation only comparable to TV and ROCK phenomena: the GODARD-STONES SYMPATHY FOR THE DEVIL synthesis was not just one film production (even as film-invention or experimental cinema): in VLADIMIR AND ROSA GODARD disintegrates speech vision is silenced in a CAGEAN way by the insertion of minutes of black leader – the hand-clawed NAGRA repeats the same course in the tennis court to the dry counterpoint of the tennis ball: both HE and the NAGRA emit a disintegrating speech: sticky syllabic: and in MIDNIGHT RAMBLER JAGGER is GODARD: have you heard about the midnight – within the silence created by the omission of the word rambler the single drumstick blow): have you heard about the boston (silence-omission-drumstick blow): GODARD – verboclast – unlike the naturalist/romantic who turns to so-called cinema verité (as if cinema were fiction) penetrates the 'weft and warp' – the very structure of cinema;

joyful the liberation of the spectator from the tyranny of image and language: BRAZILWISE experimentation is far more accessible: some individuals however became increasingly 'grave' in their 'concern with the destiny of brazilian cinema' and in their quest of 'senses' and 'significations' prerequisites of their higher ideal – the creation of a Brazilian cinematographic industry: as always the cart before the horse (unless one is deliberately going backwards) too much concern: too much searching: sans joie/ sans cocaine: plunging into shallow (uterine) waters: obscure and esoteric literature alongside flashes of insight both fresh and experimental: nevertheless GODARD outpaced all: limit question the raison d'être of a 'cinema-language' which is his own: limit taken by him to a limit not crisis but limit: to what boredom and gratuity had 'cinema-language' been reduced by the advent of teevee: HITCHCOCK's BIRDS had already announced with his usual genius (blessed fatty) such limit: WITH JOY as we recognise that cinema can transcend this NUMBNESS: spectator paralysed: how to reconcile such imprisonment with the liberation of BODY with ROCK? long for the JOY and the FRESHAIR as CAGE frees music from the greatest numbness of performance/function ever seen: but seeing is not hearing or is it? MANGUE-BANGUE followed the first less cultural more inventive experiments: why limit? it pulses with pictorial sensuality (feel the colour) and fragments into geometrically set episodes within its editing structure as if it were a cartoon strip made into sequence: whatever next? i remember rejoicing in the fact that i was not a filmmaker and consequently avoided those 'very grave' problems: i remember being loathe to edit some takes i had of various project: NEVILLE-I hand-in-hand switched from the project for one more film for CCI at BABYLKONESTS: what lightness and sure energy springs from this mere shift: to release 'unnecessary-necessities': to reject the stale so-called professional notion of audiovisual: many factors helped determine CCI's realisation on 13/03/73 and that realization which i term quasi-cinema serves to negate the unilateral character of the cinema spectacle.

one – everything started with what I later termed MANCOQUILAGENS (MANCO(CAPAC) plus MAQUILAGENS MAKE-UP): NEVILLE's invention: a parody of the artist's concerns: the COKETRACKS trace the design/pattern upon which they are laid: a demi-sourire at what we used to know as plagiarism: the MAKE-UP is the camouflage: DUCHAMPIAN sarcasm as we consider the inaccuracy and pomp of all those concepts which led to the notion of 'authenticity' in the plastic arts: plagiarism is immaterial and gratuitous: could anyone in all seriousness place competition or originality as a main motivation for creative activity? behaviour (that is having pride in being supple/light/free) becomes indispensable to anything of interest for those who aim at experimentation: the parody of plagiarism (its ambivalence) is then both subtle and fundamental: the opposite which would be the main feature of 'art professional' exists at the expense of INVENTION DISCOVERY EXPERIMENTATION and serves to restore plagiarism as an active element in a structure already obsolete: as if someone would copy a text of yours and publish it merely to 'keep ahead' of you: it is as if that which had been forgotten-plagiarism-had been unearthed and revived: the COKE copies the surface (uncritical of its plagiarising) playing playing: (petit bourgeois values lost in discussions who did this or that before...) and to think that some 'artists' submit their own work to an evaluation grounded in falsities and infantile class hang-ups: if that which is supposedly superior (presumably the work in this case) can be submitted to such discrepancies then it cannot be the work: it may well be work but it will never be SOMETHING NEW: S-O-M-E-T-H-I-N-G N-E-W...

two-the slides are arranged according to a numerical order shown on their frames: this order is a result of a semi-chance operation the order in the box may or may not be the order of shooting: each slide is taken out of the box in the order that they were put in: mayhap the order is identical... these slides are not mere 'photos from NEVILLE's arrangements' but are simultaneous with them... the slides are subject to accidental variations of operator and/or soundtrack: THEY ARE FRAMES-MOMENTS: fragmentation of the cinematic: the hand tracing the coke-track... MAKE-UP that makes itself... single/double-edge razor/blade-knife-edge honed/lick it and see: throughout finished-flat-image: film or photograph it matters not: the 'cinematic' of 'track making' and its duration are fragmented in successive static positions as frames-moments INSTAMOMENTS... crystalline one-by-one not adding up to something but in themselves are something... moments (NOWandNOWandNOWand...............)

    in a

         MAKE-UP

             process

MANCOKE-UP

.......yeah: that which is limit in all this and

    that which unites NEVILLE and I and

    that which approximates here and there experiments and

    that which may be considered the predominant element – the visual – is relative and plays with the whole it proposes to embrace: in short... IMAGE is not the works supreme motive or unifying end:

contemporary artist's experimental positing is not a mere revolt against existing art categories outside the multimedia/more the displacement of IMAGE's consistency and supremacy: that does not mean that the visual has been disposed of: it becomes enriched: it is non-unifying but becomes play-part of the fragmented game which originates in experimental positing taken to a limit: within Brazilian experimentation this game of 'NEVILLE and I' is akin to ANTONIO MANUEL'S KILLED THE DOG AND DRANK THE BLOOD: within TROPICÁLIA (April '67) i included ANTONIO MANUAL's show-table displaying the 'flongs' including the above-mentioned piece: some may have wondered about its inclusion and in what way it related to TROPICÁLIA: a 'tristesse tropiques' illustration or decay of the newly made? what made me choose this experiment instead of others close to home? TROPICÁLIA was a limit-tentative (no super realism) probing IMAGE's displacement (visually and sensorially the COMPOSITE IMAGE) through a kind of multi-media salad without the obtrusive dressing of 'sense' or 'point of view': the macaws and backyard ambience were as little 'realist' or 'meta-realist' as were the eyes in the POPCRETE poem of AUGUSTO DE CAMPOS: nothing to do with POP ART or european SUPER-REALISM: as concrete as that which it seemed to evoke: a fragmented foundation of the limits of the nonrepresentational: in ANTONIO MANUEL'S flongs we do not detect a supra-realist robustness: contrariwise they are a pseudo-technique a pun on plagiarism: nor were they a sentimental poem on the experienced realities of the tropics: they were the story-newspaper emptied of daily news: the IMAGE-grip is dislocated and a more fundamental element emerges: similarly NEVILLE's MANGUE-BANGUE is not 'search work': it fell straight into my main point: why outline into blocks – cuts cinematic flow? i also can imitate the film sequence through slides which are worked out as FRAMES-MOMENTS and this without any justification defining them as 'audiovisual' (a term which I hate: is not everything finally audiovisual and more? so why the isolation of these two senses? does it not indicate an intention to maintain IMAGE's supremacy?): the point is that IMAGE does not have the same function as before particularly relative to cinema: according to MCLUHAN teevee which has a low visual definition opens up a more participatory structure for the spectator unlike cinema which presents itself complete within the super-defined photo-sequence: the super-visual ignoring the fragmentation of reality and the world of things: but IMAGE's effectiveness as a behaviour-matrix which immobilised the spectator was not only visual: it was also conceptual: twin-sister of applied ideology and discursive demagogy: STALIN and MACCARTHY: a medium trapped withing a kind of verbi-voco-visual strait-jacket characterised by idealising constancies: a 'star-system' not improvisation: and experimentation which fragmented or threatened the supremacy of existing concepts and verbi-voco-visual order was considered subversive and decadent: HITLER towards MODERN ART and ZDANOV-STALIN: yet MAO was not reduced to that: he is the same stock as the chinese individual and not IMAGE imposing itself as immutable: he is fragmented and incorporated into the unity of each chinese individual who in turn identifies with him: similarly the glory and fall of MARILYN MONROE: where IMAGE's supposed unity fragments itself by resisting the stereotype which attempts to define and limit it leading in most cases to frustration and catastrophe: something had to happen...... MAO-MARILYN: TV-ROCK: THE BEATLES: fragmentation leading to another order of identification breaking the univocal habit: today we can laugh at the complacency of maccarthian audiences in the 50's: and we wonder how effectively the unicity of some concepts and 'points of view' imposed themselves and how foreign was the audacity of experimentation and how PARIS of latent provincialism became the very hub of experimentation mapping hitherto unknown territories: the world of objects its unity under threat would be transformable (reducible to the atom) but never fragmented in its whole: the implications of cinema as something other than sequential and linear....

so...... verbi-voco-visual constancy?...... yeah...... the skeleton in the cupboard...... and the obstruction.

BLOCK-EXPERIMENTS: slides-soundtrack-INSTRUCTIONS (as flight plan (loosely)): CC abbreviation identifies the series and should be used in the main spine of COSMOCOCA-program in progress experiments:

a) SLIDES: not audiovisual as their programming when put into performance enlarges the scope of the projected succession...... enriched as they become relative within a kind of corny environment: for me JACK SMITH was its precursor: he extracted from his cinema not a naturalistic vision imitating appearance but a sense of fragmented narrative mirror shatters: the slides displaced ambience by a non-specific time duration and by the continuous relocation of the projector framing and reframing the projection on walls-ceiling-floor: random juxtaposition of sound track (records): these BLOCKS the first five of which were programmed by NEVILLE-I replace for me IMAGE's problems consumed by TROPICÁLIA (etc.) by a level of SPECTACLE (PROJECTION-PERFORMANCE) towards which i am attracted through NEVILLE's cinema experience..........

SLIDES: FRAMES-MOMENTS: INSTAMOMENTS are a direct corollary to MANGUE-BANGUE limit: i am driven to insufflate experimentality into forms which seem to remain virtually immutable as SPECTATOR-SPECTACLE: NEVILLE's concern is to grasp environments sensorial plasticity and being above all a 'plastic artist' he finds himself driven to....... INVENT IT: the camera work in MANGUE-BANGUE acts as a sensorial glove for touching-probing-circulating: explode then into SLIDES... fragments as consequence... pretext for ENVIRONMENT-PERFORMANCE and by dint of such experimentation we are united and made to realise that 'joint work' has no more sense than individual work: NEVILLE-I do not 'jointly create' instead we mutually incorporate so that the

notion of 'authorship' is as distant as is 'plagiarism: it is........ JOY GAME born of a monumental hoax: (snorting cocaine from the cover of ZAPPA's WEASELS RIPPED MY FLESH)'who wants the eyebrows?
'who wants the lips"
'... what about the wound?' (to the accompaniment of snorting sounds) SNOW-POWDER: a parody of the plastic arts......... and

b) SOUNDTRACK: records or tape: furnished or suggested: environment incites......... DANCE......... BODY...... and

c) PERFORMANCE-GAMES plus: INSTRUCTIONS for private PERFORMANCE for small number of people indoors or outdoors and for public PERFORMANCE aiming at groupal games-experiments: to follow INSTRUCTIONS is to open oneself to GAME and PARTICIPATION the raison d'être of these CC's: to ignore INSTRUCTIONS is to close oneself and not participate in the experiment: so... where are you at?

three and four – the PRESENCE OF COKE as a prop-element in the first CC's is not obligatory (COCAINVIRONMENT... cocainvironmeans...) nor does it explicate COSMOCOCA-program in progress's INVENTION idea: just another twist in the general hoax.......... and why not? if smelling paint and other shit is part of the plastic art 'experience' then why not the shining-white COUSIN so appealing to most nostrils?.......... TO PLAY WITHOUT SWEATING... we laugh in the face of the argument that posits that it is the artist's duty to elaborate his inborn talents and to sweat out his very lifeblood 'onto the canvas (... the audience explodes With lahahahaughter):' NEVILLE-I are not in favour of sweating: not even when constructing PENETRABLES and NUCLEUS did I sweat: but it really flowssss in JOY-DANCE: PENETRABLES were invitations au voyage to the bitchy pleasantries offered by EDEN... colour... sound... languor inside tents... straw... sand: ARTAUD's poetry without blood

– ... that which emerges lifting itself above the ground... singing: ZARATHUSTIAN JOY of NIETZSCHE...... NEVILLE invents COSMOCOCA as world-name proposing not a 'point of view' but a WORLD-INVENTION program: and from my program-experiment of MARCH THIRTEENTH NINETEENHUNDREDANDSEVENTYTHREE first session-event: the making of CCI) was born the realisation of INVENTION-WORLD altering my life and behaviour and transforming the wealth of propositions of these work-years into major and radical consequences: COSMOCOCA on CONTIGUITY: OF EXPERIMENTAL WORLD-LEVELS: it is not intended to surround COKE with the so-called deifying-mystical absolutes of lsd: COCAINE neither toxic nor water: the very idea of hallucinogens as 'consciousness-expanding' (nothing could be less philosophic or constitute a greater incongruity) sounds phony.

COSMOCOCA is the supreme game-joke in which we play with SIMULTANEITY and CONTIGUITY and the multitude of possibilities of individual experience which lie within the collective-mind of MCLUHAN's GLOBAL VILLAGE: it is not a question of preaching (or its contemporary equivalent 'turning on' which should not be 'to convert' someone into our own system of beliefs (as a mode of seeing-feeling-living)) it's more a question of mutual experimental incorporation through the play of simultaneous permeating experiences: as in...... DANCING BODIES reeling and writhing never in one place long enough to form a 'point of view': nor is it a spiritual panacea for the 'general longings' what madness... each man must choose his own poison ... an extension of judeo-christian hang-ups... nobody wants to be saved contrariwise... as ARTAUD says... let the lost get lost: when BAUDELAIRE dedicates odes to OPIUM and HASHISH he is not prescribing remedies he is poisoning us with experience.... he is not preaching or promoting the commerce of the drugs (BAUDELAIRE as pusher... not the first... and certainly not the last)... he was WORLD INVENTING...... yes.... proposing a new and major order... A COLLECTIVE ONE... of participation.... carrying his poetry into new spaces flying by those nets of literary tradition.

NEVILLE-I in another situation within JOY-WORLD... becoming concrete (ROCK OF AGES)... have discovered something in common.... the omniscient generating nucleus of this proposition-program.... THAT WHICH IS PROPOSED IS ALWAYS GIVEN AS PLAY... CHANCE-PLAY... BY THE THROW OF A DICE AND NEVER AS A FIXATION ON EXISTING MODELS: PARTICIPATION AS INVENTION: SCRAMBLING OF THE ROLES: JOYFUL...... WITHOUT SWEAT.

five-the classification of these CC's serves to indicate the openendedness of the BLOCK-EXPERIMENTS: moreover there are other propositions in progress......

...

Chapter 30

The Early Days of Video Art in Brazil (2000)

Fernando Cocchiarale

The history of video art in Brazil began in 1974. In the second half of that year, experimental artists from Rio de Janeiro made the first works in the country with that technical medium invented a decade before. Many of those who participated in this pioneering experience had begun their trajectory a few years earlier. They were typical representatives of a small section of the generation that emerged in Brazil in the 1970s. It was characterised more by their interest in investigating new media and new concepts for art than by the references inherited from the Brazilian avant-gardes of the previous two decades.

Variously tuned to the international art issues of the period, these artists could not find institutional spaces for the regular distribution of their work, except for the Museum of Contemporary Art of the University of São Paulo (MAC-USP) and the experimental area of the Museum of Modern Art of Rio de Janeiro (MAM-RJ).[52] Even though these museums had different institutional profiles – the former focused on the making of national and international collective events, the latter on the diffusion of national values through individual exhibitions – they have remained in the memory and curriculum of the best Brazilian artists of our days.

Directed by Walter Zanini, MAC-USP organised, at that time, group shows that were crucial for the renovation underway: the seven editions of the exhibition *Jovem Arte Contemporânea* (JAC) [Young Contemporary Art], held between 1967 and 1974; Prospective 74; and *Poéticas Visuais* [Visual Poetics] in 1977. But only in the 8th and last edition of JAC (1974) would there be a first public exhibition of artist videos made in Brazil. Its participants were the same pioneering artists who experimented with the medium in Rio de Janeiro earlier that year. The only exception was Ângelo de Aquino, who made a video work by himself around that same time, showed it during the JAC exhibition, but didn't pursue the investigation of the medium. Anna Bella Geiger, Ivens Machado, Sônia Andrade and I (who started in the arts as an artist and not as a professor, critic or curator) were part of a group of artists with very different poetics but with a common interest in the investigation of the creative possibilities of new technologies. In 1975, Letícia Parente, Miriam Danowski and Paulo Herkenhoff, who belonged to the group as well, also started using video. We continue to work with video and other nonconventional media, and this work has been shown in this and other editions of the JAC as well as in the other exhibitions mentioned above.

These first experiments blend together with the lonely beacons represented by MAC-USP and MAM-RJ. Anna Bella Geiger, by then an established artist, had become a kind of informal consultant for Zanini on the experimental production in Rio de Janeiro. Thanks to her fondness for artists dedicated to new media experimentation, both here and abroad, Zanini would become one of the main Brazilian interlocutors with international institutions with contemporary art profiles.

In 1974, the Institute of Contemporary Arts of the University of Pennsylvania in Philadelphia asked Zanini, then director of MAC-USP, to nominate Brazilians to participate in the greatest show of artist videos ever held. Through Anna Bella Geiger, MAC-USP invited artists from Rio de Janeiro, while Zanini was responsible for recruiting participants from São Paulo. Geiger and three of her many former students (Ivens Machado, Sonia Andrade and I), motivated by the opportunity to participate in the North American event and curious about the experimental possibilities of the new technological medium, went out looking for equipment. Jom Tob Azulay, a Brazilian filmmaker who had just returned from a season in Los Angeles with a Sony-Matic portable camcorder, was contacted and offered to record our first experiences, just as he had done with Ângelo de Aquino. On the same day in the second semester of 1974, the videos by Geiger (*Passagens* [Passages]), Andrade (untitled) and myself (*You Are Time*) were recorded. Later, Azulay recorded *Versus*, a video by Ivens Machado. These were the Brazilian videos that participated in the North American *Video Art* show (Antonio Dias also participated with a video he had made in Italy). For reasons I don't know, the artists invited directly by Zanini didn't get access to the necessary equipment and were absent from the show.

Organised by Suzanne Delehanty, *Video Art* was shown in Philadelphia in 1975 and toured three other American institutions: The Contemporary Arts Centre, in Cincinnati, Ohio; The Museum of Contemporary Art, in Chicago, Illinois; and the Wadsworth Atheneum, in Hartford, Connecticut. Just like the Brazilian videos made for the 8th JAC integrated the Brazilian delegation of the show (with the exception of Angelo de Aquino, who didn't participate), so would the 32 North American artists present in *Video Art* later participate in the 13th São Paulo International Art Biennial in 1975, and soon after in the MAM-RJ show.

However, one can only grasp the meaning of these pioneering experiences by looking backwards. It is important to consider the artistic and aesthetic questions that were being raised in the background, both nationally and internationally, since the beginning of the previous decade, and their role in a daily life dominated by the discretionary political presence of the military dictatorship. Additionally, one must consider the deeper historical effects of the industrial revolution, which made possible the invention of technological media such as photography, cinema and videotape that could produce and reproduce images without requiring any manual skill.

Intersections: The Context of Plastic Arts

... Setting the stage for the pioneering video art experiences in Brazil, the combination of international art trends and the specific Brazilian cultural conditions created an apparently prosperous social environment in the first decade of the military dictatorship (1964-1974). Under the military regime, TV became a contributing factor for national integration and a means to legitimise discretionary power. Televised media became part of daily social life. Thus, contrary to what some art critics and artists of the time had supposed, it was not strange for Brazilian artists to make a poetic-critical use of this medium.

All video exhibitions that characterise the beginning of this history had full or partial participation by artists from the Rio group. After the first public video exhibition in the 8th JAC (MAC-USP, 1974) and *Video Art*, several others took place: the *1st Experimental Art Exhibition of Super 8 Films, Audiovisual and Videotape* (Maison de France, Rio de Janeiro, November 1975); *Vídeos* (MAM-RJ, 8th and 9th November, 1975, held in parallel to the *Video Art* show, which represented the United States at the São Paulo Biennial); *Fourth International Open Encounter on Video Buenos Aires* (Centro de Arte y Comunicación, December 1975); *Vijfde Internationale Videodagen* (Internationaal Cultureel Centrum, Antwerp, Holland 1976);[53] *7 Artistas do Vídeo* [7 Video Artists] (a show of the pioneering group at MAC-USP, May

1977);[54] *Vídeos by Sônia Andrade* (MAC/USP 1977);[55] and *Ciclo Fim de Semana com Arte* [Art Weekend Cycle] (Museu Nacional de Belas Artes, Rio de Janeiro, 1977).[56]

These exhibitions constitute the only existing record of the early uses of this new imaging technology in Brazilian art. They culminated in the country's 1st International Video Art Meeting of São Paulo (1978), which was attended by 25 artists living in Brazil, including: Anna Bella Geiger, Carmela Gross, Donato Ferrari, Gabriel Borba Filho, Gastão de Magalhães, José Roberto Aguilar, Julio Plaza, Letícia Parente, Marcello Nitsche, Miriam Danowski, Paulo Herkenhoff, Regina Silveira, Regina Vater and Roberto Sandoval. The future would show that some artists did not continue to explore the medium, while others simply didn't continue to produce art. This was true even among the members of the pioneer group, such as Miriam Danowski, Paulo Herkenhoff and I, who around the beginning of the 1980s reoriented our activities towards critical reflection.

Chapter 31

Testimonial: Regina Silveira (1984)

Regina Silveira

I believe that Julio [Plaza] and I have played some sort of a role in the pluralisation of the artistic modes of operation and dissemination, and that it coincides with our move to São Paulo from Puerto Rico, where we worked for four years at the Mayaguez University campus. But, truth be told, when we arrived here and began to organise and participate in some manifestations, we already found artists moving in this direction, or at least who had this predisposition. Otherwise, it would have been a completely artificial 'deployment', wouldn't it?

In Puerto Rico, especially in the last few years, we started an activity connected to Mail Art by exchanging artistic material by mail with several artists from many countries. This material would arrive at our university's Art Department, already establishing a type of international circulation. We felt quite provoked by the possibility, so open and unusual at that moment, to establish contact with artists worldwide and to have first-hand knowledge of their work.

This collaborative venture was sometimes organised by artists or art groups through publications such as Klaus Groh's German *International Artist's Cooperation*, a monthly bulletin where artists expressed themselves and invited others to the exhibitions they put together. Then we also started submitting works and receiving works in return.

Ulises Carrión did something similar in Amsterdam, where he organised exhibitions and publications through Other Books & So. These were private artist-run initiatives held in varied venues, drawing people to shows and events. In 1970, '71 and '72, as Mail Art movements intensified worldwide, there was a very stimulating communication network.

In Puerto Rico, we took advantage of all this material to start a trend, getting the university to host a large international exhibition completely received by mail. Julio was the curator of this exhibition, which was called *Creation, Creación, Criação...* and featured a huge participation of artists from all over the world, including Brazilians. The exhibition took place in the university's Art Room.

This international communication between artists continued even after we returned to Brazil. Not only did we participate in exhibitions and publications abroad, sending work by mail, but we also organised exhibitions here, like the ones Julio coordinated at MAC-USP with [Walter] Zanini. I curated the show *Printed in Brazil* abroad, an exhibition that brought together artists' books, poets and visual artists, and that was held at Other Books & So in Amsterdam in 1978.

When we arrived in São Paulo, what first came up was the idea of organising independent, collaborative productions, with the participation of artists with whom we now had contact. At that time, we were already working at the Armando Álvares Penteado Foundation (FAAP) and so many of the project participants were artists who were teaching at FAAP. The outcome was *ON-OFF*, a publication that ran three issues and circulated from hand to hand, with a completely anomalous distribution structure that was subversive with regard to the current systems of artistic promotion. The magazine was produced in collaboration with the artists, each doing their part, printing copies where they could; that is why the pages are of different sizes. In the first volume, we used envelopes to collect the works; the second one consisted of a series of postcards; in the third, we went back to envelopes. I'm not even sure how we distributed it. Each artist had their copies, which were usually given away in a rather marginal type of circulation. But many copies were also sent by mail, sometimes in exchange for other works, and participated in exhibitions in various places.

That was one mode of operation. Another, more institutional one, was in partnership with the Museum of Contemporary Art. The director was Zanini, who was extremely interested in this kind of artistic expression. With Julio's collaboration, Zanini organised important exhibitions with works coming by mail. *Prospectiva* [Prospective] and *Poéticas Visuals* [Visual Poetics] had this prerogative. It's worth remembering the space that MAC has given to multimedia art for many years.

The main practice in my first years as an artist, up to 1966, was painting. I went from figuration to an expressionist, almost abstract, kind of representation. Then there was a short period of about two years when I worked with processes with three-dimensional objects made from industrial materials. In 1969, I resumed printmaking, starting with serigraphy, my most consistent medium until 1976.

My first serigraphs were already characterised by the use of photographic images and geometric structures in perspective, showing a clear influence of constructive resources developed in the previous works. It is in these prints that, even today, I'm able to find some of the qualities I would develop throughout my activities in the 1970s in other graphic media.

As for my personal involvement in multimedia, it must be said it was related to my work in printmaking. Because, as you know, my practice has been connected to graphic media for years, even though I don't consider myself a 'printmaker'. My works in the area are very unorthodox; I have always used graphic media in a free and untraditional way and only to the extent that they could serve my ideas. It doesn't mean that I have been personally against traditional modes of printmaking. Printmaking as a whole can be quite traditional. The issue is what one does with the medium. For instance, it was silkscreen printing that brought me closer to other technologies like heliography, as I used silkscreen to make the necessary transparencies. I made my first heliographs in 1973 to participate in the circulating exhibition *Imágen y Palabra*, organised by CAyC [*Centro de Arte y Comunicación* – Centre for Art and Communication] in Buenos Aires.

Shortly afterwards, I started using offset, which would become a large technical field, especially after 1975. Offset was used to produce the Art Games series shown at the *Gabinete de Artes Gráficas* [Graphic Arts Cabinet] in São Paulo in 1977.

In a way, I was responsible for introducing offset in lithography classes here in São Paulo, both at FAAP and the University of São Paulo (USP). My interest in the technique came from my contact with [the pharmaceutical company] Hoechst do Brasil. Soon after becoming settled in São Paulo, Julio and I visited their reproduction labs, where the technicians demonstrated how to make transparencies from pre-sensitised positive plates (which we already knew), as well as how to draw directly over the plates under safety light for a more 'artistic' effect (which was a novelty for us). In the lab, we also saw manual printing on a proofing press. I was thrilled and wanted to apply the procedure at FAAP's lithography classes right away. I got FAAP to install an offset proofing press in the studio, which they brought from the print shop, and soon the students were combining offset with lithographic techniques, following the intended syntax of their work, often in combination with stone lithography made directly on manual presses.

My unorthodox behaviour as a printmaker also made me organise unconventional graphic arts shows, such as *Artemicro*, made entirely with microfiche. Microfilming is done with a camera that reduces images as much as needed to make them fit the microfiche. This process was done at IMS (Information, Microforms and Systems), whose director, Fredric Litto, was also a professor at the University of São Paulo. Rafael França and I planned the exhibition. We chose thirty two artists with experience in graphic media and each one made twelve images, constituting the fourth part of a microfiche. Bell & Howell lent us the necessary reading devices, which enlarged the images twenty-four times.

Artemicro has always been shown in installations with several of those readers, first at the Museum of Image and Sound in São Paulo, then at the University of Caxias do Sul in Rio Grande do Sul and, finally, at the Museum of Modern Art in Rio. In Portugal, it was shown at *Cooperativa Diferença* in Lisbon and at Coimbra's *Círculo de Artes Plásticas*. A year later, in 1983, it was also shown at the Bach House Cultural Centre in Dallas, Texas. Shipping *Artemicro* around was very easy because the eight microfiches fitted into a small, light envelope. It was fun to see how readers exploded the size of the works during the exhibition, giving it such a large presence. I believe that the exhibition was absolutely original not because it used microfilming to document art (which is itself unusual) but rather as a means for artistic production. However, among the participating artists, very few had direct contact with the process and saw how microfiches were made. After they accepted our invitation, Rafael and I gave them some technical 'tips', explaining how to prepare their originals: keeping the contrast high, having the correct size, using a certain line thickness – in short, not very different from preparing originals for photocopying.

My involvement with video also emerged from this curiosity about media and 'talking a walk' across them. I even believe I have always used video in a very graphic way, thinking of the representational plane as if it served for drawing. The time of the work also was almost always the real-time of the performance, invariably accounting for that visualisation plane. That's a kind of graphic behaviour, isn't it? All my videos were like that. Now, my production was scarce.... My first video works are from the same period as the first artist videos in Brazil, but they are only a rough attempt, since it was very difficult to make videos back then. Video equipment was available at the Police Academy, at FAAP and I don't know where else, but it was hard to get access to it. Donato Ferrari, Julio, Gabriel Borba, myself and some other artists have tried. The first videos were finally made after Zanini acquired equipment for MAC-USP. These were black and white, short, silent works, which generally depicted minimal actions, recorded with a fixed camera. There was no way to edit them, which soon became a big problem.

After a three-year gap, I made three more videos while working at the Aster Study Centre. The Centre, run by Julio, Zanini, Donato Ferrari and I, was short-lived: it lasted a little over two years. During some of this period, Roberto Sandoval rented the front room to set up his video studio. This made video, once again, very 'available' to us. Sandoval's studio was well equipped with editing possibilities. I made all three videos in colour, with sound and editing. In retrospect, I feel that only the last one, *Morfas*, shown in the video section of the 1981 São Paulo Art Biennial, still seems somewhat sophisticated in how it connects an idea to its execution. *Morfas* dealt with the deformation of everyday objects when examined up close.

Chapter 32

Testimonial: Anna Bella Geiger (1984)

Anna Bella Geiger

...

I began making videos in 1974 and invited some people to study with me because I realised I wasn't interested in doing and exhibiting individual work. I was interested in a kind of production that involved several individuals, leading to discussion among the participants. In this, I had, of course, a very formative role, since later these students would follow their own paths in philosophy and art, to become art teachers spreading the information across a network.

I made my first video *Passagens* [Passages] at the end of 1974. It depicted a performance in which I walked through spaces with stairs... I climbed these stairs in different ways and they would change. I would be transported from one to another by the magic of video editing, without the audience noticing.

... I wouldn't always make a video, since we had awful materials and had to deal with challenging working conditions in addition to a busted camera...

... But many people, chiefly in Rio and São Paulo, began to operate and work in these mediums, to think their work within them. At the same time, I stopped teaching in the museum. I found it very hard to convey any kind of information in only one semester. In 1973, I started to work much more slowly with people and groups, studying the development of their own work. The participation of other people who used to work with me in these discussions, like Fernando [Cocchiarale] and Paulo Herkenhoff, lent dynamism to the group...

In 1976 I made a series of postcards, *Brasil Nativo / Brasil Alienígena* [Native Brazil / Alien Brazil] in which I wanted to contrast my image and actions with those of indigenous people. The work alluded to many questions at different levels. I was working with imitation, sometimes as parody and sometimes as accompaniment, that resituated Native Brazil in a postcard – that is to say, Native Brazil not as a paradisiac home of Indigenous people, but rather as a place where Indigenous people are mistreated and have their culture eradicated....

During that period, I made very little work with technical media. However, I developed many projects and annotated drafts. I would only go on to make these projects after I felt they all fitted together, that there was some common logic there, at least in my mind.

Afterwards, I returned to video. I made a series called *Mapas Elementares* [Elementary Maps] ... at that point, I realised I could make all my criticisms and questions fit onto the map, the geographic chart. Formally, I was delighted by these maps. But it took me a while. Around 1976, I started distorting them and seeing in these distortions of images and measurements something related to arts systems. The distortion of a map has always been an ideological issue. I did a series called *O Pão Nosso de Cada Dia* [Our Daily Bread] in which I ate bread and a map. As I ate the bread, a map appeared in the empty space of the loaf. This was related to issues of ideology, our political situation, art...

There were other people working in a similar way. It was a very interesting period in Brazilian arts, but poorly understood by critics and artists, who didn't want to accept change, didn't want to give up on the art object, on the values of the market... didn't want the values of artistic production and artistic creation to be different.

It's a double mistake because our system is driven by a mechanism that is not fully capitalist. The gaps are wide, and artists must wear themselves out to work in many different ways. They become much shyer and lose their courage to produce new work due to self-censorship. This is not entirely surprising, since the punishment for going against cultural rules is often physical and economic misery. What became of the artists who worked in the 1970s? Very few of us are still working in the arts. Many found institutional jobs in order to survive and became sophisticated and critical towards art making. But it doesn't always have to be like this; each person followed their own path.

The criticism and scepticism about their own situation led many people to stop working. They lost their spirit, stopped producing; their works were no longer published or exhibited in any significant way.

Newer generations were moved by the always provocative inquiry into the meaning of the arts and their function in society. Abroad, this question had its own origins; in Brazil, it reflected our own political and cultural situation, our destitution...

This was therefore the nature of the work: more ephemeral, made without proper funding and materials (to which we didn't have access anyway), working more with ideas and concepts than with a finished product. In this sense, our most contested medium wasn't drawing or printmaking (which in fact went unscathed in Brazil) but rather painting, the medium best understood by the market.

At the time, some artists said that painting was preposterous. I always thought that the issue wasn't painting itself, because it was a medium as unknown here as any other. For me, the issue was no longer in the medium, but rather in the artists' ways of doing thing, which had become systematic and crystallised.

... All these years, these artists have been criticising the bankrupt art system, which is doubly bankrupt in the case of Brazil, where it doesn't even yield the same positive outcomes as in the capitalist countries. They have criticised the market ideology that dominated art discussions in the 1960 and '70s. They broke into the field of criticism to make certain statements. It was a cleansing, like taking nitric acid and purging the system's guts. If art had not been put in conceptual terms in the 1970s, calling into question the intelligence of the artist as well as of the audience (who sometimes didn't want to understand some things) and accomplishing this radical cleansing, the issue of media wouldn't have been as forcefully discussed and demystified by now. A new understanding of painting and its bi-dimensional qualities could only have been achieved because these elements had been thoroughly discussed in the 1970s and completely turned inside out by the criticism of artists looking for other languages beyond the retina.

Chapter 33

Videoart: The Brazilian Adventure (1996)

Arlindo Machado

Video arrived early to Brazil. It soon found practitioners and rapidly became one of the principal means of expression for the emerging generations of the second half of the century. Late in the 1960s, only two or three years after its commercial appearance in other countries, portable video equipment was being used by Brazil's video pioneers. This equipment had been put on the market by the Japanese electronics industry for private use in corporate employee training schemes. But there was nothing to stop it being put to other non-industrial purposes, given the right circumstances. The very availability of the equipment opened the way for the appearance of what Rene Berger called 'microtelevision': radical television, produced and broadcast on a closed circuit, independent of the economic and cultural models of conventional broadcasting (Berger 1977).

The precocious appearance and rapid spread of video in Brazil can be explained by a set of factors, of which I will discuss two most important ones. The first one is cost. Of all contemporary audiovisual forms, video offers the best options in terms of production costs; this makes it possible for independent authors and non-profit groups to explore autonomous cultural projects. The electronics industry tends strongly towards progressive price reduction so as to keep up with the competition. The result is that electronic equipment and processes – high-resolution cameras and digital post-production resources, for example – are accessible to small producers today. Not more than five years ago, these resources were available only to large television networks. However, cinema – a close relative of video – is the opposite in terms of the economic tendencies of capitalist industry. The growth rate of production expenses has been calculated at about 16% per year (Carbonara and Korpi 1991); what weighs most on this figure is the increasingly astronomical cost of film. As the cost of cinema production spirals upward, production on a more modest budget becomes an impossibility. National cinema industries (Brazil's included) teeter on the edge of bankruptcy, and the independent and experimental schools are caught up in a bitter process of extinction. In a poor country such as Brazil, the stampede of audiovisual creators towards video formats is thus nearly inevitable.

The second factor, more broadly cultural in its nature, concerns television. Brazil is a television-centred country; the formative role of television is so decisive that few comparable phenomena are to be found anywhere in the world. But we must not forget that for the generations that have come of age from the 1970s on, television is a primary point of reference, with its fragmentary language, its swift rhythms and its images in metamorphosis. Many of the groups from the 1980s on that took up the technology of video to express a different view of the world had television as the horizon of their cultural universe. Television was in their heads, and they wanted to turn it into reality, but not necessarily a reality that would coincide with what was found on commercial TV channels. Unlike the previous generations, which believed (and sometimes still believe) that television bears the stamp of some sort of original sin and that it is condemned to incarnate the power structures of modern technological society, young Brazilian video-makers believed in the possibility of casting television in a different mould, one that would be more creative, more democratic. They kept alive the hope that electronic media, with their immense capacity for technical intervention, might come to express an emerging new sensibility.

The First Generation: Pioneers

We have records of Brazilian artists working with video since the end of the 1960s (Machado 1985). Yet they can hardly be classed as video-makers. They were, for the most part, artists concerned with the search for new structures for their work. From the mid-1960s on, many artists attempted to break away from the aesthetic and commercial schemas of conventional painting and seek out more dynamic materials to provide form for their artistic ideas. Some went to the streets and intervened in the state of the urban landscape. Others used their own bodies as foundation for public performances. Still others opted for mixed media and for blurrier frontiers between the arts in the form of hybrid objects and spectacles, installations and happenings. And then there were those who sought innovative aesthetic experiences by using industrial techniques for generating images, such as photography, cinema and, above all, video. Here was the birthplace of video art, an aesthetic at first limited to the universe of fine arts, whose only exhibition space was the elite circuit of museums and art galleries. This, at least, was the case with Brazilian video art; in other countries, the history is perhaps quite different. In the United States, for example, video art was at first linked to experimental music (Nam June Paik was originally a composer), dance, theatre and experimental cinema.

In Brazil, the first generation of video creators was composed of well-known or emerging names in the world of visual arts: Roberto Sandoval, Antônio Dias, Anna Bella Geiger, Jose Roberto Aguilar, Ivens Machado, Leticia Parente, Sônia Andrade, Regina Silveira, Paulo Herkenhoff, Regina

Vater, Fernando Cocchiarale, Mary Dritschel, Paulo Bruscky and many more. Video was born as an expansion of the fine arts, as one medium among many others; it never came to be regarded by artists as an exclusive creative process. Indeed, it was sometimes difficult to understand video artworks outside the context of the artist's work as a whole. There was still no search for a language specific to video, except in a few isolated cases. There was nothing in Brazil like the distortion and disintegration of figurative imagery (Machado 1984; Machado 1988) that came to be the dominant line in video art in many countries in the northern hemisphere (exemplified by the works of Paik and Emschwiller in the United States).

Most first-generation works in Brazilian video were recordings of artists' gestures in performance. The basic device was almost exclusively the confrontation between the camera and the artist; for example, artist Leticia Parente, in one of the most disturbing works of that time, embroidered the words 'Made in Brazil' on the soles of her own feet, her actions recorded by a camera in an extreme close-up. In some respects, the initial Brazilian experience echoes one of the directions taken by North American video at the same time, represented by people such as Vito Acconci, Joan Jonas, Peter Campus and others, whose work (as observed at the time by Rosalind Krauss in 1978) consisted of placing the body of the artist between two machines – camera and monitor – so as to produce an instantaneous image of the performer, like Narcissus looking at himself in the mirror.

The technology was precarious, yet some powerful works were produced during this period. The most provocative were perhaps those of Sônia Andrade. From 1974 on, Andrade made nearly a dozen short experiments that can be considered among the most mature of her generation. One video shows the artist's face, totally deformed by nylon threads; she then mutilates herself in small ways, removing body hair with a pair of scissors, fixing her hand to a table with wire and nails. These are works of latent self-violence, half-real, half-fictitious, through which Andrade discourses on the tenuous limits between lucidity and madness that are characteristic of the creative act.

Of this pioneering generation, most soon gave up video and went on to other experiments in the larger field of art. Very few kept their faith in the basic principles or continued the tradition of video during the following decades. Of those who continued the aesthetic project of their forerunners (formal simplicity, moderate use of technology, 'narcissistic' insertion of the performer into the image, public self-exhibition), the most important name is certainly that of Rafael França, who started to make videos in the early 1980s. Part of his work was done in São Paulo and the other part in Chicago, where he lived, studied and worked for a time. His *Fighting the Invisible Enemy*, for example, was made in Chicago in 1983. The fact that he lived outside Brazil and had close contact with video art abroad turned França into an important link between Brazilian and international video. He was the first to make a systematic effort to draw Brazilian video out of its shell. França wrote for newspapers and art magazines. He curated important international exhibitions of video art in Brazil and it may safely be said that the new generations of Brazilian video artists have developed thanks to the ideas and paths he sketched out.

As with almost all the works of the pioneers, the principal character in França's videos is himself. In video he found a suitable means for meditating and reflecting on his own inner conflicts and, above all, on his greatest obsession: the inevitability of death. His very personal work also centred on a dramatic inquiry into homosexuality. França died of AIDS in 1991, after leaving us with his most authentic witness to his faithfulness to himself. His last video, *Prelúdio de uma Morte Anunciada* [Prelude to an Announced Death] (1991), was finished only a few days before his death and it reflects his agony during the worst moments of his illness.

The Second Generation: Independent Video

At the beginning of the 1980s, a new wave of creators rerouted the trajectory of Brazilian video. This was the generation of independent video, which consisted largely of young people recently graduated from college, who sought to explore the possibilities of television as an expressive system and to transform the electronic image into a fact of contemporary culture. The horizon of this generation's world was television, although for a long-time independent video was absent from television proper, which systematically ignored it. For these artists, the elite circuit of museums and art galleries now belonged to the past. Symptomatically, this new wave was opposed to early video art in that it tended towards documentary and social themes. Video came noisily onto the stage; it began to leave its cultural ghetto and win over its first publics. Video festivals were held; the first video projection rooms made a timid appearance; strategies were sketched out with a view to breaking the stranglehold of the commercial TV networks.

In order to correctly evaluate the contribution made by independent video, one would have to identify the nature of the rather different perspective it has on Brazil, the country and its people. This generation rejects wholesale representations; its doubts and the partiality of its interventions are made clear in its work. It questions itself as to the limits of its enunciating capacity and its ability to really know others. For these artists, the person who points a camera at someone else is no longer necessarily in a privileged position as a producer of meanings; they are no longer authorised to tell the entire truth about the person represented, nor are they in a position to bestow an impossible coherence on the culture in focus. The makers themselves are no longer absent from the audiovisual 'text', nor do they hide behind the camera under the pretence of neutrality. Instead, they see the production of meanings and the legibility of new videographic products as dependent on the capacity to create new relationships between the parties involved. Their real intent is less to tell the truth about the other -- to reveal the other, to 'translate' the other into our canons of intelligibility – than to try to build a bridge between cultures, so that they can at last enter into a dialogue.

Different groups have employed different strategies to reach this point. Let us look at TVDO. This is a fairly radical São Paulo-based group that has had the effect of renewing the expressive resources of video in Brazil. If we look at their *Caipira In (Local Groove)* (1987), it would seem to sum up the anxieties of the group. At first sight it looks like yet another of those works aimed at the preservation of popular culture – a film commissioned by some official institution for the conservation of the cultural image or the good of national heritage. The explicit idea is to film a popular religious feast that takes place annually in the small town of São Luis do Paraitinga. Yet the video negates the camera's recording function; it establishes a distance between subject and object, between observer and observed, and eliminates almost entirely the voices and statements of those of whom it speaks. Electronic studio effects corrode the *in loco* images of the cameras; the montage breaks up any possible coherence that might 'explain' the event; even the sounds recorded live during the feast are electronically processed until they are no more than pallid vestiges of themselves.

In fact, *Caipira In* is less a documentary about a religious feast than a reflection on the distance between two irreconcilable cultures – or, to be more exact, a demonstration of our inability to live the experience of another person. The 'reading' is revealed as one version among an infinite number of others. The makers interfere; they display themselves as a clearly deforming presence. When they focus on someone else's culture they do not negate themselves, they do not renounce their own world, their own values, their own culture; nor do they allow themselves to be dissolved into the culture of the others. No pretence at objectivity hides the fact that the subject in the representation, faced with someone else's feast, brings along their own world, their own past and their own cultural references. On the basis of such filters, they approach the other culture. *Caipira In* is a comment on this distance, a statement of awareness of it, a questioning of the insertion of the analyst in a reality that is not theirs. TVDO's video serves as a deconstruction of the documentary illusion, in which the intervention of the videomakers becomes a criticism of the ability to represent reality (Machado 1991).

How then might we imagine a strategy for building a bridge between two cultures? A further group of video-makers, *Olhar Eletrônico* [Electronic Gaze], has tried to answer this question, and has taken a direction rather different than that of TVDO. Their search is not for a radical separation, but for a negotiation, for an exchange, perhaps for a chance of a dialogue. Theirs is an exercise in polyphony that will allow the multiplicity of voices to assume their place again. Now the artist aims at placing their work within a process of communication in which they are just one among the many voices in conflict.

And so *Olhar Eletrônico*, in its more notable works, seeks to break down any relationship of knowledge or authority that may exist between the makers and the protagonists of the video. Attempts are made to avoid the superimposition of any discourse with pretensions to truth upon images of the subject and to create devices whereby the subjects themselves can reply, in their autonomy, to the inquiries of the makers. Fundamentally, this is an inversion of the falsifying reporting schemes of commercial networks, which reduce all the ideological, cultural, linguistic, ethnic and religious diversity of the people who inhabit the country to an integrating and normalising discourse, the discourse of institutionalised television. To let people speak for themselves, to give the subject freedom to express themselves, to render the production techniques transparent to the protagonists – these are some of the guiding principles underlying the work of *Olhar Eletrônico*. These principles are evident in *Do Outro Lado de sua Casa* [On the Other Side of Your House] (1986). In this exemplary work, video-makers Marcelo Machado, Renato Barbieri and Paulo Morelli look at a daily universe of a group of beggars, living as they do at the very edge of society. But we do not find that sense of commiseration or guilt so common in a Christian or Catholic approach to the humbler part of the population. On the contrary: as the video goes on, the beggars begin to impose their own discourse and put forward, with complete independence, the singularity of their worldview. Indeed, one of the beggars ends up taking the enunciation of the work upon himself; microphone in hand, he sets out to direct the interviews with his partners. Here, in a subversive reversal of roles, the object being investigated ends up behind the camera, thus becoming the subject who investigates. In this way, any humiliation in the approach to the protagonists is avoided (Machado 1993).

The Third Generation: The Video of Creation

The third generation of Brazilian video-makers can hardly be said to represent a radical change in style, content or form by comparison with the two preceding phases. In fact, the new generation, which made its first public appearance in the 1990s, makes the most of the accumulated experience, comes to a synthesis of the work of its two generations of predecessors and sets out in the direction of more mature work, of a reinforcement of previous achievement. Most of the representatives of this generation come from the field of independent video; however, they opt for more personal, individual work that is less militant, less socially engaged. In this, they return to some of the guidelines of the pioneers. One may also perceive a certain extenuation of local concerns, an approach to themes of universal interest and a more direct link to international videographic production. Some video-makers (Sandra Kogut, for one) produce outside Brazil so as to have access to greater financial and technological resources; others (including Eder Santos) use material produced in Brazil and abroad. Names such as Kogut and Santos are internationally known; others, such as Arnaldo Antunes and Walter Silveira, although less well-known abroad, are respected within the cultural panorama of Brazil. The only commitment common to all representatives of this latest generation is the investigation of expressive forms specific to video and the exploration of stylistic resources that speak to the sensitivity of people at this century's end.

Santos is perhaps the best and most widely known of today's Brazilian video-makers. Paradoxically, his work is not accessible. Indeed, the opposite is true: Santos videos may be the most radical, the least given to making concessions, of any Brazilian videographic producer. They are generally composed of noises, interferences, 'defects', problems with the technical apparatus; at times they go to the very limits of visualisation. In many of his video installations, Santos projects his video images onto textured or wrinkled walls, piles of sand or otherwise irregular surfaces so as to disturb the intelligibility of the images or corrupt their figurative coherence. Almost nothing remains visible except for the pale traces of the images.

It is easy to understand this deconstructionist fury in relation to audiovisual works. In his videos, Santos attacks the loss of the vitality of images, their reduction to clichés worn out by the abuse of repetition. The triviality of daily life, the stereotypical behaviour of people, mass tourism, the futility of postcards: these are all material that the video-maker takes up; he builds, on them and yet against them, an implacable reflection on contemporary civilisation. The two works that best demonstrate this existential posture are *Não Vou à Africa Porque Tenho Plantão* [I'm not Going to Africa Because I'm on Duty] (1990) and *Essa Coisa Nervosa* [This Nervous Thing] (1991). Both make use of deliberate technical interference to cause the loss of vertical frame synchronicity; this makes the image oscillate non-stop before the eyes of the spectator so that it is difficult, if not impossible, to see. But work such as *Janaúba* (1993) shows the ideal that he so tirelessly seeks: to bring back the primordial energy of the visual arts, to re-establish the meaning and force of the images that are lost in the ocean of the industrial images of today. *Janaúba* is loosely inspired by an old, practically mythological film from Brazil's silent cinema, *Limite* by Mario Peixoto. It is almost a return to the origins of the audiovisual, an attempt to revive values that civilisation has forgotten.

The work of Kogut is something rather different. This artist seems to concentrate and express innovative tendencies in video art, yet at the same time she radicalises the process, initiated by Nam June Paik, of the electrification of the image and the disintegration of any sort of unity or discursive homogeneity. The technique of multiple writing that is the stamp of this work – where text, voices, sounds and simultaneous images combine and strive to form a canvas of rare complexity – constitutes in itself the structural evidence of what may be called the aesthetic of saturation, of excess (maximum concentration of information in minimum space-time) and of instability (an almost absolute absence of any structural integrity or any thematic or stylistic systematisation). If it were possible to reduce the aesthetic project presupposed in the videographic work of Kogut to a single word, that word would be multiplicity; here we have an unceasing search for this multiplicity, which expresses a contemporary mode of knowledge. The world is seen and represented as a web of relationships, inextricable in their complexity, where each moment is marked by the simultaneous presence of elements of the most heterogeneous nature: all this is in tumultuous movement that renders events, contexts and operations changeable – and almost impossible to grasp (Calvino 1990).

Take, for example, the series *Parabolic People* (1991): digital editing and processing resources allow an almost infinite number of images (or, rather, fragments of images) to be brought to the television screen; here they are combined into unexpected arrangements that are immediately rethought and questioned, ready to be redefined in new combinations. The most common technique is the use of windows in the image, in which new images can be invoked to turn the screen into a hybrid space for multiple images, multiple voices, multiple texts. Within a scene shot in Tokyo, a window opens to a shot of Dakar, then one of New York, one of Rio de Janeiro. This is not to suggest that they are all the same place; but possible readings of these simultaneous events are studied. Subtle, unthought-of, sometimes absurd links between them are discovered.

Sergei Eisenstein (1968), in a discussion of the expressive potential of montage, had already suggested the possibility of an in-frame montage in cinema, a combination of imagistic elements of contemporary times. These would relate to each other simultaneously and not just, as frequently occurs cinema, as a linear succession of shots. Naturally, taking into account the technical possibilities of Eisenstein's time, montage within the frame ('vertical' or 'polyphonic' montage, as he called it) could only be thought of and practised as an arrangement of contradictory elements and as a counterpoint between image and sound. But within the horizon of the electronic image, these limits no longer exist. Digital editing resources such as those available to Kogut for the montage of

Parabolic People make for unlimited possibilities of constructive intervention within the frame. On a single screen we can have one image occupying the whole area, and at the same time numerous windows within this image, allowing us to visualise other images or even minimal fragments of other images (hence the possibility of a 'cubist' montage), not to mention innumerable typologies for texts and a vast diversity of graphic signs (Machado 1992).

Two other key figures in the context of the third generation of Brazilian video-makers are Walter Silveira and Arnaldo Antunes. By coincidence, both started out as experimental poets. Silveira's poetry, for example, owes much of its impact to the graphic aspects of writing, the expressive use of colours and the typology of its manuscript letters, all of which often demand that the reader 'decipher' the characters in advance. In the field of video, Silveira has opted to experiment at the edge of electronic media. The best example of this is his *VT Preparado AC/JC* [Prepared VT AC/JC] (1986, created in collaboration with Pedro Vieira). The work is an impassioned homage to the composer of silence, John Cage (the JC of the title) and the poet of the blank page (AC is Brazilian poet Augusto de Campos). The makers thought up a video in which the blank screen is predominant, sometimes being interrupted by extremely rapid image flashes and, more often, by noises, impulses and distortions from the apparatus itself. The television pixel, greatly enlarged, becomes visible.

In the 1980s, Silveira became one of the founders of the independent group TVDO mentioned above. After the dissolution of the group at the beginning of the 1990s, he engaged in the daily work of a small São Paulo television station (TV Gazeta) and since then has, on occasion, directed personal interpretations of the work of other Brazilian artists: that of Betty Leiner in *Les Êtres Lettres* (1991), of Ivaldo Granato in *Painter: Model in Video* (1991), of Wesley Duke Lee in *My Trip with*

Duke Lee (1992) and of Maria Bonomi in *Elogio da Xilo* [Eulogy to the Xylography] (1995).

Arnaldo Antunes is much better known in Brazil as a singer, former leader of one of Brazil's most influential rock groups, *Titãs*. Over the last four years, after breaking off with the band, he has returned to his old passion: poetry. Three collections of his poems have been published. After 1992 he began to experiment with a new form of literature, produced with the computer and intended to be read on the television screen. Using resources from video and computer graphics, in 1993 he launched a collection of thirty impressive video poems, *Nome* [Name], which combine animated texts with changing colours, images taken with video cameras, spoken words, sounds and music. Like Kogut's *Parabolic People*, this is another step in the direction of a multimedia art that aims to combine all previous forms of art in a perfect synthesis.

Today, important experimental filmmakers such as Arthur Omar and Julio Bressane are also working with video. In addition, new video artists are slowly appearing. Video-makers such as Carlos Nader, Lucas Bambozzi, Lucila Meirelles, Jose Santos, Henri Gervaiseau, Belisario França and Kiko Goiffman have produced works that are still few in number but high in quality. It is yet too soon to determine if their collective output will constitute a distinctive new phase in Brazilian video art.

Chapter 34

The Video Theatre Project (1985)

Otávio Donasci

The Electronic Mask

The mask has always been present in the history of culture: in ritual, parties, puppets, carnival. Even in everyday life. After all, what is makeup if not that?

And in all cultures, since primitive times, the magical process of 'dressing up' as another being has recurred, having been technically perfected, but it has always kept the same original mystery: why does one human being need to be another?

When interviewed at the end of their lives, theatre actors usually say they didn't earn anything, have always worked hard, but lived several different lives on stage, and 'that's wonderful…'

Who knows, maybe the mask and theatre are themselves but exercises in reincarnation?

With the arrival of techno-images (photo, cinema, video and other graphics), humankind has a new partner to create their images – 'the black box' (which has input, a button and output) – and falls in love with the bi-dimensional realities it creates.

The world is now seen through these 'black boxes'. The photo brings me back to my father's presence, the movie makes me travel without leaving my seat and the video instantly brings the world indoors. Our entire cultural universe is now dictated by techno-images, including art. Paintings are photographed, sculptures are filmed and theatre becomes soap opera.

Television.

Video becomes a synthesis of the other techno-images and, consequently, of the realities they depict.

But what about theatre? What happens to theatre in the age of techno-images? Slide projection replaces the stage setting just like films may enrich the *mise-en-scène*. One of the world's greatest theatre set designers, Joseph Svoboda, was already projecting video close-ups of the actor on stage. And that was in 1952.

To me, theatre is the actor, all the rest just supports the actor's work. Under these conditions [of mediated representation], the actor on stage seemed to me like a strange being on a two-dimensional planet.

Techno-images are and make everything *vidimensional*.

How can theatre, which is by nature three-dimensional and live, coexist with techno-images without losing its essential characteristics?

Actors have already tried to imitate the language of cinema/TV by acting in slow or fast motion, most of the time with satirical intentions.

In short, it would be very advantageous for theatre if it could incorporate video as an instrument of dramatic language.

It would be very advantageous for human expression if we could incorporate video – the synthesis of techno-images – into theatre, which has the live actor as its core of expression.

With this in mind, video theatre was born.

Frankenstein and the Electronic Stitching

After reducing theatrical language to its bare minimum, what was left was the actor. While studying the actor's function, I focused on two kinds of expression: facial and bodily. Even though one is physically of a larger scale than the other, both are equivalent in their theatrical potential. The distance and attitude of the audience have always curbed the power of facial expressions.

Hence the reinforced make-up, the lighting that focuses on the face and the auditorium's tilted design; the whole theatre is, in short, adapted to facial expressions.

By reducing video to its bare minimum, I arrived at the tube (kinescope) and discovered that its proportions were equivalent to a face lying on its side.

From that point on, it was a matter of stitching a 'standing' tube like an orthopaedic head to an actor's body, and the first videocreature was born in good old Frankenstein style. It scares us because it's different. It makes us laugh because it's different.

With that, I was attempting a new language, a hybrid between video and theatrical language with characteristics that did not belong to either of them.

Art exhibitions in the 1960s and '70s went as far as to put heavy TVs showing regular broadcasts in place of mannequins' heads.

But this gesture has always represented a criticism of TV rather than an instrument of theatrical expression – just as, in a recent show (Frankenstein), actors were shown carrying televisions around on stage. But they did not form a cohesive unit: they were just actors carrying televisions.

Video theatre is unique:

It merges a luminous two-dimensional language (video) with a live and illuminated three-dimensional one (theatre).

The actor's facial expression has been replaced by the video-face. The face is the most characteristic part of the character, and it moves within the space of the head.

The head works over the body, which works within the space of the stage.

The space of the face is thus the smallest space of theatrical expression, which is why it was chosen to receive the video graft.

From the moment this fusion worked, everything that was shown on video was understood as a face on stage, and everything that was shown alongside the video-face was understood as a body. The possibilities of hybridisation between the two languages (theatre and video) are infinite. A huge face could have two bodies in place of legs, just as an actor could sport several different faces simultaneously. This could expand into all forms of scenarios.

A video-face could be attached to a hand and generate a glove puppet with all the expressive possibilities of a live actor. Likewise, that actor's face could be attached to a horse or another large animal and generate an unprecedented circus act.

With the possibilities inherent to television, such as remote transmission, it is possible to perform in the street, wirelessly and simultaneously in different places, live or pre-recorded. Via satellite, theatrical work can be presented simultaneously live and worldwide.

With LCD screens, video theatre takes on the dimensions of a true electronic mask, capable of being adapted directly to an actor's face.

In the future, with digital holography, it will be possible to reinvent the actor completely, using three-dimensional images that could even act along real actors.

The Video Theatre Labs

Firstly, one drafts the videocreature and its surrounding dramatic context. This leads to a text or script.

The project is developed through successive laboratories. In a facial expression lab, we explore multiple camera, lighting and editing possibilities in order to record any object or face, which will then become the videocreature's face. The recording is made for a vertical screen. The way this face will be illuminated during the show is defined during the lab. In video theatre, the light on the videoface can be dissociated from the light on the body-actor.

It's also possible to borrow faces from archival material (TV, movies, photos) and work with them in the lab, which would enable the show to feature known characters from the daily news media (politicians, artists, etc.).

In a prototyping lab, we investigate how to build video monitors and connect them to actors' bodies based on artistic and technical sketches. It is a true Gyro Gearloose lab. Successful 'stitching' requires knowledge of electronics, electronics, physics, chemistry and orthopaedics.

In the expression-with-prototypes lab, by using devices, actors improvise and create the features of previously recorded characters. They rehearse with mirrors. They also develop costumes and make electronic adjustments.

After these preliminary phases, a laboratory where the show is finalised takes place, as part of which we explore the stage space, create stage markings, light adjustments, props, etc.

Video theatre spectacles have already been performed in several spaces: theatres, streets, beaches, art galleries, dance halls, stores, etc., exploring expressive possibilities such as the theatrical play, the performance event, the show, etc.

I believe we are still in the prehistory of video theatre. Our methods are always experimental and change alongside new technology and techniques of scenic performance.

A Brazilian Project ('Who Would Have Thought!')

Video theatre wasn't born in Germany or the United States. It doesn't use ADO or WAX post-production from California.

It's made on VHS (how terrible!), in black and white. The father of the creator of video theatre does not work at Globo, nor does the creator himself.

It doesn't have a sponsor or patron (yet...). It's not made to be watched on TV ('hey, but isn't it video?')

It's not erudite, hermetic or boring. It can be made in Brazil, with Brazilian equipment and labour (or smuggling, alas!).

It has no equivalent in France, the USA, Germany or England. Its roots are, on the one hand, in the circus, the variety show and street performances; on the other, in cinema, musicals, TV and radio programming.

Its playing field is the stage, the scene, the street. An actor's space.

It's not afraid of marketing; it doesn't run away from advertisers (it actually has a plan for them).

It's not afraid to face a larger and less initiated public. It has plenty of room for other creators to work, along with actors, producers, technicians, etc.

In short, it's a video performance project (one of the few that can be called such) that has been fairly successful. And it deserves support.

Including to be shown abroad.

The Future: A Theatre of Real Images

Video theatre is the beginning of a theatre as fluid as thought.

Every artist's dream is to express their ideas, put their imagination on stage (imagination comes from images, thinking through images) without the requirement of physical devices as heavy as projectors, screens, films, books, etc.

Electronics allow people to create images with almost the same efficiency as the brain. However, currently available means can only generate two-dimensional images.

Only now, with holography, have we been able to recover the three-dimensional world, which our thoughts wanted to express but didn't know how.

Theatre would be the most complete expression if it didn't have to rely on such solid physical devices in order to express itself (stage, setting, actors).

We yearn for a theatre in which everything flows like a dream, where actors play along with incorporeal beings, dissolve on stage, fly, turn into animals. In short, a theatre that is able to do everything we can think of.

Or a theatre that would be as we really *are*, not as we *seem* in the mirror.

Chapter 35

Video as a Utopian Television Project (2000)

Yvana Fechine

...

The implementation of national TV networks, which allowed broadcasters to reduce costs and expand the advertising market, also meant an intense concentration of production and diffusion of audiovisual products among the four commercial networks with relay branches across Brazil (Bandeirantes, Globo, Manchete and SBT). Since the power to distribute and revoke radio and TV channel concessions was then in the hands of the President of the Republic, and since the government had always allocated generous advertising budgets to the TV stations, the big networks became natural allies of the government. It was not expected, therefore, that TV stations would give any support to the kind of critical media project characteristic of independent video production. In 1980, when the government revoked the public TV concession of all Tupi Network's channels, it decided to share the spoils between the Sílvio Santos and Adolfo Bloch media groups, who were more 'friendly and reliable' than *Jornal do Brasil* and Abril, for instance.[57] Forsaken in the dispute, the Abril group (through Abril Vídeo) was founded in August 1983, a pioneering experience of independent production exclusive for TV. A partnership with TV Gazeta in São

Paulo provided the group with fifteen hours per week in the primetime slot. In order to create a kind of parallel program to the already existing commercial network for this slot, Abril Video turned to the small independent production company *Olhar Eletrônico* [Electronic Gaze], which was already working at TV Gazeta. By November 1985, when financial debts made it impossible for Abril Vídeo to renew its contract with TV Gazeta, the guys from *Olhar Eletrônico* had already set up one of the most successful convergences between TV and video of the 1980's São Paulo generation.

Historically acknowledged as one of the first partnerships between commercial television and independent video production in Brazil, *Olhar Eletrônico* was created in 1981 by a group of friends, recent graduates of the Faculty of Architecture and Urbanism of the University of São Paulo (FAU/USP), who were already making experimental videos during their studies. Initially, the group was formed by Fernando Meirelles, Paulo Morellí, Marcelo Machado and José Roberto Salatini. Renato Barbieri and Marcelo Tas soon joined them. Attending to the basic demands of video (media criticism) and television (entertainment), *Olhar Eletrônico*'s purpose was to parody TV's own structures, characters and procedures. The group deployed the same ingredients that TV networks used to keep their audience alienated (pop music, informality, humour, among others) in order to demystify TV's canons and clichés, stimulating the audience to be more critical. In 1982, the guys from *Olhar Eletrônico* won the first two awards at the 1st Videobrasil Festival at MIS-SP. In the same year, their work led to them being invited by Goulart de Andrade, veteran creator of a direct TV style, to work at TV Gazeta. For four months, they produced a nameless TV show (one of its sketches was precisely 'come up with a name for the show'). Then they were invited to collaborate on *23a Hora* [23rd Hour], a journalistic variety show that ran from October 1982 to March 1983. The core of *23a Hora* was always a grand reportage by Goulart de Andrade, with long sequence shots that were only interrupted for tape changes, pioneering a kind of *TV vérité*. The guys from *Olhar Eletrônico* produced material to be shown in between Goulart's appearances. With the autonomy Goulart gave them, they got as close as they could to making an independent production inside a TV network. In one episode, they just decided to turn viewers' TV devices into an aquarium until the broadcast was shut down, taking advantage of the fact that *23a Hora* was the last show to air on Gazeta for the day. The experiment clearly questioned the audience's passivity: it consisted of a full hour of close-ups of ornamental fish coming in and out of the screen. Every ten minutes, a voiceover invited viewers to call a mysterious phone number, and only then would they understand what was going on.

After *23a Hora*, they got an invitation from Abril Vídeo, with whom they produced two variety shows: Crig-Rá (between February and August 1983) and *Olho Mágico* [Magic Eye] (between April 1984 and November 1985). Aimed at a young audience, *Crig-Rá* dealt with themes such as love, death and loneliness. What the guys from *Olhar Eletrônico* liked the most was to 'play' with television itself, as they had been doing since they joined TV Gazeta. With sketches, fictional news and burlesque characters, they questioned TV's societal role, its unidirectional communication model and its formats. The show was hosted by Bob MacJack (played by Marcelo Tas), a kind of clown reminiscent of the other famous TV hosts of the time, such as Chacrinha and Sílvio Santos. By the end of the 1980s, when the group finally dissolved, *Olhar Eletrônico* had participated in several other experimental projects such as O *Mundo no Ar* [The World in the Air], a fictional news program 'as committed to the truth as any other'. It aired for four months as part of the *Aventura* [Adventure] show (Manchete Network 1986). Even after *Olhar Eletrônico*'s dissolution, their aesthetic approach remained influential, reverberating in Brazilian TV through the individual careers of its former members. Marcelo Tas and Fernando Meirelles, in particular, are still active in the audiovisual market as a high watermark of quality TV, the intelligent kind of TV advocated by video-makers.

At the height of *Olhar Eletrônico*'s career, one of the group's members, the reporter Ernesto Varela, who appeared in each one of its shows, synthesised the group's whole approach to intervention in broadcasting television. Played by Marcelo Tas and starring in countless sketches directed by himself and Fernando Meirelles, Ernesto Varela was the prototype of the TV anti-reporter. Disingenuous and clumsy, sporting a silly face and seemingly naive behaviour, Varela embodied a parody of conventional TV journalism. Although he was not a 'real' reporter – since Marcelo Tas was, above all, a performer – Ernesto Varela never engaged in purely fictional situations. On the contrary, his reportages focused, from a critical-satirical perspective, on the most polemical themes of the time, such as the Brazilian external debt (*Dívida externa*, 1983), the gold rush in Serra Pelada (*Varela em Serra Pelada*, 1984) and the ballot of the Dante de Oliveira amendment, which foresaw direct elections in the country (*Varela no Congresso*, 1984). Varela reinvented the TV interview, provoking his interviewees with (seemingly) obvious questions ('Mr. Nabi Abi Chedid, are you Brazilian?' addressed to the controversial federal deputy and manager of the Brazilian Soccer Federation [CBF] during the 1986 World Cup), unexpected comments ('Mr Deputy, do you believe in the words you say?' addressed to Nelson Marchezan, one of the leaders of the PDS party, during the historic vote of direct elections in 1984), and even 'preposterous' questions, such as the one addressed to the then-Presidential candidate Paulo Maluf, supported by the military junta in 1984: 'Is it true, Mr. Maluf, that you are a thief?'.

With such interventions, Varela provoked similarly unusual reactions, breaking down the whole repertoire of clichés, ready-made answers and predictable behaviours that are characteristic of sports and political coverage. Instead of 'directing' his interviewees, Varela attempted to stimulate them to take on an autonomous, authentic position, one that would be conscious of the mediating apparatus involved in a recording for TV. Varela deconstructs the univocal discourses of conventional reporters who try to reduce all socio-cultural and politico-ideological diversity and the plurality of viewpoints to the authority of their own speech. In the most diverse situations, Varela not only gave the word back to the people but also tried to adopt their perspective. As someone who didn't always seem to realise what he was doing, the clumsy and scruffy reporter rebelled, in his own way, against all hierarchy; there was no relationship of authority between interviewer and interviewee. The critical power of Varela's reportages came precisely from the seeming naivety through which he demonstrated, whether in a conversation with an illiterate street vendor or a renowned sociologist from the University of São Paulo, the contradictory aspects of Brazilian reality. This critical yet good-tempered attitude; this incisive and simultaneous down-to-earth behaviour; the deliberate 'unmasking' of TV's narrative models adopted by Ernesto Varela and his inseparable cameraman Valdeci (Fernando Meirelles) were above all an expression of the values that guided *Olhar Eletrônico*'s TV production.

In the guise of Ernesto Varela, Marcelo Tas participated in shows at TV Gazeta, SBT and Record networks between 1983 and 1986. Varela would return to the screen between 1990 and 1991 as the main character of a new series by MTV Brasil:[58] *Netos do Amaral* [Amaral's Grandchildren]. The title already hints at the parodic spirit of the series. It was a direct reference to the 1970s show *Amaral Neto, o Repórter* [Amaral Neto, the Reporter], which, following the military government's nationalist and vainglorious project, aimed to bring Brazil's natural beauties to national TV in the most conservative telejournalistic format of its time. With a radically opposite proposal and attitude, Ernesto Varela also travelled the country, but with the goal of irreverently showing the contrasts and contradictions of Brazilian socio-cultural reality. The Brazil through which Varela guided us, following in the footsteps of independent video production, was a mixed country, 'acculturated', the perfect expression of the 'nation without neckties' that Glauber Rocha already evoked in his controversial TV interventions during the show *Abertura* [Overture, Opening].[59] Co-directed and edited by Eder Santos, one of the most legitimate voices of the third generation of video directors in Brazil, *Netos...* combined *Olhar Eletrônico's* critical-satirical spirit with the new filmmakers' skills in digital editing: strong appeal to simultaneity, image manipulation and the exploration of graphic-visual resources (design, logos, letterings, animations). All these bricolage elements characterised the 'MTV style', heir to an aesthetic legacy built partly by the video artists sheltered within North American TV networks.

In Brazil, the 'MTV style' that was indebted to the fragmented, anti-narrative and non-linear discourse of music videos seemed perfectly in tune with the production of more contemporary video artists such as Sandra Kogut, who also collaborated with television shows. Along with Santos, Kogut is one of the most renowned artists of the third generation of Brazilian video-makers. Although they were already making videos in the 1980s, they only emerged publicly in the 1990s with more personal and more authorial work that was disconnected from the social engagement characterising the independent video movement (Machado 1998). This new generation took up some of the concerns of the video pioneers. They were interested in thinking of the TV screen itself as a form of design and in exploring the plastic properties of electronic images, now enhanced by easy access to editing and digital video processing resources. Kogut's *Parabolic People*, aired by MTV in 1991, is one of the best examples of how TV welcomed the aesthetic of saturation, excess and instability (the absence of thematic and stylistic systematisation) that Arlindo Machado identifies in the most contemporary videographic production (1997). Produced at the *Centre de Création Vidéo Montbéliard Berfort* (France), *Parabolic People* consists of a series of eleven segments, up to three minutes each, designed to be inserted randomly in the program of TV stations worldwide. Pierre Bongiovanni (1993) defines these segments as 'haikus' *for* and *about* television. From a formal perspective, *Parabolic People* achieves the limit of the possibilities for polyphonic video montage; from a content perspective, it can be interpreted as an authentic manifestation of McLuhan's 'global village' forged by electronic media.

Following this radical exploration of TV and video's technical-expressive resources, Kogut took on a remarkable project by a commercial TV station as the director of *Brasil Legal* [Cool Brazil] (Globo Network, 1994-1998). In this new project, produced by the country's largest TV network, Kogut resumed the proposal of series such as *Netos do Amaral* and *Programa Legal* [Cool Show] (Globo Network, 1991-1993 – which also featured Tas as a screenwriter) with her own distinctive style. In *Brasil Legal*, the actress Regina Casé had a role similar to Ernesto Varela in the MTV series: she travelled across different regions of the country, showing the huge cultural diversity of the rarely seen regions of Brazil. The big stars of the show were funny and intelligent real-life people like Mário Pezão, ex-street kid and rapper; Dona Flora, granddaughter of Indigenous people and herb seller; and Glauber Moscabilly, a 1960s rock fan. Their curious stories revealed, metonymically, the values and experiences of all Brazilian people, highlighting the big Latin American cultural 'melting pot', particularly when articulated by the metalinguistic and intertextual references scattered throughout the show. Like Marcelo Tas, Regina Casé embodied a mix of interviewer and performer who attempted to undo the hierarchy between the interviewees and herself. Interviewees were made comfortable to speak their mind and, in a certain way, even drive the conversation. By becoming more intimate with them, Regina Casé relinquished the 'TV celebrity' role. She encouraged people to open up as she herself did. In a new style for TV, following the old postulates of independent video, their interpersonal interaction became the main subject of the show.

Though sparse, Sandra Kogut's interventions in TV[60] draw from and expand the experience of another group that, alongside *Olhar Eletrônico*, is considered one of the most influential among the independent video generation of 1980s: TVDO. Willing to find a place within the broadcast industry for alternative production, the video-makers connected to TVDO worked in the boundary between low and high culture, incorporating certain elements from videoart's editing techniques and delirious discourse into more commercial TV formats. Their first works on TV were made in its most radical format: the music video. Together with Nelson Motta, already a highly respected music producer at the time, the guys from TVDO directed and edited the music videos featured in *Mocidade Independente* [Independent Youth], a show that opened space on TV for more contemporary Brazilian music (Bandeirantes Network, June-August 1981). As a group, TVDO also collaborated in the creation and production of *Fábrica do Som* [Sound Factory] (Cultura Network, (1983-1984), another musical show that introduced emerging bands such as *Ultraje a Rigor, Paralamas do Sucesso* and *Titãs*, while also featuring avant-garde artistic presentations such as the concrete poetry of the brothers Augusto and Haroldo de Campos. *Fábrica do Som* was presented by Tadeu Jungle and directed by Pedro Vieira, two of TVDO's most active figures. The group also included the video-maker and poet Walter Silveira, who, after years working at TV Gazeta, currently holds the position of a programming director of the Cultura Network, securing a space for experimentalism within that company.

Fábrica do Som was so visionary that it would be relaunched by TV Cultura in February 2000 under another name, *Musikaos*, keeping the same director and practically the same format and proposal. Though it didn't have the same impact, the new show strove to reproduce the anarchic spirit that TVDO first brought to TV: creating from precariousness, turning junk into special effects and leaning into the 'dirtiness' of the material as a source of style. Tadeu Jungle's aggressive behaviour as host of the show, delirious and 'messy' when compared to other TV hosts, led to comparisons to Glauber Rocha's segment in the now extinct *Abertura* (Machado 1993). Arlindo Machado wasn't the only one to highlight Glauber's influence over the young video-makers from the 1980s. According to Regina Mota, Glauber had contaminated this generation with a deliberately unorthodox way of making TV shows, stemming from the weekly sketch he created for the show directed by Fernando Barbosa Lima in 1979. Glauber would air 'almost raw' material; he would relinquish script and direction, bet on chance and the heat of the recording moment, incorporate the camera as a character and create around it a *happening* that would become the very show to air on TV. It was also Glauber who first brought to the screen, as his interviewees and guests, people like [the left-wing politician Leonel] Brizola, a Black *favelado* connected to *jogo do bicho* in the suburbs of Rio de Janeiro;[61] or Severino, a semi-illiterate man from the Northeast of the country who worked as a cable operator for Tupi Network. Through the unkempt and bearded Glauber of *Abertura*, TV opened space for every kind of performer who challenged 'preppy aesthetics', turned themselves into a character and mixed information with fabulation (Mota 2001)....

Chapter 36

Videobrasil and Video in Brazil: A Side-by-Side Journey (2000)

Solange Farkas

Since its inception, electronic art has introduced tension into the existing axes between art and communication, narration and information. It has done so by experimenting with different ways – singular and regional, mediated and subjective – of placing markers of the narrator in the story, markers that speak to their identity and particular territory. Thus, the electronic image focuses on the individual in front and behind the camera: a uniquely identified individual, connected to their society.

The image that video art brought forth emerged in the context of the opening of Brazilian democracy in the early 1980s.Videobrasil arrived in 1983 to organise, exhibit and legitimise the field of independent and accelerated production fostered by the technical and creative versatility of electronic and digital media. The electronic image allowed for unparalleled expressive freedom within the context of the new democracy, exploring the technical and narrative frontiers of all preceding audiovisual forms.

The Videobrasil festival was founded in 1983 to consolidate this intellectual field, creating a space for exhibition, recognition and exchange within the sectors of audiovisual production that are challenged by video. It operated as a platform for the spontaneous articulation of local production and facilitated its connection with international art, especially after 1985. However, in the dialectics of this internationalisation, Videobrasil has always been more concerned with the search and self-determination of our audiovisual identity as Latin Americans people and, more broadly, as producers from the Southern Hemisphere.

The transition from the festival to the Videobrasil Cultural Association demonstrates that working with memory is necessary to build the future of audiovisual art. This future necessarily stems from the criticism and reflection of the most daring and fertile independent production ever known to Brazil.

The collection of works exhibited in the festival reveals that video 'thinks the other audiovisual media. These intermediations determine, precisely and paradoxically, the poetic specificity of the electronic image. This specificity – brought about by a montage that transcends naturalistic speeds – has promoted and provoked fruitful and surprising contaminations within Brazilian audiovisual production, contaminations that we can appreciate today in the most significant innovations of local television and cinematographic language.

Simultaneously, while encouraging the poetic specificities of video, Videobrasil has since 1990 consolidated a space for the circulation and legitimisation of works more strictly connected to the artistic (rather than communicational) production of the electronic image. The emphasis that the festival has placed on performances, installations and experimental videos, as well as the organisation of workshops, conferences and retrospective exhibitions of the great creators of national and international video art, has opened a portal within the context of interdisciplinary production involving visual arts, theatre and poetry.

Timeline

The first edition of Videobrasil took place in August 1983 at the Museum of Image and Sound (MIS-SP), thanks to a partnership between Fotoptica and the São Paulo State Secretary of Culture. This first edition intended to showcase the pioneering works of Brazilian video, which, at the time, had a strong desire to situate itself within the television universe. This led to a moment of intense criticism against the monopoly held by a few TV networks. In addition to single-channel videos, the festival included an exhibition of installations and performances. Video was still looking for a place to express itself in its own language, but it already constituted a desirable space for independence and experimentation that seduced young directors and visual artists in tune with the avant-gardes. Theatre director José Celso Martinez Correa was Videobrasil's first winner, demonstrating that artists from other areas, such as theatre and the visual arts, were also working with video.

In the following year, video-utopia was on the agenda: the end of the military dictatorship prompted discussions around the democratisation of TV stations. The political-economic perspective that emerged along with the 'video market' promised to bring video and television together within the festival. Independent video continued to try to get closer to the seemingly inaccessible universe of TV networks. Once again, in addition to competitive screenings, the festival presented a great diversity of activities, such as lectures and a market aimed at the electronic industry, sponsors and producers. At the national level, a variety of independent production companies were consolidated: *Olhar Eletrônico*, TVDO, Telecine Maruin, Videoverso. The international showcase included works by Nam June Paik, among others.

The third edition was held at the Sérgio Cardoso theatre and covered three major thematic axes: the entry of independent production on TV, video theatre, and diffusion and dissemination – touring local productions in the interior of the country and abroad. *Olhar Eletrônico*'s shows were being sold to TV Globo and aired during *Fantástico*, the prime time of Brazilian TV. These were the first signs of stabilisation and territorial conquest by independent video in Brazil. Likewise, TV Cultura, Bandeirantes and Gazeta began to show works from this generation of video artists in their schedules, which no one had expected before. The monopoly of TV networks was still the main topic of discussion. New possibilities were brought up, such as UHF channels and cable TV. The screenings aimed to scrutinise video's specific language, featuring programs such as *Odisséia dos Sons* [Sound Odyssey] and *Holografia* (Holography). The Videobrasil video library was born.

As of its fourth edition, Videobrasil had consolidated itself as an essential space for video exhibition. The screenings were no longer categorised by genre, only separated between the U-Matic and VHS formats. There was a decline in the production of fiction pieces and an increase in experimental and documentary works. Despite this edition's large number of entries, we had more criteria in our selection process than in the previous years. There was a large international showcase made in partnership with the Video Data Bank of Chicago, large-scale performances such as Roberto Aguilar's unpacking of the Museum of Image and Sound, experiments with video-photography and computer-generated graphics, a showcase of music videos and parallel screenings from several countries.

In November 1987, in its fifth edition, Videobrasil featured the first TV shows influenced or created by the video art generation, such as Tadeu Jungle's *Fábrica do Som* [Sound Factory]. This was supported by TV Cultura, which offered wide news coverage and made a special show about the festival. National production has become professionalised and specialised, leaving amateur works out of the festival selection. Established directors showed more mature works, with ever increasing technical quality. Narrative-wise, there was a renewal of televisual language: documentary and experimental works became the main kinds of output, since the video image enhances their technical qualities with visual texture, musical editing and camera interactivity. *Uakti*, by Eder Santos, is the paradigmatic example.

The sixth Videobrasil hosted the first edition of *Videojornal*, made in partnership with TV Gazeta; it was directed by Hugo Prata and presented by Astrid Fontenelli. It was the first time a TV network did a live coverage of the festival and included the prize-winning works in its schedule. Participation in the competitive screening was increasingly demanding; there were fewer submissions and they were of a much higher quality. For the first time, the festival had international guests (Aysha Quinn, Ira Schneider and Daniel Minahan from *The Kitchen* in New York) and established a partnership with media centres to award scholarships to the prize-winning artists.

International relations were crystallised in the festival's seventh edition, as it attracted important foreign guests such as Pierre Bongiovanni from the *Centre International de Création Video de Montbeliard* (France) to host an exchange for artists such as Sandra Kogut, Eder Santos, Roberto Berliner and Lucila Meirelles. Also present were festival directors such as Tom Van Vliet from the World Wide Video Festival (The Netherlands) and Sandra Lischi from Ondavideo (Italy), as well as representatives of television networks such as Canal Plus from France, RTBF from Belgium and Channel Four from England, among others. This edition enabled a great number of connections to be made between distributors, exhibitors and television networks. Thus, the electronic image's centre of attention and expressive possibilities expanded: television and video art were already on the horizon.

In the eighth edition, the festival went international once and for all, with several world showcases introduced by their curators and workshops with guest artists such as Tim Morrison from Britain, Yoichiro Kawaguchi from Japan, Dominik Barbier from France and Marcelo Tas from Brazil. The space for video installations grew with works by Marcel Odenbach, Sandra Kogut and Tadeu Jungle. Brazilians such as Eder Santos, Sandra Kogut, Marcelo Machado, Roberto Berlíner and Renato Barbieri were widely known and became recognised as international artists. It was the first expressively mature generation, incorporated as it was into the global video art circuits. The competitive exhibition and its jury were international for the first time. Television was no longer the main target; we became aware of the independent international circuit that was more connected to visual arts through work in genres such as performances, installation, experimental TV and computer graphics. The Southern Hemisphere stood out in screening competitions, while works from the USA and Western Europe were featured in informative showcases.

It was however in the ninth edition that Videobrasil took its leap toward the international electronic arts circuit. This massive transformation began with the venue change from MIS-SP to Sesc Pompéia. The festival became a biennial and turned from a video-maker competition into a major space for showcasing the electronic art of the South. With a record budget, the competitive exhibition significantly expanded and reached the milestone of showcasing 200 works. With these changes, the festival also became international, taking advantage of the growing demand for internationalisation from Brazilian outputs (which represented only 60% of the 300 submissions). Great names from video art theory and practice worldwide, such as Bill Viola, Peter Callas, Gianni Toti, Jean Paul Fargier, Tina Keane, Jorge La Feria and Julien Temple, came to the festival, presenting lectures, workshops, installations and performances, demonstrating the broad spectrum of electronic-digital expressions.

The change of the title to Videobrasil International Electronic Arts Festival took place in the tenth edition, when the competition began to focus on artists from the Southern Hemisphere. The competition categories were video art, documentaries and animations, while fiction and television were left out. Once again, documentaries represented some of the most experimental works, along with audiovisual poetry, whose sensibility was displayed in many historical international panoramas. The big highlights were thirteen installations and three performances commissioned by the festival, which generated a record-breaking audience for the whole event, leading to an extension of the exhibition period to one month.

A little over ten years after its creation, Videobrasil began to focus its competition on the outputs made within the specialised art circuit by artists from developing countries. That was a definitive change in the festival's profile, which would become recognised worldwide for bringing together works from outside the United States-Western Europe axis. Intermedia contamination, previously prevalent across video and its relations with cinema and television, now took place between video, poetry, installation and painting. To celebrate thirty years of international video art, Videobrasil organised the most comprehensive retrospective of Nam June Paik in Brazil, who made a special edition of his work *TV Moon* for the event. The festival also crystallised its priority to be a promoter of performances, such as those made by Eder Santos and Paulo Santos, Stephen Vitiello and Steina Vasulka, Isabelle Choinniere and Marcondes Dourado.

Increasingly, Videobrasil's goal is to enhance its competitive exhibitions as well as its international retrospective and informative showcases. Originally, the festival had been a foundational gathering space for local producers and for the articulation and generation of new projects and venues. On the brink of the 21st century, the festival reinforces its role as a disseminator and educator for specialised audiences in the electronic and digital arts, both Brazilian and international, as it focuses on the regional production of the continent. In its latest edition in 2001, the festival held a retrospective of Gary Hill's installations and, for the first time, digital and Internet artworks as they converged with the most experimental trends in electronic imagining.

Since Videobrasil's 14th edition, video and new media works have competed in the same category. As a unifying and catalysing force, the festival remains committed to being a critical and generative platform for the most daring experiences in the audiovisual field, prioritising curatorial excellence and the conversation between Brazil and the world. And the work developed by the Videobrasil Cultural Association reinforces the desire to assist in building the future of Brazilian audiovisual media by preserving the festival's memory.

Chapter 37

Exploded Video and its Shards Hovering Above Us (2008)

Lucas Bambozzi

...

Many of us have devoured Arlindo Machado's *A Arte do Vídeo* [The Art of Video] (1988) as if it were a school primer. Arlindo's definitions of the nature of the videographic image have inspired many of the works made between the 1980s and 1990s. Under his influence, no one used open shots or left important details to the corners of the screen. (TVs had much more rounded corners then.) We explored the tactile surface of the image exhaustively. (The impossibility of using depth of field would bring us to video, to the surface – as Brakhage would have wanted, as Machado taught us and as Jean Paul Fargier lyricised [1993].)

In the 1990s many years were punctuated with speeches and rhetoric in defence of video. We spoke about how video was necessary for understanding contemporaneity. We tried to raise a flag for our supposed movement in the most diverse places (there would have been something revolutionary behind all this). In an environment populated by images, teaching their language would allow for a kind of visual literacy – as we often said during the ForumBHZvideo festival of 1991.[62] Day-to-day visual literacy would raise our level of understanding through a plural syntax that was capable of uniting written, verbal and visual expression. We expected the ensuing euphoria to be like the one caused by the potential expansion of perception brought about by telematic networks, or by the charms of an art driven by biology or nanotechnology, or even by the impact of mixed reality games.

Video was and continues to be something more than a title or a concept: it is a term that grows semantically. It doesn't seem like the most comfortable context for those who seek a safe language in which to ground themselves.

Undeniably, just as the set of art-related practices was much smaller ten or fifteen years ago than it is today, the universe of ideas and practices associated with video has grown over the years. There is a consensus around the vast potential of video shared by the researchers and filmmakers who have dedicated themselves to the production and reflection of electronic media, such as Eduardo de Jesus, Carlos Nader, Roberto Cruz, Francesca Azzi, Rodrigo Minelli, Patricia Moran and Christine Mello, among others.

The theoretical production of the time, lacking the channels and references that would come with the Internet, was late in legitimising many works that deserved visibility – despite the efforts of people like Arlindo Machado and Jorge La Ferla. (1997). Throughout the 1990s, it was essential to create an audience so that a consistent circuit outside of TV channels could exist. Art criticism would then have become interested in the medium and 'making video' would have turned into a spontaneous practice – whether it would be called video art, experimental video or authorial video.

If it's even possible to characterise the video-makers of the 1990s as a consistent generation, I'd say that what brought them together was the 'urge' to work, as pretentious as it may sound, since the times were not very hospitable.

All the glamour and hype had been dispelled during the 1980s. There were working models to be followed, but no specialised audience, no production grants (even worse than today), no legal incentives and no interested curators. The so-called generation of the 1990s recycled the 1980s references in more personal projects that were more in tune with micro- rather than macro-politics: more domestic and solitary narratives, travelogues, notebooks, intimate accounts. But some have broken away from these commonplace projects with brilliance: for instance, Kiko Goifman, who digested the anthropological documentary form into exercises of visual poetics (not only in *Teresa*, but also in *Clones Bárbaros* [Barbarian Clones], *Replicantes* and some of his installations); and Carlos Nader, who anticipated the invasion of privacy and the manipulation of reality in *O Beijoqueiro* [The Kisser] and *O Fim da Viagem* [End of the Journey]. These rich qualities punctuate the generation. Not everything is a daydream, not everything is solid and objective.

Colleagues from other, slightly different fields would join the group after the turn of the decade. A series of 'small' technical and procedural revolutions took place when the computer effectively became a tool for video-makers around 1998, with the introduction of the IEEE 1934 protocol (firewire port, that connected cameras to computers). Nonlinear software invited a new way of thinking about editing and visual effects. Most notably, professionals in design, photography, animation and visual poetry began to work in video, expanding not only techniques but also concepts. Many people would become part of this early 2000s 'class' or generation....

Discourse *Versus* Practice in the 1990s

When I moved to São Paulo to coordinate the video department at the Museum of Image and Sound (1993-95, on the invitation of filmmaker Amir Labaki), there was already a more mature and competitive scene in the city, with a genuine intersection of multiple generations and aesthetic sensibilities. This made me realise how rich the instability of language and convictions could be. I lost my excessively baroque accent thanks to Jurandir Muller, Renato Barbieri, Lucila Meirelles, Walter Silveira and Marcelo Machado, among others.

During that time, I got almost irreversibly involved with cultural promotion. Some of the exhibitions and permanent events we created at MIS-SP[63] with the goal of stimulating authorial production have succeeded in creating a space for continuous and official confluence between video-makers. In the MIS-SP's hallways, there was a kind of spontaneous, face-to-face interaction that now only seems to take place on online mailing lists. The notion that we were a generation born there, driven by events that promoted hybridisation and were not restricted to narrow definitions of cinema, video and art. Some one-off events hosted at the time were important for giving international visibility to that generation, such as the Southern Cone Festival, organised by Sergio Martinelli at the museum, and the itinerant showcases of the Franco-Latin American Videoart Festival (FFLA).[64] Of course, the field had been generously prepared by Videobrasil, which had been privileging the Southern Hemisphere since the previous decade. In comparison, the biggest merit of both the Southern Cone Festival and FFLA was the fact that they went on tour. The broad programming of these festivals accentuated the disparity and relative physical distance between the neighbouring Latin-American countries, while opening the possibility of communication in a language beyond any conventions, free from the pitfalls of cultural misunderstanding. With video, we might have had the opportunity to learn from our differences and create other kinds of dialogue, moving away from the high rates of inflation, illiteracy and poverty caused by local dictatorships. Our goal was to undress culture in the realm of the imaginary – a *slogan* shared by many colleagues in Paraguay, Uruguay and Colombia, but mostly in Argentina and Chile. Our connection to filmmakers such as Claudia Aravena and Guillermo Cifuentes throughout the '90s, guided by thinkers such as Nestor Olhagaray and Jorge La Ferla (having French thinkers like Robert Cahen, Alain Bourges and Jean-Paul Fargier as counterpoints), have taught us more about our cultural differences and allowed us to better identify possibilities of dialogue among South Americans.

Black Holes in Contemporary Art and the Poetics of Space through Video

I have seen a lot of things happen and fail ever since. I have been pulverised in the murky constellation of contemporary art following various audiovisual trends, some still noisy and rather intangible.

At some point, the institutional exhibition circuit seemed less exciting than the clashes taking place within the video scene, since the medium was new and less settled (and more naïve, too). For some of us, those circuits came together in the making of video installations. At some point, this was true for me as well as for Eder Santos, Luiz Duva and Carlos Nader; and, more recently, for Raquel Kogan and Rachel Rosalen (in addition to Rejane Cantoni and Daniela Kutschat, not working in video so much as in interactive real-time image processing). The incorporation of space into the work, along with the ensuing compression/dilation of time, consists in an incipient and conflicted syntax, an incomplete chapter in the field of electronic images. Even today, the correct way to present videos, their specific lighting conditions and the methods to reconstruct projection spaces, are still under debate....

Misunderstanding contexts was not typical in the 1990s, before the Web. (I still believe we need to go back to texts of that time and re-examine their aesthetic proposals.) After that, everything changed. Dissonance increased explosively across multiple circuits. So another chapter begins: a new history, different practices, many of which were shared across generations, giving rise to even more complex circuits. During the 1990s, some kind of unity was still detectable. Video experiences were more consistent and clearer. In the discourse of Raymond Bellour, Wim Wenders and Nelson Brissac, one could see video being shaped by the concept of *passage*, by being considered a transitional vehicle and a place of intersections. It was a medium contaminated by all forms of image culture. (To define plurality as a source of unity requires more theoretical precision.)

What we can say for sure is that our definitions of the term 'video' soon started to seem very narrow. In order to speak of the more immediate expansion of video, researchers and curators found it necessary to find ways to translate the term as 'media art' (a translation recently crystallised as *artemídia*). Even though it wasn't used as commonly, the term signified, to many of us, the idea that video was no longer the most important ingredient in the melting pot of digital and electronic arts. The language of video, in continuous transformation, promoting and suffering all sorts of promiscuities, has always resisted attempts at specificity. Though it has gone through (or caved in to) various fads, video ultimately spread through society and within culture in a stealthy, efficient and seamless manner....

IV

Personal Computers

Chapter 38

Personal Computers

Gabriel Menotti and German Alfonso Nunez

After the dissolution of the military junta in 1985, Brazil would go through a rapid and deep transformation. The military government had left the country in tatters, with persistent and enduring inequality, systemic hyperinflation and an outdated industry. A new federal constitution was written from scratch and promulgated in 1988, in an attempt to remedy many of these problems. In the following year, the country held its first free elections since the 1964 coup. It was a turbulent fresh start for Brazilian democracy. In two years, the elected president Fernando Collor de Mello would resign in order to avoid being impeached on corruption charges. His brief tenure (1990-92) marked the beginning of important economic changes, moving the country away from the nationalistic policies of the junta. For the next decade, Brazil would favour a neoliberal agenda, which involved the privatisation of public services and the opening of the country to imports.[65] These and other policies had an enduring impact on the national art and culture sectors.

For our story, the most significant consequence was the slow yet steady introduction of personal computers into people's lives. The previously existing ban on imports meant that many artists never had the resources or connections necessary to employ computers in their practice. That's one of the reasons why artists like Eduardo Kac had to move abroad to pursue this line of work. Only in the mid-1990s, after the opening of the national market and the stabilisation of the currency carried out through Itamar Franco's (De Mello's vice president, 1992-1994) and Fernando Henrique Cardoso's (1995-2002) tenures, did personal computers become affordable in Brazil. Soon after, commercial Internet also became available in the country, intensifying the feeling that Brazil was finally catching up with the rest of the modern world. This sentiment was expressed in an array of popular media, from telenovelas to journalism, from popular music to, of course, the arts (Nunez 2019; 2023).

The arrival of personal computing in Brazil would be followed by the growth of cultural institutions and events dedicated to digital media, leading to the further development of a circuit for technological art forms in the country. These activities built upon the avant-garde traditions discussed so far. The pioneering Web art exhibition in the country, *Arte Suporte Computador* [Computer Medium Art], was hosted at Casa das Rosas, a cultural centre in São Paulo dedicated to concrete poetry. Its organiser, Lucas Bambozzi, was an important artist and cultural agent of the video generation, which circulated both in museums and across TV channels. But, despite these genealogical connections, there were some crucial changes for the media arts field in Brazil. For starters, it finally came into being as its own genre.

Up until that point, Brazilian 'media arts' existed in the same institutional spaces as other local art forms. In the 1990s, the novel conditions created by corporate sponsorship and a rapidly expanding academic system would enable the flourishing of an ecosystem detached from the contemporary arts circuit, devoted to the promotion of emerging technological aesthetics. This ecosystem encompassed exhibitions, publications, festivals and awards organised under labels such as 'new media', 'electronic arts', 'art and technology' and 'art and science'. A stricter, almost dichotomous separation between 'traditional' and 'technological' art forms took hold in Brazil, closer to what already existed in other Western countries. While some local artists resisted this stigmatisation, others celebrated this new identity and the opportunities it created for them.

The final section of our book, 'Personal Computers', attempts to provide a comprehensive view of this era of expanded opportunities. One of the main aspects to consider is the emergence of a contingent of 'outsider artists' associated with the university. Ironically, this influx of academics was also a consequence of the military government's policies from the 1970s onwards. Further investment in higher education and a restructuring of graduate programmes during the dictatorship would eventually led to the creation of various graduate programmes in visual arts and sprung new artistic research laboratories and groups (e.g. Poéticas Digitais/USP, SCIArts/UNESP, Corpos Informáticos/UNB) (Prado 2009; Prado, Sogabe and Guasque 2018).[66] Concrete poets themselves would establish a Communication and Semiotics graduate program at the Catholic University of São Paulo in 1971 (PUC-SP). Expanding on their influence, the discipline of Semiotics would become a safe haven for media artists to explore the specificities of their practice, providing a frame through which artists could think and talk about technopoetics. Here, one cannot overstate the towering contribution of Lucia Santaella, a specialist in the work of Charles Sanders Peirce who, over decades of her career, advised multiple generations of artists and intellectuals working with the poetics of new technologies. Their employment as research professors would also enable artists to become financially independent, develop their practice away from the art market's pressure and spread their ideas. This was especially true for media artists who, by and large, have always found it difficult to commercialise their works.[67] What's more, the university could provide access to the expensive equipment and Internet connection required to produce technological art forms. Thus, it is not surprising that several Brazilian digital art pioneers from the 1980s and 1990s – such as Gilbertto Prado, Artur Matuck, Suzete Venturelli, Rosângela Leotte and Beatriz Medeiros – would come from the academic context.

However, it was not only from within the university that Brazil's new 'media arts scene' would emerge. Corporate sponsorship also played a very important role in the process. During the military years, the Brazilian economy was heavily regulated, with a number of state-owned companies in strategic areas of basic industry, aimed at producing raw materials and generating energy. The newly elected democratic government, the first one in more than two decades, aimed to open the economy and modernise Brazil's internal market. The liberal policies of the 1990s attracted a whole new set of investors to new industries, such as telecommunications (once solely in the hands of the government) and computing (now freed from import barriers). The Information and Communication Technologies (ICT) companies that sprung in the country were eager to promote – via arts and culture – their services among the population. The development of these sectors, along with the financial sector, would result in private support being lent to media arts.

Celebrations of technological art forms were a tried-and-tested form of cultural marketing borrowed from the USA and Europe (Sutcliffe 2009; Dyson 2006; Turner 2014; Shanken 2005), and soon adapted to the post-1990s Brazilian reality. The Itaú bank, for instance, had a homonymous Cultural Institute that ran many projects that commissioned and exhibited new media artworks, including the electronic arts biennial *Emoção Art.Ficial* [Art.Ficial Emotion] (2002-) and the *Rumos* commissioning program. It should also be noted that, via Itautec, their branded PCs and computing services, Itaú was heavily invested in the promotion of digitisation in the country.[68] In the 2000s, mobile phone companies would also become important sponsors of local media arts festivals. It could be argued that these events were meant to popularise new technologies among a population that most likely only had access to them in their workplaces, if at all.

The dissemination of digital tools among independent musical producers and activists would foster even more forms of technological expression in Brazilian popular culture. In parallel to the rapid institutionalisation of new media arts in the country, a vibrant scene dedicated to the principles of free software and culture came into being. Much of its spirit can be traced back to the *mangue bit* movement that broke out in the city of Recife in the early 1990s. Their manifesto, published in 1992, clamoured for technological solutions to socio-economic stagnation, evoking antennas sticking out of the mangroves that populated the city and crabs remixing *Kraftwerk* using a computer.[69] Multimedia collectives such as Re:combo, FAQ/Feitoàmãos, Media Sana and Frente 3 de Fevereiro, often connected to local chapters of the Independent Media Centre Network, developed politically engaged practices based on media interventions and interactive video performances. Created in the mid-2000s, platforms such as *MetaReciclagem* [Metarecycling], *Estúdio Livre* [Free Studio] and the online magazine *Rizoma* became forums for the advancement of technological thinking that took into consideration the country's subaltern position vis-a-vis neoliberal globalisation. These critical influences had begun to affect federal policies after 2003, when Lula (from the Brazilian Worker's Party) was elected president, making Gilberto Gil (legendary tropicália musician) the country's Ministry of Culture. Free software and tactical media were suddenly in power and, along with them, the media arts tradition that came from the concrete poets via Tropicalism. Later in that same year, the Tactical Media Festival, also hosted at Casa das Rosas, brought Gil unexpectedly into contact with cyberlibertarian John Perry Barlow and media theorist Richard Barbrook.[70]

Around this period, growing efforts towards the periodisation and theorisation of Brazilian technological art forms gained traction. As demonstrated by Arantes' *Arte e Mídia*, mentioned in the introduction, and Morais' essay *Art Machines*, included in this section, these attempts aimed at legitimising emerging new media production by underscoring its connections to the works and ideas of established artists from previous generations. These genealogies would find their footing in the claims of the unlikely media arts pioneers from the 1950-60s who had computer and digital media on their radars since before these technologies were widely available in the country (Campos 1997).

Overall, in the years leading to the new millennium, Brazil became a rather stable and functioning democracy. Though most of its socio-economic inequalities remained, it was among the fastest-growing countries in the world. It would soon be one among the BRICS: the five major emerging economies in the 21st century. An increasingly mature cultural and arts market provided strategic leverage for Brazil's entrance into the global era as a developing nation. In this context, the technological aspirations of the country's late avant-gardes seemed to have finally come to fruition. From an international Web arts award promoted during *Arte Suporte Computador* to the collaboration between local tactical media groups and the Creative Commons Foundation (Rebālo 2002), new media figured as one of the components of Brazil's newfound internationalisation.

Chapter 39

Investigative Poetics (2005)

Christine Mello

Poetic investigations of new media follow the logic of action-thought applied to art and technology, like so many living, experimental laboratories where knowledge production and artistic production meet. This is what creators like Júlio Plaza believe. The questions surrounding digital poetics and their processes of hybridisation run through his entire research project. Beginning in the late 1960s, Plaza, who died in 2003, developed a critical-sensorial discourse at the intersection of art, science and technology. He is one of the most original representatives of conceptualism in Brazil. His dogged interest in languages in hybrid contexts drove him to explore a new way of thinking art: intersemiotic translation.

As an intersign translator in close contact with concrete poets Augusto and Haroldo de Campos and Décio Pignatari, Plaza began his career in visual poetry before moving on to new media research in the 1980s. His work can be placed in the fields of videotext, electronic advertisement billboards, sky art, holography, digital imaging and interactivity. He is a strong presence in the Brazilian art scene, as an artist, theorist, curator, critic and professor who served as academic advisor for several artists. He has done relevant theoretical and curatorial work on digital-electronic languages and he is a pioneer in Brazilian experimentation in interactive and telematic contexts, all of which makes him one of the most stimulating and curious personalities of the 1980s and 1990s.

Plaza's trajectory is similar to that of other artists such as Philadelpho Menezes, Diana Domingues, Regina Silveira, Eduardo Kac, Gilbertto Prado, Silvia Laurentiz, Suzete Venturelli, Tânia Fraga, Artur Matuck, André Parente, Kátia Maciel, Analívia Cordeiro, the SCIArts group (Fernando Fogliano, Milton Sogabe, Renato Hildebrand, Rosangella Leote), the Poéticas Digitais group (affiliated with the University of São Paulo's School of Arts and Communication) and Daniela Kutschat and Rejane Cantoni. These creators are in touch with the scientific field, favouring an experimental approach to technological modalities that place their work at the forefront of innovation in new media.

Philadelpho Menezes is a creator whose work, like that of Julio Plaza, originates in visual poetry. He makes interfaces by mixing artistic modalities, as is the case with his sound poems, the videos *Antologia poética da língua das vogais* [Poetic anthology of the language of vowels], *Nomes impróprios* [Improper names], *Canto dos adolescents* [Song of teenagers] and the CD-ROM *Interpoesia* (with Wilton Azevedo), in which the verbal, the visual and the aural aspects of poetry interact in videographic, telematic and digital contexts. Menezes passed away in 2000, after making a career out of modifying the poetic system, creating a new relationship, or a new property, for the components of a statement: a poetics made from the interpenetration of languages that expands technological particularities.[71]

Diana Domingues is head of the research group Artecno at the Caxias do Sul Federal University. In her work, she expands strategies for connecting our bodies and technology. In 1991, the 21st São Paulo Biennial featured her video installation *Paragens*, made of three parts: *Olho* [Eye] (a reflecting pool), *Clareira* [Clearing] (seven monitors, representing the seven days of creation) and *Muro* [Wall] (a video-window in the shape of a 28-inch screen showing landscape scenes). In 1994, at the National Museum of Visual Arts in Rio de Janeiro, Domingues presented the video installation *In-viscera*, showing scientific images sourced from laparoscopic surgeries. In 1997, she produced the interactive video installation *Trans-e: my body, my blood*, in which prerecorded video images mingled with images created in real-time, in collaboration with computer systems that generated interactions between the spectator and the work. In 2002, she began the project *Ouroboros*, set in three virtual reality environments: in *Village*, she explored remote environments; in *Serpentarium*, robotics and telepresence; and in *Terrarium*, artificial life. The metaphors engendered in these pieces related to ideas of movement, of exchanges with the unknown and of displacements in new relationships with virtual environments.

In that field of the *unterritories* known as telematic networks, where geographic distances hold no sway over space and time (Rush 1999), we can witness some experiments in real time made in Brazil by artists like Eduardo Kac, Gilbertto Prado and Bia Medeiros, and the *Corpos Informáticos* group [Informatic Bodies]. For them, new media plays the role of a gesture, an action or an opportunity for communication in the work. Live performances happen online, often mediated by telepresence and webcams.

Eduardo Kac is another artist who hails from the world of visual poetry and whose technological investigations have led him onto an international path. In his 1996 interactive installation *Teleporting an Unknown State*,[72] anonymous people from all over the world pointed their webcams to the sky and transmitted sunlight, via the Internet, to the inside of an art gallery, where the photons captured by the webcams were directed towards the growth of a plant. These images, captured in real time from remote locations, were 'devoid of any pictorial, representational, formal or plastic value; they are simply a means of conveying waves of light' (Donati and

Prado 1999, 88). Kac thus recycles and subverts the uses of technology while simultaneously offering new meanings for it. In one of the first iterations of this piece, the entire process of the plant's growth was shown on the Internet for the whole world to see, allowing participants to witness the results of their own intervention. More recently in 2004, the piece was revived in São Paulo for the exhibition *Emoção Art.ficial 2*, curated by Arlindo Machado and Gilbertto Prado. Much of its poetry lies in its exploration of the nature of codes, simulated vegetable life and human communication within intelligent synthetic environments.

Gilbertto Prado, an artist and researcher who has been working with communication art since the 1980s, has made a career out of finding different strategies for action using real-time and artistic networks. In August 1991, for the group exhibition *Luz Elástica* [Elastic Light] curated by Eduardo Kac and held at Rio de Janeiro's Museum of Modern Art, Prado created a *telescanfax* project consisting of, in his own words, 'a handheld scanner used to scan a television screen, then sending these transformed images somewhere else via fax modem'. As Prado explains, the combined motion of the handheld scanner (digital) and the interlaced video (analogue) resulted in decomposed, jumbled, enigmatic-looking images (1995). This piece, called *La vendeuse de fer à repasser*, was sent from Paris to the artists in Rio de Janeiro.

Gilbertto Prado's 1992 project *Moone: La Face Cachée*, created for the exhibition *Machines à Communiquer - Atelier des Réseaux* at the Cité des Sciences et de l'Industrie in Paris, is another example of his exploration of the hybrid core of art networks. Its first images were made between the Electronic Cafés of Paris and Kassel (Documenta IX) in Germany. For Prado, the proposition made by this piece was 'the construction in real time of a hybrid and composited image in collaboration with a distant (and possibly unknown) partner. This ambiguity is at the root of what is asked by the piece: the creation of an ephemeral relationship, one in which the growth and composition of the work depends on the exchange dynamic that is established' (Prado 1994, 43).

In 1995, Gilbertto Prado created an interactive installation at the University of São Paulo's Museum of Contemporary Art featuring a video camera which allowed spectators to see themselves from the position of voyeurs. In 1998, he exhibited the Webinstallation *Depois do turismo vem o colunismo* [After tourism, comes social columnism] at São Paulo's Paço das Artes, consisting of a portal monitored by two video cameras connected to the Internet.

Through experiments in real time such as these, Prado expands the meaning of moving images, transmuting them to hybrid spaces and using them to (re)connect different dimensions between physical and virtual space. He also does this in his piece *Desertesejo*, a multiuser interactive virtual environment built in VRML and made available on the Internet. Inverting the usual logic of video games, the piece transforms the public space of the Internet into a space of *poiesis*, into a dialectic and oneiric search for the Other. Its interface promises sensorial engagement to its users. In its multiuser environment, desire and the desert hold as much fascination as the sounds, its tendencies towards silence and the dynamics of interaction in smooth spaces, under different views of a world shared in real time.

The work of Bia Medeiros and Corpos Informáticos exemplifies another field of research developed in the 1990s that was equally concerned with the body and the intersections between video and new technologies.[73] Created in 1991, the group focus on the body as a site of lived experience, materialised in live digital performances, video installations, net art and telepresence through the mediation of video cameras or webcams. In 2002, the group presented *Macula@corpos*, a telepresence performance shown in São Paulo during the first Centre of the Earth Scenic Arts Circuit. In the performance, webcams interacted with spectators' bodies, and these interactions were simultaneously transmitted to an internal circuit of video and computer screens (placed inside the theatre) and to the Internet.

Daniela Kutschat broke new ground in digital video with her 1998 *Vôo cego I* and *Vôo cego II* [Blind Flight I and II], animations made from video images generated by the hybridisation of analogue and digital procedures. The video camera shoots various dimensions of a single space or of different spaces in movement, and this footage is then digitally manipulated. In Kutschat's own analysis, these 'images are full of noise which, were they sharp, would immediately be perceived as collages or superimpositions. Dim and fuzzy as they are, however, by virtue of the way they were edited and assembled, they become synthetic "neo-realities"' (Kutschat Hanns 2001, 61-63). It is interesting how the very titles of Daniela Kutschat's pieces point to conceptual issues relating to the confrontation of the analogue with the digital. The title 'blind flight' might be thought of as relating to a metaphorical discussion of the capacity of seeing, capturing and recording images from the physical realm (thanks to optical systems like the one in the video camera) and the inability of synthetic imaging to do the same. The computer is known to do precisely the opposite: instead of extracting images from the real world, it engenders them and constructs them directly through its own numeric-symbolic constitution, using languages such as virtual reality.

In 1987, Rejane Cantoni created what is probably one of Brazil's first experiments with video installation in the context of a class at the University of São Paulo's School of Art and Communications with the Catalan artist Antoni Muntadas. It is *Ao vivo* [Live], a work in which the participant, upon entering the environment, sets off an alarm and a video system. A screen then shows a gun pointing to the user, who becomes a victim of their own gaze. As soon as the gunshot is heard, the title of the piece appears onscreen and a light pointing to the exit is turned on.

In 1999, after conducting several research projects and creative experiments, Rejane Cantoni produced, with Daniela Kutschat, the installation *Máquinas de ver I* [Machines for seeing I] at São Paulo's Paço das Artes. In this piece, images shot and shown in real-time via closed circuit video system incorporate the spectator and the physical environment into the artwork and are both simultaneous and opposite to each other.

In the first decade of the 21st century, Daniela Kutschat and Rejane Cantoni also collaborated on a piece titled *OP_ERA*. According to them, this work is a computational world made up of four dimensions interconnected by passages which can be explored by the visitor. Taking the shape of a progressive mathematical space, this project unfolds in several meaningful ways. It is about using tactile and aural interfaces to submerge the body performatively and interactively in a sensorial space, through a rhythmic, kinetic and vibrational experience. It expands the aesthetic experience beyond the confines of the artwork, and towards life and our relationship with the machinic, virtual 'other'. This is an experience which takes place mainly in the field of language, where meaning is created and transformed.

In dialogue with ideas put forth by Merce Cunningham, since 1994 the researcher and choreographer Ivani Santana has worked at the intersection of dance and technological mediations. Her choreographic piece *Gedanken* (2000) is about a body's trip through imaginary experiences. In it, the physical body takes on many dimensions in various forms of existence. As Santana explains, it's a trip that begins before its materialisation onstage, since the public is greeted by projected bodies that turn both the stage and the audience into a large-scale installation. In the work, she uses two tiny video cameras, one attached to her knee and the other to her eye, connected to a real-time closed-circuit system. Also projected are images made with the *Life Forms* software, with which the show's movement phrases were created. Another software package, *Image-ine*, is used for processing images in real time and projecting the images and texts sent by Internet users.

More recently, we have had examples of artworks in the shape of interactive mobile phone systems where music, the body and movement come together, such as Analívia Cordeiro's 2005 pieces; or in the form of interactive videos or videogames, like the ones made by Márcia Vaitsman with support from Germany and Japan, in which the user inhabits a mutant, fluctuating viewpoint.

These creators are part of a group of Brazilian artists inventing strategies around their shared experiences of exploring time in the context of digital and telematic art. Calling our attention to media practices emerging from the confluences of gaming, dance and multimedia performance contexts means addressing hybrid media poetics in real time; poetics that are impermanent and transitory, and that expand our ideas about media flows in dialogue with the wide array of current creative procedures at play in the realm of digital culture.

Throughout this range of examples, we notice diverse interdisciplinary investigations and different circumstances of artmaking; ideas are transformed by mechanisms of contamination and hybridisation between technological media. Through their poetics, these creators directly engage with the ubiquitous time of cyberspace, engendering a series of artworks which subvert/alter/expand the primary meanings of electronic-digital technologies, whether through reflections on time or new forms of artistic experimentation. They manage the difficult task of reconciling the art world with media networks.

These procedures aim to bend the temporal dimension of art towards new realities, introduce new criteria of authorship (now shared with the public) and argue for lived experience as an intrinsic part of the artwork.

Analysing methods of artistic creation, Julio Plaza and Monica Tavares highlight the fact that 'artistic operations are processes of invention and production'. They focus their analysis on ten or so ways of using new technologies. Among them is the limit method, which consists in 'exploring the laws, norms and rules that define a project in an attempt to acknowledge the limits of their field of action in order to then transgress those limits' (Plaza 1998, 97). If, for Plaza and Tavares, creation depends on breaking the boundaries imposed by the medium in which an artist is working, such rules are being constantly updated by the creators discussed here, who search for experimental processes at the limits of the languages of new media.

Chapter 40

Time Capsule (1997)

Eduardo Kac

Introduction

Time Capsule is a work-experience that lies somewhere between a local event-installation, a site-specific work in which the site itself is both my body and a remote database, and a simulcast on TV and the Web. The object that gives the piece its title is a microchip that contains a programmed identification number and that is integrated with a coil and a capacitor, all hermetically sealed in biocompatible glass. The temporal scale of the work is stretched between the ephemeral and the permanent, i.e., between the few minutes necessary for the completion of the basic procedure of the microchip implantation and the permanent character of the implant. As with other time capsules that lie underground, this digital time capsule projects itself into the future by getting under the skin.

The Procedure

When the public walks into the gallery where this work takes place, what they see is a medical professional, seven sepia-toned photographs shot in Eastern Europe in the 1930s, a horizontal bedstead, a computer connected to the Web, a telerobotic finger and additional broadcasting equipment. I start (and conclude) the basic procedure by washing the skin of my ankle with an antiseptic and using a special needle to subcutaneously insert the passive microchip, which is in fact a transponder with no power supply to replace nor moving parts to wear out. Scanning the implant generates a low energy radio signal (125 kHz) that energises the microchip to transmit its unique and unalterable numerical code, which is shown on the scanner's 16-character Liquid Crystal Display (LCD). Immediately after this data is obtained I register myself via the Web in a remote database located in the United States. This is the first instance of a human being added to the database, since this registry was originally designed for identification and recovery of lost animals. I register myself both as animal and owner under my own name. After implantation a small layer of connective tissue forms around the microchip, preventing migration.

Memory and Information

Not coincidentally, documentation and identification in imaging have been one of the main thrusts of technological development, from the first photograph to ubiquitous video surveillance. Throughout the nineteenth and twentieth centuries, photography and its adjacent imaging tools functioned as a social time capsule, enabling the collective preservation of the memory of our social bodies. At the end of the twentieth century, however, we witness a global inflation of the image and the erasure of the sacred power of photography as truth by digital technologies. Today we can no longer trust the representational nature of the image as the key agent in the preservation of social or personal memory and identity. The present condition allows us to change the configuration of our skin through plastic surgery as easily as we can manipulate the representation of our skin through digital imaging, so we can embody the image of ourselves that we desire to become. With the ability to change flesh and image also comes the possibility of the erasure of memory.

Memory today exists on a chip. When we call 'memory' the storage units of computers and robots, we antropomorphise our machines, making them look a little bit more like us. In the process, we mimic them as well. The body is traditionally seen as the sacred repository of human-only memories, acquired as the result of genetic inheritance or personal experiences. Memory chips are found inside computers and robots and not yet inside the human body. In *Time Capsule*, the presence of the chip (with its recorded, retrievable data) inside the body forces us to consider the co-presence of lived memories and artificial memories within us. External memories become implants in the body, anticipating future instances in which events of this sort might become common practice and putting into question the legitimacy and ethical implications of such procedures in digital culture. Live transmissions on television and on the Web bring the issue closer to our living rooms. Scanning the implant remotely via the Web reveals how the connective tissue of the global digital network renders obsolete the skin as a protective boundary demarcating the limits of the body.

Incorporating Biotechnology

To consider some of these questions, we need only to look closer at the present, not the future. If one's unique signature is in the genetic code, in order to leave an undeniable authentic mark one doesn't need to sign their name in blood. A special pen containing ink infused with one's own DNA, which is currently available to fight counterfeiting, is all that's needed. Radar tracking, or the use of tagging and tracking technology to monitor at a distance the position and behaviour of animals as small as a butterfly and as large as a whale, is also a case in point. The emergence of biometrics, with its conversion of unrepeatable personal traits – such as iris patterns and fingerprint contours – into digital data, is a clear sign that the closer technology gets to the body the more it tends to permeate it. The current and successful use of microchips in spinal injury surgery already opens up an unprecedented area for exploration, in which bodily functions are stimulated externally and controlled via microchips. For example, experimental medical research towards the creation of artificial retinas, using microchips in the eye to enable the blind to see, forces us to accept the liberating effects of intrabody microchips. At the same time, the legal seizing and patenting of DNA samples from Indigenous cultures by biotech companies, and their subsequent sale through the Internet, shows that not even the most personal of all biological traits is immune to greed and to technology's omnipresence.

Ethics and Trauma

As we experience it today, the passage into a digital culture – with standard interfaces that require us to pound a keyboard and sit behind a desk staring at a screen – creates a physical trauma that amplifies the psychological shock generated by ever-faster cycles of technological invention, development and obsolescence. In its most obvious manifestation, this physical trauma takes the shape of carpal-tunnel syndrome and backache. In its less evident form, current interface standardisation has led to an overall containment of the human body, which is then forced to conform to the boxy shape of the computer setup (monitor and CPU). It is almost as if the body has become an extension of the computer, not the other way around. This perhaps only reflects technology's general outlook, since organic life is indeed becoming an extension of the computer, as the emerging vectors in microchip technology clearly point to biological sources as the only way to continue the exponential process of miniaturisation beyond the limits of traditional materials.

The need for alternative forms of experience in the digital culture is evident. The wet hosting of digital memory – as exemplified by *Time Capsule* – points to a perhaps no less traumatic and yet freer form of embodiment. The living body wants to get out of the uncomfortable box and have unrestricted motion. Only in death should the body rest in a box. The intradermal presence of a microchip reveals the drama of this conflict as we try to develop conceptual models that make explicit undesirable implications of this impulse and that, at the same time, will allow us to reconcile aspects of our experience still generally regarded as antagonistic, such as freedom of movement, data storage and processing, moist interfaces and networking environments.

Chapter 41

Itaulab Research: Paulista 1919, Abadia Virtual and Policarpo (2008)

Marcos Cuzziol

Experiences with the construction of 3-D virtual environments have formed part of the research of Itaú Cultural since 1998, the year in which the first virtual versions of the exhibitions of the Institute were recreated via the Web in VRML (virtual reality markup language). In 1999, the development of *Imateriais* [Immaterials] required the deployment and customisation of a game engine (a program used in the creation of commercial games) and resulted in the mastery of techniques for producing multiuser virtual environments. The experience acquired with such projects was subsequently applied to the technical development of works such as *Desertesejo* [Desertdesire] by Gilbertto Prado and *Descendo a Escada* [Descending the staircase] by Regina Silveira.

With the creation of Itaulab in November 2001, research was directed towards interactive narratives in virtual environments. The objective was to generate knowledge for the creation of 3-D spaces, which may develop dynamic stories in accordance with the actions of a participant. For this purpose, two separate lines of experimentation were initiated. The first has the objective of optimising the techniques for building 3-D environments and it has resulted in the products *Paulista 1919* and *Abadia Virtual* [Virtual Abbey]. The second, the initial result of which is *Policarpo*, aims to develop characters which can interact with the public in a sympathetic way, possibly in order to direct dynamic screenplays. This text deals with these three projects and some of their practical results connected to the research initiated in 2002.

3-D Environments

Paulista 1919 was based on intensive iconographic research, in particular into the photographic archive of the city of São Paulo of Banco Itaú, which included old maps and house plans. Since the photographic material was only available in black and white, the colours of the buildings raised particularly interesting challenges. Construction and finishing techniques were consulted for the approximate recreation of colours. In the same way, surviving buildings were compared with period photos serving as references. Characteristics of the photographic film used can also provide information on the original colours. Orthochromatic films, very common at the time, were very sensitive to greens but not to reds. As a result, the intense greens appear very clear, the reds are almost black, and the yellows, especially those rich in red, appear as dark grey. Postcards of the time, carefully coloured by hand, complete the colour references.

Other results of this survey that discussed the origin of street names and curiosities about the avenue were included in the final output as explanatory narrations accompanying the virtual visit.

Abadia Virtual [Virtual Abbey] required a different kind of preparatory work, since the church attached to the Monastery of St. Benedict still exists. Plans for the library of the Monastery served as a basis for the virtual reconstruction, while models and textures were created on digital photographs of the location. Developed two years after

Paulista 1919, the *Abadia Virtual* project focuses on the optimisation of illumination and texturisation techniques. Details of the paintings and of the roof, images of saints and inscriptions in Latin were reproduced with great care. However, this did not require the creation of high-resolution models and textures. Contrary to what one may think, detailed 3-D models (featuring large numbers of polygons) and textures of large dimensions in pixels do not necessarily contribute to a better image result in a real-time 3-D environment. The principal causes of this apparent paradox are the processing optimisations required to ensure that such environments can be rendered as final images, which occur several times per second. Under these conditions, exaggeratedly detailed elements usually degrade the final effect, generating shimmering and other glitches in the image. For this reason, the level of detail of each element of the abbey was determined in accordance with its average visualisation distance, i.e., in accordance with the perception of the visitor, always using the smallest texture file size and the fewest number of polygons possible. The experiences with different texture sizes led to the discovery of a very simple but effective effect: it is possible to call attention to certain objects by giving them textures with resolutions slightly superior to those around them. Accordingly, the 3-D models of the saints and of the side altars received textures with a slightly better resolution than the walls and columns. As a result, such objects attract the eye of the visitor in a subtle way without the need for some cruder techniques found e.g. in video games, in which objects are illuminated or highlighted in vivid colours.

Environments in 3-D such as *Paulista 1919* and *Abadia Virtual* allow for interesting experiences of immersion in different eras and locations. Applications of virtual reality are still tentative in this sense and, without doubt, there is a great deal of possibility for simulations and historical recreations. However, the narrative possibilities of such simulations are limited. These are environments to be explored, perhaps in a form similar to an architectural work. The narrations of *Paulista 1919*, for example, recount details on the avenue and the city, but the narrations are fired off in absolute linearity, depending merely on the place where the visitor's avatar is located.

For a genuinely interactive plot to be developed in a virtual 3-D environment, something else is necessary: agents which are intelligent enough to carry out a dynamic story in real time.

Characters

A great deal has been written and much research has been conducted on artificial intelligence for virtual characters, particularly over the last ten years. There are sophisticated algorithms, capable, for example, of controlling the emotional state of a character. Various games from the newest generation use similar algorithms, but the richness of reactions provided by them is normally lost, in part on account of the low degree of expressiveness of the characters themselves, in part due to the lack of empathy between them and the participant. The main objective of the *Policarpo* project is to explore both the expressiveness of the character and its potential for empathy.

In characters from so-called realistic games, the absence of empathy may often be explained by the hypothesis of the 'uncanny valley', created by the Japanese roboticist Masashiro Mori.

The graph that describes the uncanny valley has as its horizontal axis the degree of human appearance, and as the vertical axis the level of familiarity which we feel with the creature. The uncanny valley is the region of the graph where the creature has a very human appearance but evokes extremely low familiarity. Such creatures create an accentuated feeling of estrangement, destroying any possibility of human empathic response. This effect is particularly observable in newer-generation game characters; as realistic as these virtual creatures may be, there is something disturbing in certain details, particularly in the eyes and facial movements – details which immediately draw our attention when we interact with other human beings. At the same time, it is perfectly possible to feel empathy towards creatures with a less human appearance, such as animated cartoon characters or characters of less realistic graphic simulations, for example those in *Shrek* or *Toy Story*.

Principles of empathy and the desire to avoid the uncanny valley defined the appearance of Policarpo, a rodent with a fragile body and enormous head, eyes and ears. Its planned behaviour is extremely simple: shy and stressed, Policarpo reacts in an exaggerated way to the movements and the approximation of individuals, but his fear is in constant conflict with a curiosity about what is going on around him. The artificial intelligence code developed for Policarpo was merely schematic, without emotional variables or other subtleties, in order to highlight the influence of his expressiveness on the perception of his behaviour. In fact, the program merely detects the signal of movement sensors and, depending on the signal's frequency, triggers the corresponding animations. Thus, it is the animations (triggered at the correct moments by the code) which are chiefly responsible for the feeling of intelligence which Policarpo arouses in its interactors.

Policarpo certainly appears to generate empathy with individuals who approach him. A survey of the reaction of the public in the first weeks of the exhibition recorded behaviour which strengthens this impression. Visitors initially tend to frighten it with brusque movements. After some time, however, visitors' movements become more subtle, and with the absence of signals from the movement sensors, Policarpo reapproaches them hesitantly. Many visitors then tend to avoid any sudden movements, shifting their position only with great care, as if they did not wish to bother the timid character any further.

Chapter 42

Technology and Contemporary Art: Bringing Politics Into the Conversation (2005)

Arlindo Machado

In his recent book *Politizar as Novas Tecnologias* (2003) [Politicizing new technologies], Brazilian sociologist Laymert Garcia dos Santos endeavours to express a growing feeling of dissatisfaction with the glorification of technology, the praise of scientific progress, the promotion of consumerism and the outright advertising of industrial products, all of which have become commonplace in international events dedicated to discussing the relationship between art, science and technology. In a country like Brazil, geographically distant from the global producers of technology and where access to tech products is still limited and classist, a serious discussion on the topic of new technologies must necessarily reflect those dislocations and this difference, in ways that resonate with independent, disruptive and critical thought and experiences taking place marginally in various places across the world, mostly outside the hegemonic centres....

Despite their impact on everyday life, on environmental policies and on the geopolitics of international domination that rich nations exert over poor ones, new technologies are still implemented through political decision-making exclusive to the State or by private corporate strategy, without any input from society. Society at large is left by the wayside due to negligence, lack of knowledge or the lack of critical capacity. The centrality of new technologies, be they electronic, digital or biogenetic, is also hardly ever questioned in events dedicated to them, least of all in the field that most interests us here: *contemporary art*. A rather naïve legitimising discourse is still predominant in the world of electronic arts or technological poetics, oblivious to the risks inherent in the adoption of technologic acceleration as a strategy. If it is true, as Martín-Barbero (2004, 22-37) points out, that the last fifty years have seen a hollowing-out of politics, leaving a void that has been slowly filled by the hegemonic discourse of technology, it is on the other hand also true that technology has been converted into a fertile new ground for utopias. Doctrines of every kind now rely on algorithms and machines for their promises of emancipation, progress and collective happiness, promises that were once confined to the realm of politics.

Some cyberspace analysts have suggested, for instance, that the way computer networks connect their users and allow their distribution inside that network has profound consequences for intersubjective relationships and human sociability, as well as for the very nature of the self in its relationship to the other. British artist Roy Ascott, one of the leading proponents of this line of thinking, goes so far as to say that the Internet is creating a 'planetary consciousness', which is a synthesis of all subjects present in cyberspace (Ascott 2003, 236). Integrated with the body of interfaces, the Internet user is no longer a mere passive spectator, incapable of interfering with the flow of energy and ideas; on the contrary, users multiply through the nodes of the network, spreading themselves all over, interacting with other participants and so engendering a kind of collective consciousness. Ascott seems to advocate for something like a hypertrophy of cyberspace, making it out to be a privileged 'space', a sort of virtual agora in which, unlike in depauperated, degraded real space, the promise of a true democracy can finally achieve its ultimate expression. For him, you're either inside the network or you are nowhere. And if you are inside, you are everywhere.

Ascott is hardly the only representative of this line of reasoning. We witness nowadays a hyperinflation of the new utopian discourse which credits tech devices with a nearly 'revolutionary' potential to boost ideas of universal democracy so ardently pursued by humanity throughout its history, while also unleashing mutations in humans' actual biological nature, elevating Man to the status of *Übermensch* ('superman' or 'overman') in the Nietzschean sense – escaping human frailty and the perishability of the body through electronic prosthetics and genetic engineering. Derrick de Kerckhove in Canada, Peter Weibel in Germany, Pierre Levy in France and Nicholas Negroponte in the United States, to name but a few, all represent the intellectual avant-garde of techno-utopianism, a doctrine that has rapidly spread to all corners of the planet. Still, it is curious that this neo-positivism, understandably popular in Europe, Japan and North America, has gained considerable traction in some corners of Latin America, where the reality that surrounds us is constantly calling its tenets into question. In Brazil, where Roy Ascott's ideas are laced with a folklorised, ultimately colonial mysticism (a return to shamanism, to tribalism and to the therapeutic effects of indigenous drugs such as ayahuasca, which are supposedly 'primitive' forms of immersion and 'Web-surfing' similar to what we experience in cyberspace and with virtual reality gadgets), the large-scale importation of ideas and models for action from other socio-economic realities has hindered the development of our own alternative outlook on new technologies. Blindly, uncritically, we follow the global hegemonic project.

On the other hand, our critics have not yet broached a full discussion about new technologies that takes into account all of their complexity, being often limited by a technophobic tendency that is just as naïve and just as imported – this time, from European and North American apocalyptic thought (Paul Virilio, Jean Baudrillard, Fredric Jameson, among others). For starters, as computer applications become ever 'friendlier' and more potent, it becomes increasingly difficult to discern between original contributions from true creators and mere demonstrations of a program's virtues. What we witness now is an unravelling of the meaning of value, especially when it comes to art: value judgements become flaccid, and we become complacent when confronted with artworks made with technology, since we lack sufficiently mature criteria to evaluate an artist's or a collective's contribution. As a consequence, our sensibility turns numb, judgement loses rigour, and any rubbish whatsoever seems exciting so long as it appears up to date with regard to current tech. Beyond the comforts of technophilia and technophobia, what we really need is to politicise the discussion on technology, on the relationship between science and capital, on the meaning of heavily tech-mediated artmaking.

Flusser's Contribution

Among the many Western scholars of technology who came to prominence in the second half of the 20th century, Vilém Flusser is perhaps the one whose reputation has grown the most in the last few years. What first strikes us when reading his works is how he assumes neither the technophilic nor the technophobic positions prevalent today. Born in Czechoslovakia and raised in a Jewish family, Flusser had to leave his country in 1939 to escape the Nazis. After some time in England, weary of Europe's descent into the darkness of its archaic myths of race, power, ideology and nation, Flusser emigrated with his wife Edith Barth to Brazil, believing he would find a civilisation unconcerned with the values of the Old World. That is not exactly what he discovered. Though he managed to draw into his orbit many of the most independent intellectuals in the country, he faced hostility both from the military dictatorship which ruled Brazil between 1964 and 1984 and from the local left, which, in the words of Sérgio Paulo Rouanet, 'was unable to grasp a way of thinking so anarchic, genuinely subversive and free from cliches' (Rouanet 1997, 5). Flusser lived in Brazil for 31 years and was perhaps the most important intellectual mentor for several generations of Brazilian artists who faced technology's challenges head on. Even after his return to Europe and until his death in Prague in 1991, he was a fixture in Brazil's intellectual milieu; he had left in the country not only two children but also many disciples. His studies on the impact of electronic and biogenetic technologies on contemporary civilisation started very early, in the 1960s, during his time in Brazil. In addition to his first writings on technical images and his controversy with Brazilian concrete poets, Flusser became very close to Brazilian artists working with new technologies, with mutually influential results. Many of these artists were his students or colleagues at São Paulo's Armando Álvares Penteado Foundation (FAAP). We can therefore draw a line extending from Flusser's nascent ideas about our technological society to the art world.

All the postmortem notoriety Flusser has been receiving over the world can be explained, among other reasons, by the fact that he is an incredibly canny thinker when it comes to analysing cultural, social and anthropological mutations happening in our current world, and he is extremely convincing when warning us about the risks we face. In fact, the Czech-Brazilian philosopher can think of only one historical period comparable to our own: antiquity, when humankind moved from a pre-historic, mythic stage into a historical, logical stage because of alphanumeric writing. In our current stage, which Flusser calls *post-historic*, 'writing' is made with and by machines, and essentially consists of an articulation of images – ultimately, of images which are digitised, endlessly multipliable and mouldable at will, which can be distributed instantaneously to the entire planet. Characters become bytes, lines of text become lines of pixels, means and ends give way to chance, rules give way to probability and reason gives way to programming (Vilém 1978). It is true that many contemporary thinkers – from McLuhan to Kerckhove, from Debord to Baudrillard, from Ong to Lévy – have tried or are still trying to express similar ideas through other pathways and using other arguments, but Flusser not only did it first, he also did it with a clarity, precision and radicality that makes all other paths seem more winding, arid, rhetorical; more compromised and less strategically efficient.

One can't bring up Flusser without first of all speaking about *Filosofia da Caixa Preta* [Philosophy of the Black Box], his most dense work – and also his best known (Vilém 1985a). This book has a singular history. First published in Germany in 1983, its Portuguese-language version is no mere translation, but a revision of the German edition. Starting with the title: while the first version was titled *Für eine Philosophie der Fotografie* ('Towards a philosophy of photography') (1983), a title that has remained constant in all its translations into other languages, the Portuguese-language version had its title changed to *Filosofia da Caixa Preta*, which better represents the book's conceptual realm and its purview. These changes were provided by the author, who wrote the Portuguese version himself after reconsidering some of his arguments.

In 1984, likely the year in which the Brazilian version was written, Flusser was conceiving his *Ins Universum der technischen Bilder* [In the Universe of Technical Images] (1985b), which was, in fact, a continuation of his *Philosophie* and a response to the many criticisms the philosopher received upon the prior book's release. It was inevitable, then, that immersion in this new discussion affected his Portuguese 'translation' of the book. That is why the Portuguese-language translation of Flusser's magnum opus is unique and uniquely different from all other translations (which are all based on the German version). A simple comparison between the German and the Brazilian versions is enough to see how much was changed. The preface was entirely reformulated for the Brazilian version, the glossary is filled with new terms absent from the German version and several sections of the book's main essay were rewritten to lend greater precision and consistency to the argument. In this sense, for true fidelity to Flusser's ideas only the Portuguese-language version (and not the German one) should be considered the definitive text of the *Philosophie* and, consequently, it should be the basis for all subsequent translations into other languages.

The title change is crucial. Though photography is the book's main object for reflection, it functions more as a pretext through which Flusser can gauge the inner workings of our 'post-historic' societies, societies defined by the decline of the written word and the hegemony of images. Among the various media of our time, photography occupies a strategic place, since current machines of symbolic audio-visual production are built on the basis of the semiotic and technologic definitions of photography. Photography inaugurates a new paradigm in human culture, one based on the automation of production, distribution and consumption of information (any information, not just visual), with gargantuan consequences for processes of individual perception and for systems of social organisation. But it's the arrival of electronic images (broadcast via television) and digital images (disseminated in so-called cyberspace) that has brought these changes into sharp focus, making them ostensive enough to warrant critical-philosophical responses from a section of the intellectual community. Readers of Flusser's book should not therefore expect a classic analysis of photography.

Photography is viewed through the lens of informatics and serves as a basic model for analysing how just about any technological or media apparatus works. This is why 'philosophy of the black box' better represents the work's ambitions than the laconic title *Towards a Philosophy of Photography*....

Flusser warns us about the dangers of undertaking actions that are purely external to the black box. In the age of automation, the artist, incapable of inventing or (de)programming the equipment which they need, is reduced to an operator of prefabricated apparatuses, a functionary of the productive system who is bound to the possibilities already predicted by the program and who is unable to establish new categories within the boundaries of a preset game. Indiscriminate repetition of the same possibilities inevitably leads to stereotyping, that is, to homogeneity and predictability of results. The multiplication of prefabricated models generalised by commercial software leads to an astounding standardisation of solutions, to generalised uniformity and, ultimately, to absolute impersonality, as is made apparent by so many international gatherings dedicated to electronic arts, where so much of the work exhibited looks as if it had been made by the same designer or communication firm. It may be natural and even desirable that a washing machine should repeat the same, invariable technical operation when washing clothes, but that is not what should be expected from devices whose purpose is to intervene in our imagination, or from semiotic machines whose basic function is to produce symbolic goods destined for human intelligence and sensibility. Stereotyping in machines and technical procedures is the main challenge to be met in the field of informatics, its most dramatic limit that must be overcome by every conceivable means.

The Role of Art

We can now introduce our main problem: the relationship between technology and contemporary art. Flusser doesn't specifically address this issue in *Philosophy of the Black Box*, which is primarily concerned with the more banal uses of technology in everyday life by the functionaries of production, but he does ponder it in his sundry writings published in various journals.[74] Though it may be commonplace to say that art (any art, at any time) has always been made with the technical means available at a given time, the way it appropriates a technical apparatus of its era is significantly different from the way other sectors of society – such as, in our case, the consumer goods industries – do it. Generally speaking, devices, instruments and semiotic machines are not made for creating art, at least not in the secular sense of the word, as it came to be understood in the modern world from about the 15th century on. Semiotic machines are almost always conceived with the principles of industrial productivity in mind, with the intention of automating procedures for large-scale production, never for the purpose of making singular, 'sublime' objects.

Photography, film, video and the computer were conceived and developed according to principles of productivity and rationality, within industrial frameworks and obeying the logic of capitalist expansion.[75] Even appliances made specifically for artistic creation (or at least what the industry understands as creation), like computer graphics, hypermedia and digital video applications, can only formalise an already-assimilated set of procedures inherited from established art-historical sources. Through them, the 'computable' portion of the constitutive elements of a given symbolic system, as well as its rules of articulation and its modes of enunciation, are inventoried, systematised and simplified for the convenience of a generic, disposable user – preferably a non-expert – allowing for large-scale production to meet industrial demands.

Current algorithms for image compression, used in nearly all digital video formats, best exemplify the 'philosophy' underpinning most progress in the field of audiovisual technology. They start from the premise that every image contains an extremely high rate of redundancy, which is how identical areas inside a single frame and, in the case of moving images, areas which repeat from frame to frame are understood. Eliminating redundancy using a specific codec means significantly reducing the size of image files, which allows for lighter storage use (using up only a few kilobytes of memory capacity) and quick image retrieval (allowing for real-time visualisation). This premise is problematic since it can only be applied to the most banal everyday usage for which it was developed. It cannot be applied to contemporary art images such as action paintings or North American experimental flicker films (in which every individual frame is different from the next) – digital compression ruins artworks of this nature. I recently tried burning a DVD anthology of Stan Brakhage films that he made by hand-painting the film strip with no regard to the boundaries of each photogram, and the DVD burner simply shut down. Because there was no image redundancy, the files could not be compressed. Experiences of this kind highlight how aesthetic responses that are central to contemporary art such as defamiliarisation, uncertainty, indeterminacy, hysteria, collapse and existential discomfort are rarely if ever taken into consideration by the market and by corporations, which tend to favour positivity, optimism and banality. Algorithms and applications are industrially produced for conservative, commonplace usage, not for pushing boundaries and disrupting the status quo.

There are several different ways of using commercially available semiotic machines. The artistic way is certainly the most deviant of them all since it intentionally breaks with the original machine's program to such an extent that it entails a total reinvention of the medium. When an artist like Nam June Paik, with the help of powerful magnets, causes a detour in the flow of electrons inside the cathode-ray tube of a television set in order to corrode the figurative logic of its images, we can't say that he is operating within the programmed and predicted limits of the medium. What he is actually doing is breaking the boundaries of the semiotic machine and radically reinventing its programming and its purposes. He is, in other words, doing what a true creator does: instead of submitting to what was determined by the technical apparatus, he is continually subverting the machine or the program's function, handling it in a way that is opposed to its programmed productivity. Perhaps it could be said that one of art's most important roles in a technocratic society is to systematically refuse to submit to the logic imposed by tools, or to refuse to fulfil the industrial expectations of semiotic machines, instead reinventing their functions and goals. Rather than allow itself to be enslaved by the rules of standardised communication, truly groundbreaking art reinvents the way a technology can be used.

Art and Technology: The Brazilian Experience

In Brazil, the history of technological poetics as a field spans fifty years. Ever since this story began in the 1950s, with Abraham Palatnik's first experiments in kinetic art, and in the 1960s, with Jorge Antunes's first forays into electroacoustic music and Waldemar Cordeiro's pioneering use of computers in art, technological poetics in Brazil quickly assumed two defining characteristics: 1) synchronicity and attunement to what was being made outside the country, meaning Brazilian artists were up to date and even ahead of their time in some instances; 2) at the same time, paradoxically, a difference in approach compared to international contexts mainly due to the critical stance taken by a significant portion of the art made here, given our tragic social reality and oppressive political situation during the military dictatorship, which made Brazilian artworks distinct from their foreign counterparts. The generations that followed made forays into the realms of video art, computer art, computer music, communication-art, holography, intersemiotic poetry and the intersections between art and science (to name only the fields which flourished the most in Brazil during the 1980s and 1990s). They were a bit freer from political constraints, but still held fast to the principles established by the pioneers while expanding the field of experimentation to encompass nearly the whole range of tech poetics.

We can't help but wonder about the precociousness of this qualitative expansion of technological poetics, a truly puzzling phenomenon when we consider that few other Latin American countries (with the possible exception of Argentina and Mexico) matched our level of development. The Brazilian artworld was, luckily, quite receptive to computers from the outset, thanks mainly to the enthusiasm of the concrete poetry scene, from where the first global examples of computer-generated poetry emerged in the 1970s, conceived by Erthos Albino de Souza. Additionally, although most of the pioneers in computer art came from Europe and the United States (for the obvious reason that these were the places where research in computer science was most advanced), a Brazilian artist was among the inventors of this artform: Waldemar Cordeiro, a concrete artist who came to prominence, in Brazil and abroad, for incorporating digital imagery into his work. In partnership with Italian physicist Giorgio Moscati, Cordeiro's most significant contribution was incorporating a critical stance to computer art by supplementing his image-making with social commentary that was lacking in most global artistic output. As an outspoken militant communist, Cordeiro did not endorse the myth of miraculous technology, but attempted to discuss, with great originality, Brazil's sociopolitical disaster. The development of computer arts in Brazil was greatly boosted by the fact that Cordeiro organised one of the world's first international conferences for computer art: *Arteônica*, held in São Paulo in 1971, which attracted the most important names in the field and placed Brazil on the map of creativity with regard to the artistic use of computers.

Here in Brazil, we believed for a while that electronic and digital technologies were introducing new problems of representation to the field of meaning-making practices, unsettling old epistemological certainties and consequently demanding that normative aesthetic concepts be reconsidered. We supposed, at the time, that the ideas springing forth from the realms of engineering and the 'pure' sciences such as physics and mathematics would push art to a new cycle of reinvention to keep up with the times. Back then, when we were still a rather small group, when technology and science were still seen as a more or less strange and, to a certain point, undesirable intrusion in the established artworld, we felt that we needed to join forces in order to implement in Brazil what was already being established in other countries – namely, a new field of aesthetic invention. We also needed to lend legitimacy to artistic practices that were then regarded with suspicion by the hegemonic sector of the cultural sphere. Ideas spawned in video art, holographic art, computer art, Web art, telepresence art, interactive environments, multimedia installations etc. were gradually introduced into the Brazilian artworld, from the heroic days of Abraham Palatinik and Waldemar Cordeiro until their legitimation as forms of artistic expression now that informatic and electronic technologies have become widespread. Much has changed since then. Technological poetics lost its marginal, almost underground character and quickly reached hegemonic status in the art world. In the last few years, we have witnessed multiple festivals, conferences and exhibitions exclusively devoted to the intersection of art with science and technology pop up all over the planet. Artists increasingly resort to computers as a tool for making images, music, written pieces, built environments; videos are practically inevitable in installations; interactive audience responses are the norm (or obsession) in any artistic endeavour that purports to be up to date and in synch with the cultural moment.

We realise all of a sudden that tech-heavy artworks have sprung up everywhere. But that initial promise of intense discovery and invention soon turned into banalisation of rote art-historical procedures or a return to conformity and integration with mainstream values. The unifying trait of the vast majority of artworks made today is their standardisation, their generalised uniformity, their participation in what seems to be an aesthetic of merchandising, where each piece has the sole purpose of demonstrating the qualities and potentials of a particular hardware or software. We realise, on the other hand, that our criteria for judgment and critique have not matured enough to allow for a proper assessment of these artworks in terms of their real importance and effective contribution to the redefinition of artistic and cultural concepts.

What appears to be happening in many instances is a subtle but implacable loss of art's more radical aspects. Nowadays, whenever we visit an event dedicated to electronic art, digital music or interactive writing, or leaf through any specialised magazine, it is easily made apparent that aesthetic discussion has been supplanted by tech talk, that issues relating to algorithms, hardware and software have replaced creative ideas, subversion of norms and the reinvention of life. The tech boom has reduced art – with the exception, naturally, of a few powerful and unsettling experiments – to professional evaluation, where technical skill takes precedence over radicalism. Where the relationship between art and technology is concerned, few events thus far have managed to go beyond a mere overview of algorithms, computer languages, programming and electronic circuits – all of which is inevitably framed by the interests of the industry

– and to face the deepest and most dramatic questions of our time. It all indicates that the time has come to draw a clear line between a mere industrial production of pleasing designs for multimedia celebration on one hand, and the search for an ethics and aesthetics for the age of informatics and genetic engineering on the other.

What we really need to reestablish, first and foremost, is the missing link between the current state of art and the tradition of nonconformity that is contemporary art's best feature, a link that has been artificially severed by a number of obtuse theses on postmodernity. Nothing is more inconceivable than the current generation of uninformed yuppies who make multimedia pieces, use nonlinear editing devices and design their own webpages, but have never seen a film by Vertov, have never read Artaud, never heard of Beckett or touched one of Lygia Clark's *Critters*. Secondly, we need to find stricter, more rigorous criteria to sort the wheat from the chaff in the tricky terrain of technological poetics, so we can single out and celebrate artworks that leave their mark on history, that make an effective and lasting contribution, that point towards invention, freedom and knowledge. In Brazil, a number of events dedicated to new technologies have been trying for some time to reintroduce an attitude that has lately been sidelined back into the art world and have for this reason made it their mission to bring together unaligned intelligence and talent from different regions of the planet, especially those regions that seldom take part in the global strategies of technological insertion. Among these events, we can cite the two editions of *Emoção Art.ficial*, a biennial held in São Paulo that is preoccupied precisely with these issues, so much so that the last edition in 2004 was called *Technological Divergences*. Another example is the *Videobrasil International Electronic Art Festival*, also held biannually and currently in its 15th edition, which equally makes space for divergent experiences in tech, especially those taking place in locations outside the hegemonic centres, such as Latin America, Africa, Southeast Asia, Eastern Europe, the Middle East and Oceania.

There is a huge range of issues waiting for critical intervention from the arts: new forms of domination based on gender, class, race and nationality (imperialist wars, genocides, terrorism, international migration, xenophobia etc.), universal surveillance, predatory globalisation, the conversion of life into spectacle, environmental degradation. Concurrently, new forms of direct social engagement emerge based on telematic networks, tactical media, the employment of multiuser distribution systems to create truly collective artworks, the search for new body politics, the expression of different cultural identities and so on. It's a question of interrogating where the insertion of new technologies in art introduces a qualitative difference or produces truly new situations in terms of expressive means, contents and forms of experience. In other words, it's about searching for the small-scale revolutions, what Félix Guattari called 'molecular revolutions', that are nowadays clearly identified with digital creation and new biological scenarios.

The technologies, artifices and apparatuses which artists use to conceive, build and exhibit their work are not simple, inert, easily replaceable tools or innocuous mediations, indifferent to the results of their use. They are loaded with meaning and with history, derived from specific productive, economic and geopolitical conditions. Technological poetics, like any other art form strongly determined by technological mediation, place the artist before the permanent challenge of rebelling against technological determinism, of refusing the industrial project embedded in machines and devices, of not allowing their work to become propaganda for the productive goals and the global hegemony of high-tech society. Far from submitting to the rules of labour, to standardised modes of operating and relating to machines; far from being seduced by the feast of effects and cliches currently dominating mass entertainment, an artist worthy of their name endeavours to reappropriate digital and biogenetic technologies in innovative ways, making technology work for the benefit of truly contemporary aesthetic ideas.

Chapter 43

Make Way for Tactical Media! (2003)

Ricardo Rosas and Tatiana Wells

A spectre is haunting culture – the spectre of tactical media. Defiant, playful, iconoclastic and politically conscious, tactical media don't mince their words when it comes to challenging the standards of good taste, social apathy, the artistic practices and ideological innocuousness present in new media.

With the advent of cheap technology in the 1980s, a new form of activism emerged. Enamoured by ideas of nomadism and resistance, new movements aim to rethink the transgressive role of communication, often via the route of aesthetics. They borrow features from both 1960s countercultures and from European strands of avant-garde revolutionary aesthetics. The avant-gardes moved art out of the gallery and into the streets, reintegrating art with the praxis of life; but cultural experimentation cannot belong to a single political inclination or to a single movement, just as art no longer needs to be a higher expression of moral superiority.

'Tactical media' as a concept reached maturity in the 1990s through the work of media activists and new media festivals in Europe and the USA. Its basic tenet is 'Do-It-Yourself', an exhortation to put in practice the alternative potentials of communication enabled by the growing accessibility of media equipment and materials.

Detached from the whims of the market and the ideological agendas of large media companies, tactical media lend a voice to those excluded from corporate vehicles: the underclasses, minorities (racial, sexual, etc.), alternative communities, political dissidents and street artists, among others.

Tactical media don't rely exclusively on the usual channels of communication but make use of public space, they don't cosmetically alter urban surfaces but rather respond to issues of general interest: hence their hybrid nature which mixes together popular culture, oppositional culture and even mass culture. Hence also the vast array of weapons in their arsenal from repurposed traditional media like TV, radio, video, print and the arts in general to websites, software design and all kinds of electronic media – including, as necessity might dictate, performances, DJ sets and street theatre. The street = an alternative public sphere which allows for greater interaction between artwork and audience. Media can be the fulfilment of its own creative potential, as a critical process that raises awareness against the deformations of hegemony.

This does not mean that tactical media are synonymous with alternative media, for it is a concept created precisely to escape dichotomies – amateur versus professional, alternative versus mainstream – and take full advantage of the flexibility of its extensions and responses, and of collaborative work and mobility between different media. What matters most are the temporary connections it allows us to forge.

But what is the point of a 'Tactical Media Laboratory' in Brazil?

It just so happens that a lot of people have been practising tactical media here, even if they're not always aware that there is a name to what they're doing. Whether it is urban interventions, tactical uses of art, the Web, pirate radios, fanzines and so on, the fact is that in Brazil we are witnessing a real boom in indie media. It's impossible not to notice it. Besides, we urgently need digital inclusion for those who can't, for example, afford a PC. The concept of tactical media can be adapted to Brazilian reality in our search for alternatives forms of mobilisation that propagate interdependent circuits. The search for autonomy is about education, inclusive technological dissemination and forging relationships between the centre and the periphery.

We anthropophagise media practices not only to promote collectivity and autonomy in relations of production, but equally to acknowledge the periphery (and we are all peripheric in relation to the Empire) as the marginalised reality and, above all, as the primary expression of the colonised logic of Latin American cultures.

The study of these practices in a laboratory would demonstrate how we use, consume and push forward these representations, since we already know that our use of them is far more creative than we might suppose. We understand the 'laboratory' as a space for experimentation, for the exchange of information and experiences, as well as a place where unexpected chemical processes happen. A laboratory for tactical media is a space where we are all artisans of our own media, where all of us can create, interfere, recombine, inform our ordinary reality and so return to small everyday myths. Tactical media practitioners are those who not only produce their local stories, their dramas, joys and concerns, but who are also the protagonists.

> Be your own media, that is our motto!
> And, to paraphrase the anthropophagist-in-chief,
> 'Our independence has yet to be declared'.

Against social reality, well-dressed and oppressive, catalogued with statistics and characters from soap operas. Against holy wars, reality shows and the traffic of dreams disguised through the connivance of the tabloids before the numbness and blindness of those who see only this side of their self-imposed cages – reality without complexes, without madness, without prostitution and without the penitentiaries of another possible world.

Chapter 44

Gambiarra – Elements for a Reflection on Recombinant Technology (2006)

Ricardo Rosas

The street finds its own uses for things.
— *William Gibson, Burning Chrome*

Two episodes of our times: in March 2004, in Madrid, bombs go off in train and subway stations, killing thousands of civilians. Between the 12th and the 16th of May 2006 in São Paulo, the PCC (Primeiro Comando da Capital)[76] uses cell phones to organise a series of attacks on several spots in the city, spreading panic among the population. Both situations terrorised society and had a deep impact on how everyday life would be lived in the two cities.

Beyond the fact of urban terrorism, there was another element that is common to both occurrences, an element that was perhaps essential to the structure of these events, without which they might not have worked. An element so subliminal and imperceptible in their arrangement, although so crucial to their execution, that it may have gone unnoticed: the actions were probably carried out using paltry, precarious resources, improvised apparatuses – in other words, *gambiarras*.[77]

A sizeable fraction of the cell phones used in prison before, during and maybe even after the PCC's attacks, were stolen devices adapted for likewise stolen chips, which is the standard procedure in phone cloning. The Madrid bombs were made of dynamite and nitro-glycerine connected to a mobile phone.

So maybe, hopefully, it's not all bad news. The era of *gambiarra* bombs is also the era of *gambiarra* solutions, of *gambiarra* recycling, of scrap parts and electronic waste, and the debris of consumerist society repurposed as *gambiarra* artworks.

But what is, after all, *gambiarra*? The definitions we find in dictionaries like the Houaiss link it to electricity theft – 'fraudulently hooking into power cables with the purpose of stealing electricity' – or, in a less accusatory tone, as 'a long electrical extension cable with a lamp attached to the end'. But the ordinary common-sense application of the word refers to any deviation or improvisation in the use of spaces, machines, wiring and objects originally destined for other functionalities, or when those objects are used 'correctly' but in a different context, due to a lack of resources, time or manpower.

But there is more to it: as a concept, *gambiarra* has great cultural resonance, especially in Brazil. It often means a quick fix, using whatever resources are at hand at a given moment. This significance has not escaped the art world, where *gambiarras* have led to many creations. The arts have shed light on other aspects of the *gambiarra* and its symbolic/cultural meanings. In an essay on the *gambiarra* in Brazilian art titled 'The Juggler and the *Gambiarra*', Lisette Lagnado suggests that the idea of *gambiarra* has become a lightning rod for certain types of discourse. As an assemblage of stuff that has been banished from the functional system, the concept of *gambiarra* 'involves transgression, fraud, ruse – without ever eschewing order, but a very simple order' (Lagnado). As a mechanism, *gambiarra*, according to Lagnado, has a political as well as an aesthetic inflection. Stemming from a lack of resources, 'there can be no *gambiarra* without nomadism or collective intelligence'.

Gambiarra is likewise associated with the concept of bricolage as formulated by Claude Lévi-Strauss in 'The Savage Mind'. If we define the bricoleur as 'someone who works with his hands and uses devious means compared to those of a craftsman' (Lévi-Strauss 1989, 32), the tools and materials of their labour cannot be determined beforehand by the project they are working on, as in the case of an engineer, but only by their usefulness at a given moment. The bricoleur gleans and hoards the bits and scraps that make them say, 'this may come in handy'. They create without a preconceived plan, with little regard to well-established technical processes and norms, using ready-made fragments of materials. Their creations amount to new arrangements of elements whose nature is modified only as they find their place in the tool set or in the final composition. Lévi-Strauss's distinction between the bricoleur and the engineer is crucial to understanding *gambiarra* – this free-form creative act that eschews user manuals and goal-oriented project restrictions – as essentially a form of bricolage.

Most of all, in order to understand *gambiarra* not only as social practice and popular creation but also as art or intervention in the social sphere, we must keep in mind a few key elements, namely: precarity of means; improvisation; inventiveness; the back-and-forth with local realities and communities; the potential for sustainability; a shaky legal status; and technological recombination via the reutilisation or the repurposing of a given technology, to name a few. All these elements need not always be present. But a combination of some of them always shows up, depending on the circumstances.

Besides, there is always a degree of unpredictability that allows things to be what they seem – or not. The present state of technology also infinitely amplifies the possibilities for recombining technical devices and apparatuses in ways that broaden the concept and definition of what can be classified as *gambiarra*.

Since our number of pages is limited, we will focus exclusively on Brazilian and Latin American examples. We could start with the truly popular *gambiarras*, the ones found on the streets. *Gambiarras*, by their nature and origin, are undoubtedly vernacular. They are born out of spontaneity, the daily need to improvise as a struggle for survival, sometimes as the result of piracy and illegality, sometimes as a means to add a little creativity to the surrounding chaos and poverty. Their scope is huge, but we can sketch a tentative cartography of devices and configurations.

Gatos or *puxadinhos*, that is, electricity theft via direct line; *'gato TVs'*, illegal interception of cable television content; 'electric bikes', loudspeakers attached to bicycles, used for popular advertising in the city of Belém do Pará; Mr. Pelé's *Triciclo Amarelinho* [Little Yellow Tricycle], which, according to Gabriela de Gusmão, boasts a three-in-one stereo system, TV set, headlights, battery, raincoat, alarm clock and Christmas lights; the well-established *trios elétricos*,[78] trucks/floats equipped with high-power sound systems; and the sound systems used in Rio's *baile funk* (among other types of party), modified to the point where they resemble spaceship control panels.

There are a few artworks that depict the world of popular *gambiarras*, some of which veer towards documentation or studies in design, as is the case of Gabriela de Gusmão Pereira's photographs, Christian Pierre Kasper's recordings or Cao Guimarães photos and videos.

Subtle and sophisticated reinterpretations of the world of popular tech, *gambiarras* are the province of Brazilian collective Bijari, whose works are steeped in popular imagination and informed by research conducted with street vendors and scrap collectors, like their current research project on 'resistant technologies'.

And of course, we have to mention the usual tactics deployed in the digital arena and catalogue practices like digital piracy, software cracking, wardriving (unprotected wireless network invasion), making wi-fi boosters out of cans of Pringles, etc. The same goes for the growing community of free and open-source software developers. Exchanging codes and information via highly active networks, these creators improvise configurations and invent new usages and applications in a true *gambiarra* fashion, making programs that are open to interference and improvement by anyone who might be willing.

Artists and activists also make *gambiarras* out of existing machines, which they tweak, pervert or repurpose. The connection between art making and the invention or alteration of machines is hardly new. Artists have been imagining or making contraptions for centuries – think of Leonardo da Vinci or Athanasius Kircher, just to a name a couple of particularly remote examples.

One such machine that is very interesting, but not necessarily functional, is the Brain Decoder Plus, invented by the Recife-based artist Moacir Lago. This thought-decoding device is licensed by the Obsoletch Brasil corporation – another of the artist's creations. It purports to do what technology so far has been unable to accomplish: decode our most intimate thoughts and desires. Using irony, Lago wants us to think critically about the ethical implications of scientific and technological advancement and about the relationship between new tech and everyday life. The artist believes technological inventions create consumer desires, making current appliances seem obsolete in comparison to new, more modern gadgets. Besides questioning art's reliance on technology and vice versa, the artist wants us to discuss how knowledge can be appropriated and democratised in the realms of science and art. Challenging the institutional powers that legitimise art, he transformed the gallery at Recife's Joaquim Nabuco Foundation into the offices of Obsoletch.

On the sound research side of things, Paulo Nenflídio is an inventor of gizmos and gadgets made from surprising combinations, such as a berimbau/computer mouse/doorbell solenoid combo, as well as wind-powered musical instruments. As an intervention in public space, his Maracatu Bicycle is definitely the flashiest of his contraptions. It consists of a bike coupled with a mechanism attached to an agogo[79] connected to the pedals, so that it plays maracatu music whenever the bicycle is ridden. Equally classifiable as musical *gambiarras* are the installations and concerts by the music-art collective Chelpa Ferro. Among various sound machines, two stand out: the piece *Jungle* – a motorised plastic bag that plays a rhythm similar to the dance music style known as jungle, and the installation *Nadabrahma* – a mechanical rattle made from dried tree branches and seeds.

Hailing from the media art scene, Lucas Bambozzi is often guilty of technological transgressions. Of special interest here is his recent *Spio Project*, a Roomba robot vacuum cleaner equipped with wireless infrared high-sensitivity CCTV cameras and a light-emitting diode (LED) for tracking in the dark. Spio transmits images in real time according to the robot's position, as a kind of continuous and autonomous generator of images without human authorship, while the robot's movements are followed by two additional cameras. In a partially intentional 'short-circuit', the robot's behaviour and movement tends to become erratic, to the annoyance of the spectators. One of the project's goals is to address the nearly imperceptible invasion of our homes by seemingly innocent gadgets that might well be equipped with surveillance apparatuses and remote tracking devices. Spio alludes to the new practices emerging in digital culture, like sampling and remixing, and to the ineffectiveness of the intentions behind interactive artworks, the changing frameworks for understanding authorship and the continuous transit between high and low tech. Obviously Spio's big target is the ever-encroaching surveillance of everyday life, here spoofed by a humorous and dysfunctional little gadget, equal parts endearing and annoying, which represents the archetype of the electronic eye of surveillance societies.

Without much of a fuss, Etienne Delacroix is an artist who, perhaps more than any other, addresses most of the issues discussed so far. A Belgian living in Brazil, he moves in the grey area where art and engineering, tech inclusion and creativity, *gambiarra* and design, cultural activism and education, appropriation and reinvention, theory and practice all mingle. A computer bricoleur, Delacroix is a type of artist who is far more interested in the process than the product. Trained as a physicist, he attempted to implement his 'nomadic workshops' at the Massachusetts Institute of Technology, where participants would create a low-cost interface between traditional artistic gestures and the fundamentals of computer science and electrical engineering. Bringing together students of engineering, computer science, arts, communication, design, architecture and music on one hand, and a growing heap of electronic waste on the other, this project only took off when it was implemented at the Universidad de La Republica in Montevideo. There, in his studios, old computers were taken apart and the still-working components were picked up to be repurposed not just as parts for new computers, but also for huge art installations. The project isn't about 'recycling' machines for the purposes of digital social inclusion, but about experimentation, about a technical process involving aesthetic sensibility in a more complex manner while still evidencing a concern for social inclusion.

There's nothing new to the observation that the practice of *gambiarra* is 'endemic' to Brazil. This begs the question:

why has there been no theory derived from this praxis so far? This paper is only a first step in that direction. Maybe we can find reasons for this absence by looking at the contexts in which theory on technology, electronic art, art and technology, and media arts flourish in Brazil. We should therefore look around us and turn our attention to the streets instead of only trying to catch up with what's trending in Europe and the USA. More importantly, perhaps, gaining an understanding of tech *gambiarras* would demand that we abandon the assumptions, biases and prejudices still dominant in some of these scenes. Above all, we should watch out for the occasional excesses of self-complacency or snobbery towards popular practices. Mirroring the stance of 'art for art's sake', art and technology creations often risk the ostracism that comes with 'art for technology's sake'.

In the meantime, we overlook phenomena that are abundant not only in the popular imagination and on the streets of cities large and small, among street vendors or in slums; but also disseminated (although with different names) in geek culture, in endlessly creative new media products and as the bread and butter of the activities and machinery of media activists and practitioners of tactical media.

In geek culture, how could we not notice common practices in the free software community, like installing systems and new software trials, for example, and the way in which they promote continuous reinvention? And we haven't even mentioned the hardware modifications made by users, the culture of customisation, game hacking, robot hacking, etc.

Gambiarra is undoubtedly political praxis. Such politics can't be reduced to activism (or to a tool for activism) because practicing *gambiarra* is political in itself. Intentionally or unintentionally, *gambiarra* often opposes the logic of capitalist production, fills a lack, fixes a shortcoming, diminishes precarity, reinvents production, offers a utopian glimpse at a new world or at a revolution; or simply attempts to heal some of the open wounds of the system, giving comfort or a voice to those in need. *Gambiarra* itself is a voice, a cry – for freedom, in protest, or simply in affirmation of existence, of innate creativity.

Gambiarra doesn't necessarily result in a finished product. It is also process, work in progress. The process, in fact, may be what's most important, precisely because a *gambiarra* is never over; there is always something to add, some tweak to be made. And there's more. As our examples from Brazilian activism show, *gambiarra* is also about the method. It's a *modus operandi*, it's tactics, it's guerrilla, action, transmission, dissemination. This can be seen not only in the way media activist groups operate, but also in the work done by art collectives and alternative networks. All over Brazil, alternative spaces like São Paulo's Casa de Contracultura, the now defunct Gato Negro, Espaço Insurgente, Espaço Impróprio and Espaço Estilingue are not just meeting places but, like so many anarchist 'processual *gambiarras*', they also promote artist residencies, occupations, exchange programs for activists and other collectives, while implementing self-sustaining strategies for their continuing existence.

The present state of technology has allowed the proliferation of devices, of possibilities for connection and convergence and of increasingly interconnected online and offline networks in which mobile devices, wi-fi, remote tracking gadgets, GPS, RFID and other systems exchange information and allow for analogue and digital technologies, whether low-tech or high-tech, to intermingle in what scholar Giselle Beiguelman calls cybrid culture (Beiguelman 2004).

This intense tech-convergence has, in turn, coincided with a true boom in invention (or reinvention) in the world of new media as well as art and technology, with the growing use of preexisting tools and apparatuses generating myriad weird widgets, gadgets and gizmos that do all sorts of things, from new ways of communicating to new strategies for activism, from previously unheard of ways of dealing with urban space to innovative approaches for adapting to the likely future ubiquity of computational machines. These conditions have blurred the boundaries between the artist and the engineer, that old dream of the Russian productivists; and undone Lévi-Strauss's fixed categories that separated the bricoleur from the engineer and from the artist. All these circumstances open up unpredictable perspectives for the future of *gambiarra* practitioners and creators. We should speculate about what the future of *gambiarras* has in store. We can call upon someone who has already had a glimpse of what's to come for our familiar gadgets: science-fiction writer Bruce Sterling, whose recent writings have dealt with the objects and appliances of today and of tomorrow. In a speculative style he has dubbed 'design fiction' – a design-focused variant of sci-fi – Sterling imagines what our future will look like on the basis of our current relationships with objects. His latest book, *Shaping Things*, is a sort of diatribe on sustainable design for the future, where he warns that 'we're in trouble ... because we design, build and use dysfunctional hardware' (Sterling 2005, 54). He talks some sense into us by denouncing the exploitation of archaic, finite and toxic energy resources by our dominant classes in a regime that destroys our climate, poisons the population and leads to wars for the control of resources. In other words, this regime has no future.

In his peculiar writing style, Sterling attempts to show us an evolutionary timeline of humanity's technological journey, from the making and using of tools at a certain point in history (namely the late Mongol Empire) to the creation of machines as substitutes for tools, which turned their users into clients. Centuries later, after World War I, these clients were turned into consumers as machines evolved into products through distribution, commercialisation and anonymous uniform manufacture. This evolution led to an increasing specialisation in object production and useability, a specialisation which would become even more acute in a phase that followed, starting in 1989 with the rise of the gizmos, which in turn transformed consumers into end users in our current 'New World Disorder'. Gizmos are highly unstable, multifunctional and often programmable objects which can be altered by users. They also have a short lifespan. Gizmos have so many functionalities that it's usually cheaper to import new functions onto existing gadgets than to simplify them. The next rung on the evolutionary ladder is what Sterling has named *spime*. Technically, spimes don't really exist yet. They are new, inventive, interactive machinery,

> manufactured objects whose informational support is so overwhelmingly extensive and rich that they are regarded as material instantiations of an immaterial system. *Spimes* begin and end as data. ... *Spimes* are sustainable, enhanceable, uniquely identifiable and made of substances that can and will be folded back into the production stream of future *spimes*. (Sterling 2005, 11)

In Sterling's words, '*spimes* are information melded with sustainability' (2005, 43).

Although Sterling never directly mentions the concept of 'Do-It-Yourself', and although the spime incorporates data from the object's own history (via RFID, among other ways) – which requires a technological sophistication that is out of reach for most of our current *gambiarras* – it's hard not to see in his spimes something of the multifunctionality, the ever-present possibility of reinvention, alteration and enhancement that defines the recombinant character of the *gambiarra*. In an almost biological way, as Gilbert Simondon or Bernard Stiegler would have it, the technical object (appliance, apparatus, or what have you) can always be improved with time, generating compost, being transformed in a perhaps truly evolutionary lineage. And in this lineage, the *gambiarra* could very well be the gizmo's more creative, daring sister, a forebear of the spime. Or perhaps, who knows, the always updatable *gambiarra* is a spime already.

Chapter 45

Free Studios (2006)

Fabianne B. Balvedi, Guilherme R. Soares, Adriana Veloso and Flavio Soares

Introduction

It is not uncommon today to find the idea of open and shared systems associated with the defence of freedom in the fight against a proprietary monopoly. Based on this perspective, free software is almost always appropriated as a banner and strategic weapon in a counter-hegemonic struggle, placing it in opposition to closed models of information systems.

Although this discourse succeeds in attracting the attention of mainstream media to questions such as the inequalities present in global technological development and the consequences of patent laws, its failing is that it ignores what are perhaps the most important characteristics of the free software phenomenon: its dynamics of production, its rules for the circulation of products and the behavioural changes towards the medium brought about by the philosophy behind its use (Novaes, Caminati and Prado 2005). It is different from the proprietary model not just in the nature of its materiality, but most of all in terms of the social relations into which it is inserted. Therefore, we understand that it is not correct simply to say that free software is better than proprietary software, but rather that it is of another order that is fairer and qualitatively better than the proprietary one. According to De Ugarte, the free software movement is the basis of the first ever large-scale structure based on free property in distributed networks (De Ugarte 2005).

While the proprietary model is based on competition and holding back information, the free model is mainly motivated by collaboration and generosity. At any of the levels of interaction, multidimensional developer/user relationships are established, which constitute an alternative to the unilateral producer/consumer or provider/client relationships. As a result, the ensuing product is also a process. This process can be defined as a cumulative feedback cycle which makes the network think and is based on the sharing of information as the driving force behind technological innovation and the production of cultural goods.

It is worth observing that the coexistence of the process and product variables as the result of a continuous flow of occurrences cannot be understood within the traditional Western logic, that of Aristotle, which is based on affirming binary values. According to this logic, the result of a development process would be just a product, and not the process itself. On the other hand, fuzzy logic supports modes of reasoning which are approximate rather than exact – modes of reasoning we are naturally used to working with. Many human experiences cannot be classified simply as true or false, yes or no, black or white. This is also how *Estúdio Livre* (Free Studio) works. The Estúdio Livre project is a collaborative environment for research, development, experimentation and production in free media, based on the perspective that one of the biggest innovations of the digital world is to be found in the structure of the division of labour which takes place in an open network – and of which free software is the best example. The methodology proposed here illustrates the breaking down of the barriers between producer and consumer as an example of collective intelligence and of changes in aesthetic, economic and social paradigms in contemporary society.

The Community – Developers: Art and Science

The use of licences which allow the sharing and reuse of codes is potentially a huge trump card for the sustainability of an interdisciplinary community like Estúdio Livre, which combines art and science. Stimulating this model of production encourages a space in which science can operate more innovatively and art can become more involved in improving its techniques.

One of the big problems with the dehumanisation of technologies is the failure to question the mechanisms of repetition built into the interfaces of industrial software. In most cases, artists see the computer as a closed box which ends up dictating aesthetic paths linked to standard interfaces. Thus, the cultural producer is tied to a blind dependency on new products and formats launched by the industry.

In the case of free software, production follows a rhythm of requests and mutual collaboration in which the developers receive immediate feedback from the artists, who thereby gain more advanced knowledge about the development of their tools since they are no longer trapped within the cycle of industry secrets. This encourages the deepening of knowledge for the shaping of a personal relationship to technology. The potential for customising the production processes thus grows, bringing with it a greater interest in science and the methods which make this possible.

Scientists also find an enormous incentive for creativity in the free studio environment. Breaking down the distance between scientific technique and the artist, this environment brings the awareness that the process of producing code or designing an interface or a machine can be loaded with communicative intention and it can be as playful as making brush strokes on a canvas or strumming a guitar. A much less technocentric vision of scientific work is revived, bringing back the figure of the inventor and adding poetry to the mix.

The Community – Artists and Cultural Producers: Collaborative Means of Production

Without a doubt, the way free software is produced represents one of the most successful models of organic and participatory management of collective work ever known. The idea of producing collaboratively and using Internet-based interfaces for editing code, version control, discussion forums and email lists stimulated the construction of systems which are today so proficient for certain application niches that they have overtaken proprietary applications (as in the case of Web servers). This happens because there is also an open dialogue between the various parties; this is a more direct and intelligent way to solve problems and implement innovations than a closed approach, in which the parties isolate themselves from everything, cloaked in secrecy.

This vision has had a great influence on how artistic production is seen at the beginning of the present century (Lessig 2005). It became clear that artistic production could reach its audience directly, without intermediaries and without needing to conform to the aesthetic and marketing demands of distributors (in many cases retrograde demands that hamper creativity). This brought with it a better and more organic understanding of the artistic field of action. On the other hand, it also generated the need to look again at the question of how authorship is recognised or remunerated, since any consumer could potentially be a distributor or even a collaborator in this production.

One of the solutions proposed and encouraged by Estúdio Livre is support for collaborative production through the use of licences for sharing. Just as the free software developer shares their code using licences such as the GPL, the cultural producer gives the public the prior right to redistribute their work through licences such as Creative Commons with or without charge, and therefore makes them a partner in creative production. In this way, a relationship is established in which consumption and production are parts of the same cycle, in which the greater profit is the knowledge acquired and the establishment of social networks. Sooner or later, these same social networks will become partners in initiatives for mutual sustainability, creating a chain of production flows that breaks down cultural and geopolitical barriers, making possible autonomous niches that are much more self-referential and aware of their direction, as well as capable of reflecting both their socioeconomic influences and the role of their production.

The Environment

Estúdio Livre is a collaborative online environment that emerged from the combined perspectives of people with the most varied backgrounds, converging around the need for research into, and for deeper knowledge of, the use and development of free media. The media contextualised through this environment corresponds to communications media, that is, it refers to the instrument or the form used to carry out communication processes. Since software is an instrument for interaction which makes communication between human and machine possible, it may also be considered media, reinforcing McLuhan's hypothesis that the medium is the message (McLuhan and Fiore 1967). The main objective of Estúdio Livre is active research, supporting and encouraging the production and circulation of free cultural goods: works which can be freely distributed, remixed and retransmitted in a legal way and without restrictions on access. Both virtually and in person, Estúdio Livre's activities and participation take place in the freest way possible. Proposals are made, added or removed depending on the profile of the group in each activity. All the tools in the environment are based on the concepts of free software, open knowledge and technological appropriation. The stimulus for interaction comes from workshops, media labs, free archives, user manuals, forums, personal blogs, research groups, discussions taking place via a mailing list and other tools for collaboration. The maintenance costs for the project include a small voluntary contribution on behalf of the collective and another larger contribution which comes from its partners: the Free Software Project-Paraná (PSL-PR) and the Digital Culture sector of the Brazilian Ministry of Culture (MinC). PSL-PR was the cradle of the project and manages some of the network services, while MinC maintains the server and a small team dedicated to the maintenance of the environment. The main reason this partnership exists is to provide support to the Cultural Hotspots (*Pontos de Cultura*) that form part of the Ministry's Living Culture Programme (*Programa Cultura Viva*).

The Abstract Environment: Administration and Development

Currently the tools used for virtual interaction are located on the World Wide Web. The main ones are the public discussion list and the collaborative portal, which allow for the real-time editing of hypertexts as well as uploading and downloading documents with metadata.

The public mailing list was the first virtual environment for interaction in the community. Up to now it has been hosted on the Riseup.net technical collective's server. Although we currently have emails and discussion lists under the Estúdiolivre.org domain, we chose to maintain our main list under the Riseup.net domain in order to establish a 'knot in the network', in other words, a project that uses resources from another project and vice versa. There are people in the Estúdio Livre community who also collaborate on Riseup.

net projects, for example translating its web interface from English into Portuguese.

The Estúdio Livre website was originally hosted on Federal University of Paraná (UFPR)'s *Utopia* server and is now hosted at the University of São Paulo (USP). It is made with free software and can be developed by any person with the technical knowledge of PHP, MySQL, Smarty and CSS. It is based on TikiWiki, a content management system designed for communities and distributed under the LGPL licence. People without programming knowledge can also contribute via bug reports.

The Estúdio Livre code is a Tiki module that consists of a group of new files, patches and SQL scripts. It is managed by Polvo, a software written in Perl to carry out automatic publication on the Web from a local version on the developer's machine. This procedure is necessary to maintain the Estúdiolivre.org code separate from the TikiWiki code.

The group responsible for the development, maintenance and administration of the website; moderating discussion lists; issuing verification requests and organising information consists mainly of more experienced users, programmers, system administrators, musicians, videomakers and producers who have been using free software for some time.

The Abstract Environment: Desktop

The main aim of Estúdiolivre.org is to gather a community that researches, documents, experiments with, produces and develops free media. Therefore, different modes of engagement are available to users. One may search for information as well as add to or correct incomplete content one comes across during one's research. One may also make one's own creations available through the Free Archive (*Acervo Livre*) or download productions by other members of the website. Depending on the licence used by those files, users may also remix and reupload a new version of them. This is only legally possible because the content made available on the portal uses open licences, which facilitate the most diverse types of sharing.

Another resource implemented in the Free Archive are the live channels which make possible audio and/or video streaming. Users can listen to and/or watch someone else's transmission or host their own, as long as they have the necessary tools installed on the computer that will generate the stream.

Access to all of these tools is completely free. However, to interact in this virtual environment, it is necessary to register some personal details on the site. By doing this, the user declares that they are aware of the conditions of the site's Terms of Use, thereby taking exclusive, irrevocable and irreversible responsibility for the information provided, as well as for any complaints from third parties about the material contributed.

The Abstract Environment: The Concrete Environment

In face-to-face interactions, proactive members of the community promote and participate in workshops and events which involve themes covered by Estúdio Livre's remit.

The first workshop experiment took place at the Fifth World Social Forum in January 2005 through participation in the activities of the Free Knowledge Lab (*Laboratório de Conhecimentos Livres*) located at the Youth Camp, which Lawrence Lessig attended and later mentioned on his personal blog. Starting that same year, the Free Knowledge Encounters (*Encontros de Conhecimentos Livres*) took place all over Brazil in the partnership with MinC.

In 2006, a partnership with the regional government of Extremadura in Spain made it possible for seven members of our community to travel to Spain to share knowledge with European activists. Workshops took place in Almendralejo and Barcelona, and they added a subtle upgrade to the project's evolution. This trip also encouraged the internationalisation of the website, which gained an interface in various languages, starting with the translation of the wiki pages. Despite its aforementioned nomadic nature, the concept of Estúdio Livre is being applied in many parts of Brazil, such as Curitiba, Rio de Janeiro, São Paulo and Belo Horizonte – or even inside the home of a member of the community.

Final Considerations

Estúdio Livre's activities focus on supporting the development and use of free software in media production as well as on encouraging sharing and collaboration. Above all it is an environment that engages a community of volunteers who share an interest in principles of sovereignty and autonomous proposals. It also encourages the participation of its more active members in the implementation of projects that require free methodologies and that use the documentation and tools available on the website. Estúdio Livre also accepts voluntary donations and partnership proposals from institutions, governments and companies that are interested in using its materials or would like to encourage specific projects within its community (e.g. documentation of a specific software, compilation of documentation, customisation or multimedia production) – as long as the partnership is aligned with Estúdio Livre's objectives and the partner or donor in question does not stand for anything that goes against its activist ideals.

Our current aim is to foster participatory cultural and technological production that will be able to elicit greater social awareness in everyone involved, as they see themselves part of an independent, open and collective process. We call this *Estúdio Livre Phase Two*, which is a phase that aspires to produce a work as impactful as *City of God* while following in the footsteps of the short *Elephants Dream,* the world's first open-source film enjoying critical acclaim.

Chapter 46

re:combo Full Use Licence (2004)

re:combo

Re:combo is a collective born in Brazil, Recife, but now of global calibre. It is formed by musicians, software engineers, DJs, educators, journalists and visual artists, whose objective is (using concepts such as translocality, dialogism and the openness of all sources) to enable the creation of music, art and film in a collaborative, open and free way.

The need for a user licence for audiovisual production was a pressing issue right from the project's inception. It was essential for us to create a licence that, just like GNU Licences protect free software, would protect our audiovisual production as well, so as it was *always* free and able to bring other projects along that path.

After a series of studies, we ended up with this first version of the document, developed by the collective with the participation of lawyer Caio Mariano.

The document's objective is to create a basis for open-source work that is coherent with our ideas of 'Intellectual Generosity', as opposed to intellectual property.

Preamble

There was a time when music was played only for pleasure, and its creation until then was collective, whether in the European villages of the sixteenth century or in the ceremonial *ocas* of pre-1500s Brazil. However, midway through the eighteenth century that changed. Art, which was free, became a commodity; and musical composition, previously linked solely to a gift or entertainment, became a product of speculation and industrial exploitation.

Taking a leap ahead in history we reach the second half of the 1980s. A new renaissance seems to show a postmodern path for music: collages made from different compositions split the doors of meaning wide open and show the road to a universe that reverberates with the experiments of Stockhausen and John Cage, with a street flavour. That crop of rap music is musically one of the most interesting ones from the 20th century.

Then came the industry, with their commercial interests and their legal and marketing devices. In less than ten years, the possibilities of open production have been all but extinguished. At the beginning of the 21st century the market-based concept of Intellectual Property (a term borrowed from other industries such as the chemical industry) took hold among musicians, turning the act of creation into a bureaucratic and tedious clash surrounded by flash grenades, with the sole intent of obscuring the true reason for all of this: the entertainment industry is sick and paranoid!

re:combo is not against the remuneration of intellectual creators for their efforts in the creative process. On the other hand, we believe that extremely restrictive institutions that are keepers of an excessive and exclusivist mindset with regard to intellectual property by the author and other deserving parties of specific artworks (often yielded in its totality to mega-corporations from the entertainment industry with indefinite usage rights) are no longer in line with the new ethics and behaviours resulting from technological advancements in the digital revolution, let alone the creative possibilities that have emerged since.

This revolution not only amplified access to creation but also raised a series of questions about the authorship of artworks created with machines, most often in digital formats. The re:combination, in that context, although not unprecedented or new as a form of cultural expression, is one of them. The current legislation and principles ruling intellectual property nowadays virtually forbid free artistic expression through the re:combination of artworks by a third party without going through bureaucratic procedures, which come with several particularities.

All these matters are evidence of a lack of coherence regarding the handling of these new forms of the use and creation of intellectual artworks from certain institutions that rule over intellectual property. The persistence of those institutions in scorning the new ethos and behaviours of digital media further hampers the traditional artistic formats used by the industry.

re:combo believes that the freedom to create is indeed directly related to a spur to creation itself, be it collaborative or not. For us it is incoherent to claim that the exclusivity an author has over their work is itself a stimulus to creation. The people and groups damaged by the limitations imposed on new possibilities of remaking, recombining and creating other artworks from an 'originary work' is infinitely larger than the possibilities of re:combination within an environment that favours intellectual castration and the ultraprotection of the author's exclusivity when it comes to the use of their work. Freedom is thus the sole key for collective and decentralised art if it is to continue to grow in the coming years.

In search of a modern and coherent cure to this issue that doesn't hurt the artists, re:combo feels the need to instrumentalise their principles and publish this Free Use Licence as a way to encourage and ensure that the circulation and use of their works remains free in a variety of ways.

Through this Full Use Licence, all audiovisual or phonographic work made by the re:combo collective (or by whoever wants to adopt the licence) becomes, in a fully legal sense within Brazilian legislation, permanently open and free so as to instigate new productions that are also open, and to secure free circulation of intellectual work in favour of Intellectual Generosity and human progress.

1. Licence

Terms and conditions for the USE, COPY, DISTRIBUTION, EXECUTION, MODIFICATION AND COMMERCIALISATION of audiovisual and phonographic works covered by this Licence. This Licence is applicable to any audiovisual or phonographic work that includes a warning, notice or mention placed by the copyright holder, making it clear that it can be freely used in accordance with the following terms.

2. Definitions

For the purposes of this licence and in accordance with its Terms, **'Work'** refers to any creation of the human intellect with the purpose of materialising (in any tangible or intangible medium that exists or may exist in the future, such as phonograms, videos, software, sound or any other media using images, moving or not, whether interactive or static) a cultural expression of the author.

Within the artistic, literary or scientific spectrum, any audiovisual pieces, phonograms, open-source or non-open-source software, programs, databases or other kinds of **derivative work** based on the original work created by the copyright holder can be considered **work** in these terms.

2.1. For the purposes of this Licence, it is understood that a **'derivative'** or general modification means a new work that contains the pre-existent **'original work'** or that, through whatever intellectual intervention, incorporates, transforms, complements, reduces, reunites or adapts, in part or in full, its content; either in its original form, with any possible alterations, or translated to another language.

2.2. **'Collaborative work'** is understood as an **original work** resulting from the intellectual effort of more than one author, gathered as a unique work or free to be combined in distinctive final works, elaborated through the individual contribution of other authors, no matter if result in independent works or not, in accordance with the Terms of this Licence.

2.3. The **source files** of a work are the best source for developing changes to it.

Complete source files mean all the sources of all the modules of content that compose the work, phonogram or audiovisual piece, such as: excerpts or audio files, animation frames, original digital video files, static images in high resolution, open-source files originated from proprietary software. Such software is the sole responsibility of the user in its acquisition and use and is not covered by this licence, unless expressly stated otherwise.

2.3.1. If the distribution of **'derivative work'** is conducted through access to a given repository, then equivalent access must be offered to the work's source files, so that interested parties have access not only to the work itself but also to the source files that compose and originate it.

Interested parties are not required to copy the sources together with the work itself. This, however, **does not exempt those who distribute or commercialise the work from the obligation to offer its source files in an open format** to be defined according to the conventionality of their use, distribution and manipulation.

3. Use

In observance of the Terms and Conditions of this licence and its previous sections, the content, structure and source codes of the utilised **work**, as received, can be freely **copied, reproduced, distributed, executed, modified and commercialised by third parties** through any media, tangible or intangible, pre-existent or yet to exist, as long as a warning, sign or mention of the adequate holders of the original authorship of this work is provided; a copy of this Licence shall be assigned to any other **work derived** from the original or from modifications made utilising such work; as well as a warning regarding the absence of guarantees on behalf of its original developers.

3.1. Anyone who utilises work encompassed by this Licence must add a file to the work, usually named 'readme', containing the re:combo Full Use Licence.

3.2. Charging fees for the physical act of file transfer or copying is allowed.

4. Permissions

Permission is granted to modify the content, copy or copies of the **original work** in any way, or even create a derivative work based on the original work distributed, as well as use such modifications according to what is allowed by the Licence, provided that under the Terms of the previous sections and the following:

4.1. There must be a prominent notice stating that the original files were altered, accompanied by the dates of the alterations.

4.2. In case of the modification of the original work by third parties, there must be a notice stating that the derivative work distributed or published is, in whole or in part, derived from a certain previous work or some part of it, as well as a direct reference to the original title and authorship thereof, which can be licenced freely and completely free of charge to third parties under the Terms of this Licence.

4.3. If derivative or modified work is performed, it is mandatory, at the beginning of its execution, to present copyright information and the absence of warranties (or that the warranty runs on behalf of third parties who may modify it), and that users may redistribute the work or program under these conditions, indicating to the user how to access this Licence in its entirety.

These requirements apply to **derivative and modified works** in general. If some identifiable sections are not derived from the **original work** and can be considered by themselves as independent parts of another work endowed with aesthetic originality, then this Licence and its Terms do not apply to those sections when distributed separately from the contents of the **original work**, its use being the responsibility of whoever is using the sections not derived from the original work.

However, when distributing those sections as part of a derivative work that contains in its final structure data or content of the original work, as defined in Section 2, its usage and distribution in any form as a whole, must, mandatorily, contain the Terms of this Licence, whose permissions extend to the final work as a whole, and not to each of its parts, regardless of who has developed them.

5. Open Source: Use of Open-Source Works

Copying, reproduction, modification, distribution and commercialisation of the work (or of a derivative work based on it) by third parties are allowed, in any existing media, supports and formats, open or not, or that may exist in the future and in the form of open code (open source), object or executable file according to the Terms of the Sections above, provided that the following is met:

5.1. Be accompanied by legible source files available on platforms that allow modification, which must be distributed in the form of the Sections above, in media normally used and directed to handle such works in their future formats of use, modification and distribution.

5.2. Be accompanied by the same information received with regard to the offer to distribute the corresponding source code (this alternative is only allowed for non-commercial distributions and only if the program received in the form of an object or executable file has such an offer, according to the subsection 2 above).

6. Commercialisation by Third Parties

Third parties are allowed and permitted to sell the works published under the terms of this Licence through CD-Rs, CDs, Vinyl Records, Cassette Tapes, VHS, VCD, S-VCD, DVD or any other tangible or intangible medium, existing or to be invented in the future.

6.1. Whoever sells the works covered by this Licence is responsible for any damage that they cause to consumers as well as for their warranty.

6.2. In addition to strict compliance with the Terms and Conditions of this Licence, the sale of the products covered and included in this Licence does not depend on any contractual or bureaucratic formalities on behalf of those interested in doing so.

7. Limitations

Copying, reproduction, modification, sublicensing, distribution or commercialisation of the original work or those derived from it are not permitted without observing the conditions expressed in this Licence.

7.1. Any use contrary to the Terms and scope of this Licence is prohibited and in that case the rights described in this Licence will immediately cease. Third parties who have received copies or rights under this Licence will not have their rights terminated as long as they remain within the terms of the Licence.

7.2. It is strictly forbidden to use the works created with this Licence for any purposes that are prejudiced in terms of gender, race, creed, sexual orientation, social class, ethnicity, language and species; and in works of sexual nature that exploit minors.

7.3. The copyright holder of the work used by third parties should be consulted regarding the use of the product in works related to politics, associations and football teams or for the purposes of advertising or commercial acts.

7.4. Each time the original work (or any derivative work based on it) is distributed, the recipient automatically receives a Licence from the original holder of the rights to copy, distribute or modify the work that is subject to these Terms and Conditions. No other restrictions can be imposed, removed or added by recipients that modify the essence or the Terms of this Licence or its main objective, namely the progress of science and knowledge through the free circulation of audiovisual works.

7.5. Formal acceptance of this Licence is not necessary. There will be no document or contract that guarantees permission to modify or distribute the original work or its derivative works. The modification or distribution of the original work or any work based on it implies acceptance of this Licence and all its Terms for copying, distribution or modification of such work, or works derived from it, on behalf of those who modify it.

7.6. Failure to comply with or breach of any provision relating to the Conditions of this Licence will result in the termination of the effects of the same and, supported by the Brazilian Legislation, will also result in the search for reparations through the legal sanctions applicable by the rights holders in the works included herein.

8. Resolutions

In the case of unappealable court decisions or allegations of improper use of patents or copyright by third parties, or if any restrictions are imposed and come to contradict this Licence, these are not exempt from its application.

If it is not possible to distribute the work in such a way as to simultaneously fulfil the obligations of this Licence and other licences that are necessary for the free circulation of the content of the works and experiments for which they are intended, they cannot be distributed and the distribution of this Licence will be null and exempt from any legal value for the purposes of copying, reproduction, execution, modification, sublicensing or distribution of the work or derivative works thereof.

9. Absence of Guarantees

Since the work is licenced free of charge, has no commercial purpose and is aimed at the contribution of third parties for its improvement and for development and progress in Science and Humanity, there is no guarantee for the work; except when third parties who modify it or use its content for the production of derivative works market it and express themselves formally in the sense of taking on such guarantee in relation to the work and the possible damages that it may cause to third parties.

Thus, unless otherwise specified, quality and performance are at the sole risk of users, the costs necessary for any changes, corrections and repairs being at their own expense, when deemed necessary.

In no event, unless required by an unappealable judicial decision or by free will, will the author or third parties who have modified the program **for non-commercial purposes and for intellectual and scientific progress through constant improvement of such work** be responsible for damages or losses arising from the use or lack of skill in its use, even if a warning about possible errors or damages has been issued in the Terms of this Licence.

End of Licence

Chapter 47

Art Machines (1999)

Frederico Morais

...

2.

This is an exhibition about machines – machines for making art. Dysfunctional, unproductive machines from a strictly economic perspective, but essential in their gratuitousness. It was conceived as an extension of the Abraham Palatnik retrospective taking place simultaneously at the Niterói's Museum of Contemporary Art. When his first kinechromatic device – the culmination of an extensive investigation into light and movement begun in 1949 – was shown at the 1st São Paulo Biennial in 1951, Palatnik became the founder of technological art in Brazil and one of the global pioneers of Kinetic Art. After his 'painting machine', in the 1950s and 1960s, the artist would go on to make kinetic objects (merely capable of movement) and playful pieces as well as games involving research on magnetism (magnets and electromagnets), Newtonian physics and the laws of perception.

Those first inventions left no direct heirs. Palatnik always worked alone, never belonging to any group or movement, only occasionally grazing their orbit. But other artists, some of whom are represented in this exhibition, have carried on and are still carrying on research in the same fields as Palatnik, exploring the aesthetic possibilities of real movement, light and sound. This is where the two shows meet, forming a single conceptual unit. What brings Palatnik and the artists shown here together is the fact that their works exhibited here all remain within the field of Newtonian physics and electromechanics.

3.

An in-depth analysis of Palatnik's work can be found in the catalogue of the Niterói show. Let's move on to the other exhibitors.

Since his return in 1963 from the two-year European residency awarded to him by the National Salon, Mauricio Salgueiro has dedicated himself exclusively to technological art. In 1964 he started his series of 'light sculptures' in which, for the first time in the world, fluorescent lightbulbs were made into raw material for artistic creation. Displaying sculptures in which the spatial dynamic is determined by coloured light, the following year he participated in the 8th São Paulo Biennial and the 4th Paris Biennial. These works received a lot of attention from the likes of Pierre Restany and Georges Orley in the November issues of the magazines *Domus* (from Milan) and *Studio International* (from the United States). As a reminder, Dan Flavin, wrongly considered the pioneer in this field, only showed his first artworks featuring fluorescent lights in 1966. Exploring the aesthetic potential of light, sound and movement through mechanical structures, Salgueiro has created what we might call a poetics of the machine. With his pulsating (*A Poça* [The Puddle], 1986), noisy (*Ordinário, Marche* [Forward, March], 1994) sculptures, he has consistently created metaphors for the organic within the machine, giving concrete shape to what was mere literary rhetoric used in futuristic modernity-worshipping circles, which was more immaterial desire than solid reality.

Sérvulo Esmeraldo was a member of the informal group of Brazilian artists who, while living in Paris, renewed the vocabulary and language of Kinetic Art, together with Argentinians and Venezuelans. In the early '60s he made kinetic pieces using magnets and engines, two of which are on display in this exhibition. In the 1970s, his *Excitables* demanded the tactile interaction of spectators. Also working in the first half of the 1960s, abstract painter Danilo di Prete added motorised moving parts to his canvases, thus justifying his inclusion in the cult of kineticism, despite hybridity being a central component of his project. In the work shown here, *Semovente Amarelo* [Yellow Semovente, 1967], painting in the traditional sense no longer exists: it's his most purely, wholly kinetic work.

João Wesley deploys engines, hydraulic pumps, lightbulbs and electromagnets to recreate the natural rhythms of water spirals, vortices, irisation or the slow and steady crumbling of soapstone into dust, like a miniature slow-motion simulation of erosion or some other natural disaster. It's as if he were attempting to devise a new alphabet and a new language for matter itself, elevating art to the very substance of nature. In this sense, João Wesley's artworks can be understood simultaneously as Arte Povera and Kinetic Art.

The origin of life is said to be the breath that was breathed into bodies made from dust. Pneumatism. Air would therefore be the first and most vital energy source. It's what sets in motion Calder's mobiles; it's the point where Kinetic Art begins. From *Bolhas* [Bubbles] to *Birutas* [Windsocks], from *Cubo de Fumaça* [Smoke Cube] to his *Fragiles*, air is Marcelo Nitsche's most frequently used material. A(i)rt machines. The artist uses wind, exhaust pipes, engines and airplanes to animate his pieces. Some of them were designed for public spaces, that is, for an open-air exhibition. A pioneer of Brazilian inflatable art, Marcelo Nitsche created his first 'bubble' in 1967.

If in Nitsche's work air is a playful material that calls on spectators to become active participants, as is the case with some of his *Bubbles*, it gets a more conceptual treatment in Pedro Paulo Domingues' pieces (*Quatro Ventos* [Four Winds], 1992), which are often more akin to theoretical treatises than to artworks. Countering the popular expression 'to the four winds',[80] Domingues strategically places twenty electric fans in such a way as to direct four wind streams at the same point in space, thus creating a clash of energy that is concentrated in the space between two opposing mirrors that reflect each other. The double mirrors infinitely multiply what is invisible, a material lacking shape and colour. Like the Gothic artist who, when erecting a cathedral, verticalises stone until it turns to cloud, Domingues manipulates matter in search of its opposite: spirit. This is his operation: to materialise the immaterial, to give solidity and consistency to what is only atmospheric.

In traditional sculpture light plays a passive role; it is external to the work, limited to revealing its contours or accentuating its volume. In *Cerca de 20 Lâmpadas* [Around 20 Lamps, 1988], Domingues 'sculpts' directly with light, creating a luminous frame for a previously non-existent space. Similarly, in Maurício Bentes's 1988 sculptures, light is at the heart of the work. The light in his pieces reaches us through cracks and slits, like bright shards cutting through the pitch-black surface – a light that, like in Goeldi's engravings, seems wrested from the depths of the night.

The Concrete (1956) and Neo-concrete (1959) movements linked poets to visual artists, drawing the two creative fields close in intersemiotic artworks. Albertus Marques exhibited his 1961 'electric poem' *Fim* [The end] at the 2nd National Neo-concrete Art Exhibition, held at the São Paulo Museum of Modern Art in 1961. In this poem, light plays a central role, for 'it is only light that makes the word appear and disappear, thus conveying the poetic charge intended by the author'.

We are also showing works by Waldemar Cordeiro, the main theorist of the visual side of the Concrete movement and a pioneer in Brazilian computer art since 1968, and Lygia Pape – a member of Neo-concretism – made in a similar vein but with much more technical and conceptual elaboration. For both artists, the printed word had proven insufficient in triggering the entire semantic range promised by the verbivocovisual[81] project. In Cordeiro's 1965 piece, *Amar(go)*,[82] light breaks the word apart, multiplying its meanings: bitter love. In Lygia Pape's 1999 work, *Sedução II* [Seduction II], the words 'vai' (go) and 'vem' (come), bobbing up and down, unleash a wide range of ambiguous suggestions. For Cordeiro love is painful duration; for Pape it's the act of making love, skin-to-skin.

This erotic component underlying the language of the machine, which has always ignited the imagination of humans when admiring mechanical structures, is equally present in Salgueiro's *A Poça* [The Puddle] and in Cordeiro's 1988 *Beijo* [Kiss], in the latter of which the systolic and diastolic movement of the photographic image suggests orgiastic sounds. Lips open and close as if moaning in pleasure – ahh! And while we're at it, let's talk about Márcia X's erotic machinations. In her works, the artist challenges sexual taboos, daringly juxtaposing objects, structures and themes from the realms of childhood, religion and pornography. She turns toys into pornographic objects, playfully perverting children's games; or, conversely, renders eroticism holy by decorating dildos with kitschy religious ornaments. Her 1995 *Kaminhas Sutrinhas* [Little Kamas Little Sutras] does not 'enshrine the coitus' in the manner of Persian miniatures or of Francisco Toledo's art, but, on the contrary, shows it as a mechanised, repetitive, industrially reproduced process. At the same time, though, this installation suggests a breakdown in the sexual/industrial assembly line, a bug in the productive system that results in a delicious anarchy reminiscent of Charlie Chaplin's *Modern Times*.

In one of his most important essays, the 1936 'Crisis of the Object', André Breton advocated for the creation of objects seen originally in dreams, the multiplication of which would result in the devaluation of all other objects whose conventional utility clutter the so-called real world. In other words, he proposed a 'total revolution of the object' that would be accomplished by deviating objects away from their utilitarian purposes, endowing them with new functions and meanings in a continuous, vivid reassessment of law and order.

In simple terms I would say that this is a good summation of Barrão's intents. There are a couple of caveats, however: 1) Barrão is not a Surrealist late to the game but is actually closer in spirit to the creative anarchy of Dada and Fluxus, and to the formal and thematic vocabulary of Pop Art; and 2) he is in no way apocalyptic: as a multimedia artist and professional, he feels quite at home in the industrial society and its mass culture. This doesn't stop him from questioning the underlying order of industrial society's productive system. He makes his art from disassembled and reassembled household appliances, automobiles and toys; through accumulation and fragmentation, unusual associations, detours and breakdowns in functionality and new configurations he sets the stage for a theatre of the absurd in which the actors are his machines.

Where Barrão has a penchant for the illusionism of consumer society, Guto Lacaz draws his poetry from the observation of the laws of physics and mechanics. Like Palatnik, he is above all an artist-inventor. In the catalogue for his 1987 show at the Subdistrito gallery, he used this quote from Karl Marx's *Capital* as an epigraph:

> Each useful thing (iron, paper, etc.) is to be considered from a double point of view, in accordance with *quality* and *quantity*. Each such thing is a totality of many

properties and is therefore able to be useful in different respects. The discovery of these different respects and hence of the manifold modes of utility of things is an historical act.

An illustration of this concept can be found in the 'unusual objects' Lacaz has been creating since 1978. In *Outravitrola* [Othervictrola] from 1985,[83] he increases tenfold the length of a record-player's tonearm, which remains nonetheless perfectly functional. He does not replace utility with aesthetics but multiplies or renews utility through art. The 1985 *Welcome-Sayonara* is a nostalgic poetic receptacle for the memories of childhood that can be equally interpreted as a counterfeit bullet train going back and forth at miles a minute. It's a portrait of a country that, attempting to move forward, goes backwards.

In the last twenty or thirty years, Carlos Fajardo's art has been minimalist. The reduction in form and the emphasis on the physicality of the materials do not exclude, from time to time, a touch of lyricism or an organic referent that insists on manifesting itself in the apparent coldness of the structure. Suddenly, almost imperceptibly, matter moves, gives off an odour, babbles an almost inaudible sound. From this moment on, an artwork that seemed neutral and devoid of meaning ensnares us in an uncanny, disquieting atmosphere. This voice of Carlos Gardel I just heard: where is it coming from?

A sizeable chunk of popular creativity is employed in creating machinery. These are primitive machines with crafty gears, operated by hand or using natural resources like water or, more commonly, air, as is the case with so many children's toys: hand-cranked kites, paper windmills, wheelbarrows, wooden dolls that move with the wind, Nativity scenes, etc. We could argue that this is something like a vernacular kineticism, or dare we say, a set of vernacular 'installations'. In the realm of popular creativity, the boundaries between art and craft are blurry. Or else what starts out as craft slowly turns into art, into worldview, into concept. That is the case of Jorge Luiz Fonseca, a railway worker from Conselheiro Lafaiete in the state of Minas Gerais, who started out by embroidering text, phrases and popular sayings, more or less in the style of Arthur Bispo do Rosário, and by collecting pictures and objects from popular and mass culture in collages and assemblages with almost invariably astonishing results. Now, only four years after his debut in regional art salons, he is a rising star of new Brazilian art. The piece shown in this exhibition, called *Máquina de Fazer Voar* [Machine for flying], is a lovely and engaging kinetic structure. It is most certainly a machine for making art.

Notes

1 As stated by the author Abraham Palatnik: 'It was not painting, or drawing, or printmaking or sculpture. So it had no place in the catalogue. There was no way for it to participate in the Biennial' (Scovino and Tjabbes 2013, 186).

2 Palatnik may have, in fact, been one the first artists to use these technologies. As Fabiana Barcinski recalls, 'during the Venice Biennale, in 1964, the Italian critic and poet Carlo Belloli sought out the artist to verify the original date of his first Cinecromático. Seeing that the date was 1951, Belloli corrected the then prevailing information in Europe that considered Malina and Schoffer to be the first pioneers of artworks employing light and movement. This correction was made in the catalogue of the *1st International Exhibition of Kinetic Art* held at Galerie Denise René, in Paris, that same year' (Scovino and Tjabbes 2013, 181).

3 As British computer art pioneer Paul Brown put it in 1996: 'For the past 25 years, computers have been the forbidden medium. It was OK for established artists like Warhol and Hockney to use them but for a young unknown it was the kiss of death' (Brown 1996).

4 Indeed, the most relevant Brazilian institutions focused on new media arts were created after Kac had compiled his timeline: Festival Videobrasil (1986), FILE – *Festival Internacional de Linguagem Eletrônica* [International Festival of Electronic Language] (2000) and the now-defunct *Prêmio Sérgio Motta de Arte e Tecnologia* [Sérgio Motta Art and Technology Award] (2000).

5 Recent scholarship has intended to map and discuss this relationship. See, for instance, Cateforis et al. 2018, McCray 2020. For a more sympathetic view, see Shanken 2006.

6 This topic has been the subject of heated debates in the country. The interplay between local elites, artists and critics, from both the 19th and early 20th century generations, respectively representing old

landowning elites and new European migrants, is explored by Sergio Miceli in two pivotal works (Miceli 2003, 2012).

7   For more information on this highly disputed movement in Brazilian cultural history, and especially in relation to its utopian project, see Viveiros de Castro 2018, Torre 2019, Azevedo 2018, Faria 2013.

8   In fact, recent scholarship has been dedicated to Zanini's role in thinking and shaping such artworks. For more information, see Zanini and Jesus 2018.

9   For an in-depth discussion of such movements in the UK, see Brown 2009. For a broader view of this optimism in Europe and the US, see Nunez 2016. For a perspective dedicated to early computer arts alone, see Taylor 2014.

10 It can be argued that 'progress', embodied by industrialisation and urbanisation, was seen as a necessary step in the quest for a new nation, towards modernity and against Brazil's rural, agricultural past. For more see: Pinto 2001.

11 'futura 9: luxo lixo'. *the idea of the book*. https://theideaofthebook.com/pages/books/814/augusto-de-campos/futura-9-luxo-lixo.

12 'rot - gesamtverzeichnis'. *Stuttgarter Schule*. http://www.stuttgarter-schule.de/rot.htm.

13 This kind of writing is commonplace across the scholarship on Brazilian media arts. By doing the muscular work of contextualising national artistic production within the internationally established theories, texts such as the one by de Campos have been instrumental for the constitution of the genre. If they do not appear more often in this volume, it is only because the topics they cover are easily available for the readership through their own primary sources.

14 Omar Khouri provides a comprehensive introduction to the uses of independent publishing by the Brazilian avant-garde and experimental poets. See Khouri 2004.

15 These letters are currently in the collection of the Institute of Brazilian Studies of the University of São Paulo (IEB-USP), which hosts Amaral's personal archives. The reference code for this specific document is DOC: AAA-C-ICAUP-002.

16 See 'Documents of Latin American and Latino Art' in https://icaa.mfah.org/s/en/page/home.

17 Here, Roberto Moreira S. Cruz's (Belo Horizonte, 1962) curatorial research on the institutional history of time-based media in the country (*Expoprojeção 1973-2013*, *Video MAC*) and Fabio FON's (São Paulo, 1979) decades-long survey of Brazilian Web art come to mind. See http://expoprojecao.com.br; https://video.mac.usp.br; https://fabiofon.com/webartenobrasil.

18 We had first-hand experience of this issue while interviewing Lucas Bambozzi. In a situation that seems fairly common among independent producers and curators, Bambozzi keeps most documentation of the projects on which he has worked stashed in cardboard boxes at home. He told us every time he moved house in the recent years, he had to throw our some of this material. The material being stored in a domestic space, coupled with the fact that it is not catalogued, makes it extremely inconvenient to access without Bambozzi's direct assistance.

19 The broad 'cryptoart' scene is characterised by employing non-fungible tokens (NFTs) to represent artworks. An NFT is a unique record stored on a public blockchain, the decentralised database utilised for the production and trade of cryptocurrencies. These tokens include metadata linking them to other online files. This process allows for the assumption that NFTs can authenticate pieces of digital art and generate the artificial scarcity necessary for their meaningful commercialisation.

20 See http://labiennale.org/en/art/2022/collateral-events/vera-moln%C3%A1r-ic%C3%B4ne-2020

21 See, for instance: Rotinwa 2021, Valenti 2021, Ferrarese 2021.

22 'Bolsa de Fotografia ZUM/IMS 2022'. *Zum*. https://revistazum.com.br/bolsa2022.

23 Ironically, the large Indigenous participation in the 2021 Biennial, which earned it the nickname of 'Indigenous Biennial' [*Bienal dos Índios*], was not part of its original plan. It mostly resulted from the pressure by the late Macushi artist Jaider Esbell, one the few Indigenous people initially invited to participate in the event. The 2023 Biennial, however, seems to have been committed to diversity from the outset, considering its direction was granted to a team that featured three Black curators: Diane Lima, Grada Kilomba and Hélio Menezes. See Domingos de Lima 2021 and Fundação Bienal de São Paulo 2022.

24 In fact, as Maria Arminda Arruda has argued, since the first decades of the 20th century, Brazilian intellectual and financial elites have made the country's modernisation their explicit goal. According to her, 'for many, [modernisation] represented the pinnacle of developmental efforts and nation building; for others, it signified the formation of an open and democratic society; and, for a few, it marked the rise of a stream of progressive cultural tendencies'. This early ambition reverberated across all cultural fields, and the changes it generated would contaminate the country's imagination of itself with the idea of progress, as expressed in the national flag. Arruda invokes Mario Pedrosa's infamous definition of Brazil as a nation 'condemned to be Modern' (Arruda 2001, 24-25).

25 The Cooke Mission was an American technical mission that arrived in Brazil during a critical period of the Second World War, after the country declared itself opposed to the Axis powers and in alignment with the USA. In collaboration with Brazil's Economic Mobilisation Commission, the mission significantly bolstered the country's industrial capabilities, aiming to enhance the production of essential goods, improve transportation and lay the groundwork for Brazil's long-term industrial development (Ortiz 1988, 45).

26 Ortiz's work discusses in detail how Brazil's cultural field developed in the second half of the 20th century. By focusing its analysis on the material aspects of cultural production, Ortiz brings to light a detailed account of how different media emerged in the country over the years.

27 For a history dedicated to the technology itself, see Patterson 2015.

28 This is perhaps most visible in São Paulo and its various postwar cultural developments, which are examined in rich detail by Arruda 2001.

29 References missing in the original (Editor's Note).

30 From a poem by Décio Pignatari, *'Eupoema'* [I-poem]: 'Eu jamais soube ler: meu olhar de errata / a penas deslindas as feias / fauces dos grifos e se refrata' [A literal translation, without accounting for the many puns: I never knew how to read: my *errata* eyes merely unravel the ugly faces of griffins and refracts]. *Olhar de errata* means here something like 'wrongful or mistaking eyes', as well as a 'correcting glance', another pun on the theme of feedback and self-correction (Translator's Note).

31 Old interjection originally exclaimed when someone is getting on or trying to control a horse or another wild animal (Translator's Note).

32 Mario Pedrosa, in his influential article 'Arte Concreta ou a Ausência de Ícones' [Concrete Art or: the Absence of Icons], *Jornal do Brasil* newspaper, Rio de Janeiro, 15 Feb 1957, has stressed the importance of non-verbal communication in concrete poetry.

33 Reference missing in the original (Editor's Note).

34 'Our intelligence needs to become used to a synthetical and ideographical understanding more so than to an analytical and discursive one', in a loose translation (Translator's Note).

35 Something that the Argentinian artists from the group Madi did before the neo-concretists, as evidenced by their reliefs and by Kosice's sculptural work from 1952, which consisted of articulated metal objects without pedestal.

36 How can we explain art dealers' lack of interest in the work of Sacilotto, whether in his expressionist or concrete phases, if not by

utter ignorance? Sacilotto is the most interesting painter of the São Paulo group, with the exception of the intuitive 'genius' of Alfredo Volpi, who is not a proper concretist.

37 Décio Pignatari, foreword to the 'Fiaminghi' catalogue, Aremar Gallery, Campinas/SP, June 17 – July 12, 1961. The contact between the already dissolved concrete group from São Paulo and the artists from Campinas occurred through the mediation of the Aremar Gallery, where concrete artists always exhibited their work.

38 Maldonado, Lidy Prati and Iommi had made contact with the group from São Paulo during the Ist Biennial.

39 A notable exception is the publication of computer-generated poems in *Código*, an experimental poetry magazine from Salvador that ran between 1974 and 1990. *Código* acted as an intergenerational bridge between the original and emerging concrete poets. The magazine was financed by one of its editors, Erthos Albino de Souza, a poet, engineer and close personal friend of Augusto de Campos and the other original concretists. Albino de Souza was also the first Brazilian to actually compose poems with a computer. For more on Souza, consult Paros 2014, 2015.

40 Teletext technology, in particular, was promoted by Telecomunicações de São Paulo S/A (Telesp), the public company responsible for the telephone system in the São Paulo state during that time. They collaborated with traditional media outlets to popularise the technology and expand their business. This public-private partnership supported the use of teletext during the 17th São Paulo Biennial in 1983, as well as exhibitions at the São Paulo Museum of Art (MASP) and the Museum of Image and Sound (MIS-SP), among other instances. For a comprehensive discussion of the history of videotext in Brazil, please refer to Netto, Zaniboni. 1986. *Videotexto no Brasil*. São Paulo: Nobel, 134.

41 For concise information on Meireles' work in English, see Salvo 2005, 138.

42 'DOPS Doesn't Want Guevara in the Exhibition', *Jornal do Brasil*, Rio de Janeiro, 22 Dec 1967, 10. Nowadays, Tozzi states that the artists' intention was to provoke the status quo or, as he told the reporter at the time, present a work such as the Guevara panel to 'explore the communicative power of this type of painting'.

43 See, for example, the stamp *Who Killed Herzog?*, a direct reference to the journalist who died in a military prison in São Paulo.

44 The installation's title, *Fiat Lux*, also refers to a well-known brand of matches in Brazil. Thus, *Faça-se a Luz* (Let there be light), in the translation from Latin acquires a double meaning, becoming ambiguous in this conceptual work by Meireles.

45 In particular the work *Morte no Sábado: Homenagem a Vladimir Herzog* [Death on Saturday: an Homage to Vladimir Herzog] (1975).

46 'VI Intervenção'. São Paulo: Secretaria de Estado da Cultura, 1981.

47 Untranslatable wordplay. 'Ver grama' signifies 'to see grass'. Individually, 'vermelha' means 'red' and 'gramática', grammar (Editor's Note).

48 A recent survey by curator Roberto Moreira S. Cruz at MAC-USP retraced the history of the museum's Video Sector and its *Espaço B* [B Space], dedicated to the promotion of video experiments. Cruz's survey recovered many of the artworks produced at the museum and yielded an online exhibition, where most of these movies can now be watched: http://video.mac.usp.br

49 For more information on the history of Brazil's computing industry, see: Motoyama 2004.

50 In 2001, our survey of experimental Super 8 production was made public with the logistical support of the Itaú Cultural Institute, which recovered and remastered around 180 titles that had been practically inaccessible since the 1970s. I was then able to see more than 450 films from among the 681 surveyed, encompassing 237 directors (a third of these being visual artists) from 21 cities (Porto Alegre, Florianópolis, Curitiba, São Paulo, Campinas, Santos, Rio, Goiânia, Belo Horizonte, Governador Valadares, Vitória, Salvador, Aracaju, Maceió, Recife, Caruaru, João Pessoa, Teresina, Fortaleza, São Luís and Manaus). Between 2001 and 2003, a traveling selection from the São Paulo show, *Marginália 70: o Experimentalismo no Super-8 Brasileiro* [Marginália 70: Experimentation in Brazilian Super 8], toured dozens of cities in Brazil and abroad (e.g., in France, *À vos Marges, Années 70*, in 2003). The São Paulo version of the exhibition totalled 125 films, and the itinerant ones ranged between 24 and 42. Among the dozens of filmmakers recovered – there were 78 in the largest showing – were Jomard Muniz de Britto, Edgard Navarro, Ivan Cardoso, José Agrippino de Paula, Hélio Oiticica, Lygia Pape, Antonio Dias, Torquato Neto, Sérgio Péo, Jorge Mourão, Rui Vezzaro, Mário Cravo Neto, Raymond Chauvin, Geneton Moraes Neto, Paulo Bruscky, Jairo Ferreira, Abrão Berman, Carlos Porto, Leonardo Crescenti, Gabriel Borba, Marcello Nitsche, Claudio Tozzi, Nelson Leirner, Regina Vater, Anna Maria Maiolino, Henrique Faulhaber, Giorgio Croce, Ragnar Lagerblad, Fernando Bélens, Pola Ribeiro, José Araripe Jr., Virgílio de Carvalho Neto, Marcos Sergipe, Paulo Barata, Robinson Roberto, José Umberto Dias, Kátia Mesel, Donato Ferrari, Marcos Bertoni, Isay Weinfeld, Marcio Kogan, Iole de Freitas, Ismênia Coaracy, Vivian Ostrovsky, Fernando Severo, Peter Lorenzo, Paulo Rocha, Hassis, Júlio Plaza, Luiz Alphonsus, Artur Barrio, Carlos Vergara, Carlos Zilio, Maria do Carmo Secco, Daniel Santiago, Ypiranga Filho, Amin Stepple, Ana Nossa, Berenice Toledo, Bernardo Caro, Marcos

Craveiro, Getulio Gaudielei Grigoletto, Henrique de Oliveira Jr., José Albino Gonçalves, Bertrand Lira, Torquato Joel, Chico Liberato, Firmino Holanda, Flávio de Souza, Flávio Motta, Luciano Figueiredo, Óscar Ramos, Luiz Otávio Pimentel and Sérgio Giraud.

51   Popular Brazilian idiom in praise of persistence (Translator's Note).

52   In 1975, 'The Museum of Modern Art of Rio de Janeiro featured among its activities a series of experimental exhibitions. "Experimental" was meant to cover new artistic production that did not find space in galleries, given its incompatibility with the market's interests. The choice of candidates did not take into consideration their curriculum, only the project they presented. Moreover, MAM was financially committed to the making of the projects' (in 'Sala Experimental'. *Malastartes* magazine, No. 3, Rio de Janeiro, April/May/June 1976, 25).

53   During which *Wireless Telephone* [*Telefone sem Fio*], the only collective work made by the pioneering Rio group, was first presented. Participants: Ana Vitória Mussi, Anna Bella Geiger, Fernando Cocchiarale, Ivens Machado, Letícia Parente, Miriam Danowski, Paulo Herkenhoff and Sônia Andrade.

54   Participants: Anna Bella Geiger, Fernando Cocchiarale, Ivens Machado, Leticia Parente, Miriam Danowski, Paulo Herkenhoff and Sônia Andrade.

55   The first solo video exhibition in the country.

56   Participants: Anna Bella Geiger, Fernando Cocchiarale, Ivens Machado, Leticia Parente, Miriam Danowski, Paulo Herkenhoff and Sônia Andrade.

57   The government had revoked the concession of Tupi Network, belonging to Diários Associados [Associated Newspapers], because of financial corruption and their debts with the Social Security. On the politics of concessions and the configuration of Brazilian TV networks, see Capparelli 1982 and Mattos 1990.

58   MTV Brasil was created in 1990 thanks to a partnership between the Abril media group and Viacom, one of the largest entertainment companies in the world. At the time of writing, MTV was the largest targeted TV channel in the country.

59   Created after the suspension of the Institutional Act 5, *Abertura* was the first news show with segments run by intellectuals who were openly critical of the military regime, such as Glauber, Ziraldo, Fausto Wolf, Vilas-Bôas Correa and Antônio Callado, among others. It was created and directed by Fernando Barbosa Lima and aired on TV Tupi from February 1979 to July 1980.

60   See more about Sandra Kogut's presence on television in Lima 1997.

61 'The animal game' – a kind of informal lottery and form of gambling (Translator's Note).

62 ForumBHZvideo was an electronic arts festival created in the city of Belo Horizonte by filmmakers and producers who intended to encourage local production and give visibility to radical experiences using video. 'We threw ourselves into the idea of respecting the filmmakers and the audience, aware that the audience deserved to get in touch with experiences and concepts that were being developed in other parts of the world, making it clear that broader phenomena were taking place with regard to the relationship between people and images in contemporary society' – as I have written in the catalogue *Retrospective of the Independent Video of Minas Gerais*, Instituto Imagens Movimento, 1995. ForumBHZvideo was run by Adriana Franca, Ana Flávia Dias, Rogério Veloso, Vanessa Tamietti, Vania Catani and myself.

63 The renewal of the video sector at MIS was characterised by activities that focused on video as an artistic medium. Long-running programs such as *Radical Video*, which exhibited first-hand works by Sadie Benning, Bruce Yonemoto, Francisco Ruiz Infante, Claudia Aravena, Gary Hill, Tom Kalin and Michael O'Reilley, were created at that time. In addition to new work releases and exhibitions of classic video art pieces, special attention was given to video installation projects and events foreseeing hybrid relations between video and other areas.

64 The event was already being held for fourteen years in Chile as the Franco-Chilean Video Art Festival. In 1990, during its 14th edition, it expanded to include Uruguay, Argentina and Colombia, becoming the Franco-Latin American Festival. Brazil joined the group in 1994. Some believe this made the festival too expensive and less interesting as a soft power vehicle for the French Ministry of Foreign Relations. Regardless, the event has largely contributed to exchanges among neighbouring Latin-American countries.

65 The collection organised by Baumann (2000) offers a good overview of the profound economic changes Brazil went through the 1990s. For an overview of the history of neoliberalism in Brazil and its region, following the work of Perry Anderson and the idea of a Washington Consensus in Latin America, see: Gennari 2002, 21.

66 For a broad overview of the forced modernisation process afflicting Brazilians universities at the time, see Motta 2014.

67 While the 1980s saw an expansion of the art market in the country, it is important to recall that most of the private resources were still focused on painting and other traditional media. For more, see Canongia 2010 and Costa 2004.

68 It could be argued that, via the digitisation of banking, Itaú synergised both ends of their business, IT and banking. For a historical account of the importance of banking for the development of IT in Brazil, see: Fonseca *et al*. 2010 and Silva 2019.

69 See https://twitter.com/emannuelbento/status/1605613731789934596/photo/1

70 The festival was proposed by Ricardo Rosas and Giseli Vasconcelos to Bambozzi, who promptly welcomed it. Gilberto Gil's opening address can be found at https://www.youtube.com/watch?v=evqUQlMIqME

71 These issues are explored in greater depth in Mello 2002.

72 Documentation of the piece is online at http://ekac.org/teleporting.html.

73 The group was led by Bia Medeiros and its current members are Carla Rocha, Cila MacDowell, Cyntia Carla, Maria Luiza Fragoso, Alice Stefania Curi, Robiara Beccker and Viviane Barros. For a better understanding of its scope and activities, visit http://corpos.org.

74 Some of those texts were compiled in Flusser 2002.

75 On the relationship between the invention of these technical apparatuses and their political and economic context, see Winston 1998 and Zielinski 1999.

76 'First Command of the Capital': a criminal organisation first established in the São Paulo prison system in the 1990s, currently spread across several regions in Brazil, where they vie for control over drug trafficking and other lucrative illicit activities with other criminal groups (Translator's Note).

77 *Gambiarra*: a popular, informal noun used to denote an improvised solution to a practical problem, usually employing whatever is at hand in a display of ingenuity and thriftiness. Somewhat similar to jury-rigging, jerry-rigging, 'MacGyvering' (Translator's Note).

78 Literally 'electric trios': trucks equipped with huge loudspeakers and a stage on top of which musicians perform for large crowds that follow these moving vehicles at outdoor parties. First introduced in the late 1940s during the Carnaval in Bahia and often associated with *axé music*, *trios elétricos* have become a mainstay in popular Brazilian festivities and gatherings, from Pride Parades to political rallies (Translator's Note).

79 Agogo: Yoruba musical bells often used in traditional Nigerian music and in Brazilian samba (Translator's Note).

80 Brazilian Portuguese idiom meaning to carelessly or deliberately spread a piece of information around to everyone; to let the world know (Translator's Note).

81 A portmanteau blending of the words 'verbal', 'vocal' and 'visual', borrowed from James Joyce's *Finnegans Wake* by the São Paulo Concrete poetry collective Noigandres in the 1950s (Translator's Note).

82 A play on the words 'amar' (to love) and 'amargo' (bitter) (Translator's Note).

83 In Brazil, the brand name Victrola came to be synonymous with record players, to the point that it dropped its capitalisation and the letter c, becoming simply 'vitrola' (Translator's Note).

Original Sources

I Code and Language

Form, Function and General Project (Décio Pignatari)
   Pignatari, D. 2014. 'Forma, Função e Projeto Geral'. In *Teoria da Poesia Concreta: Textos Críticos e Manifestos, 1950-1960*. Eds. Augusto de Campos, Décio Pignatari and Haroldo de Campos. 5th ed. Cotia: Ateliê Editorial. 153–156. Originally published in: *Arquitetura e Decoração*, No. 24, São Paulo, 1957. Translated by Leonardo Lamha and Gabriel Menotti.

Concrete Poetry – Language – Communication (Haroldo de Campos)
   Originally published in the 'Suplemento Dominical' of the Jornal do Brasil newspaper, Rio de Janeiro, 28 Apr 1957 and 5 May 1957. Translated by Leonardo Lamha.

Poetry and Modernity: From the Death of Art to the Constellation. The Post-Utopian Poem (Haroldo de Campos)
   Campos, H. de. 1997. 'Poesia e Modernidade: Da Morte à Constelação. O Poema Pós-Utópico'. In *O Arco-Íris Branco: Ensaios de Literatura e Cultura*. Rio de Janeiro: Imago. Abridged version. Translated by Leonardo Lamha and Gabriel Menotti.

Art and Technology, Part III (Augusto de Campos)
   Originally published in the 'Suplemento Literário' of the *Estado de São Paulo* newspaper, São Paulo, 18 Mar 1967. Translated by Leonardo Lamha.

On Some Aspects of Concrete Poetry (Haroldo de Campos)
Excerpt from an interview published in *Diálogo*, No. 7, São Paulo, June 1957, in response to a questionnaire posed by poet Alexandre Cravinas. Translated by Leonardo Lamha.

New Language, New Poetry (Luis Ângelo Pinto and Décio Pignatari)
Originally published in the *Correio da Manhã* newspaper, Rio de Janeiro, 25 August 1964, alongside the poems *agora, talvez nunca!* [now, maybe never!] (by Pignatari) and *terra homem* [man earth] (by Pinto). Translated by Leonardo Lamha.

The Three Sides of the Coin: Brazilian Poetry in the 1960s and 1970s (Eduardo Kac)
Self-published by the author in 1983. Abridged version. Translated by Leonardo Lamha. CC BY-ND.

Two Lines of Contribution: Concretists in São Paulo / Neo-Concretists in Rio (Aracy Amaral)
Amaral, Aracy. 1977. 'Duas Linhas de Contribuição: Concretos em São Paulo / Neoconcretos no Rio'. In *Projeto Construtivo Brasileiro na Arte (1950-1962)*. São Paulo: Pinacoteca do Estado/ FUNARTE. Translated by Leonardo Lamha and Gabriel Menotti.

The New Possibilities (Walter Zanini)
In Universidade de São Paulo - Museu de Arte Contemporânea. 1977. *Poéticas Visuais: de 29 de Setembro a 30 Outubro de 1977*. São Paulo. Exhibition catalogue. Translated by Leonardo Lamha.

International Multimedia (Walter Zanini)
In Universidade de São Paulo - Museu de Arte Contemporânea. 1979. *Multimedia Internacional: de 19 de Novembro a 16 de Dezembro de 1979*. São Paulo. Exhibition catalogue. Translated by Leonardo Lamha.

II Social Communication Systems

Art in Hard Times (1964-c. 1980) (Aracy Amaral)

Originally published in *Brazil: Body Nostalgia*, National Museum of Modern Art, Tokyo, 2004. Exhibition Catalogue. Republished in Amaral, Aracy. 2006. *Textos do Trópico de Capricórnio: Artigos e Ensaios (1980-2005); Vol. I: Modernismo, Arte Moderna e o Compromisso com o Lugar*. São Paulo: Editora 34, 318-30. Abridged version. Translated by Julia Manacorda and Gabriel Menotti.

General Outline of The New Objectivity (Hélio Oiticica)
Oiticica, Hélio. 1967. 'Esquema Geral da Nova Objetividade'. In *Nova Objetividade Brasileira*. Rio de Janeiro: Museu de Arte Moderna do Rio de Janeiro, 4-18. Abridged version. Translated by Julia Manacorda and Gabriel Menotti.

Mail Art: Art in Synchrony (Julio Plaza)
Plaza, Julio. 1981 'Mail-Art: Arte em Sincronia'. In *XVI Bienal de São Paulo: Arte Postal*. Exhibition catalogue. São Paulo: Fundação Bienal de São Paulo, 8-10.

Mail Art and the Great Network: Art, Today, Is this Statement (Paulo Bruscky)
Excerpt from a text originally published in 1977 in *Jornal Letreiro*, No. 2, and rewritten a couple of times. Our version comes from: Bruscky, Paulo. 2010. 'Arte Correio e a Grande Rede'. In *Arte e Multimeios*. Ed. Cristiana Tejo. Recife: Zolu, 11-16. Translated by Julia Manacorda.

Artistic Xerography: Art Without an Original (From the Invention of the Machine to the Xero/graphic Process) (Paulo Bruscky)
Bruscky, Paulo. 1985. 'Xerografia Artística: Arte sem Original (da Invenção da Máquina ao Processo Xero/gráfico)'. In *Arte: novos meios / multimeios: Brasil 70/80*. Ed. Daisy Peccinini. São Paulo: Fundação Armando Álvares Penteado, 131-135. Abridged version. Translated by Julia Manacorda.

Conversation with the Reader (Júlio Plaza)
Plaza, Julio. 1986. 'Diálogo com o Leitor'. In *Videografia em Videotexto*. São Paulo: Hucitec, 179-188. Introduction of Plaza's videotext monograph. Translated by Julia Manacorda.

Way of Conclusion (Júlio Plaza)

Plaza, Julio. 1986. 'A Título de Conclusão'. In *Videografia em Videotexto*. São Paulo: Hucitec, 179–188. Conclusion of Plaza's videotext monograph. Translated by Julia Manacorda.

Holopoetry and Perceptual Syntax (Eduardo Kac)

Originally published in the magazine *Holosphere*, Museum of Holography, New York, Summer 1986, Vol. 14, No. 3: 25. CC BY-ND.

Pretext for an Intervention (Annateresa Fabris)

Originally published in *Arte em São Paulo*, No. 22, April 1984. Translated by Gabriel Menotti.

Museums and New Communication Media (Walter Zanini)

Originally published in the *Estado de S. Paulo* newspaper, São Paulo, 7 Mar 1976, 23. Translated by Julia Manacorda.

Introduction to the 17th São Paulo Biennial (Walter Zanini)

In *Bienal Internacional de São Paulo*. 1983. General catalogue. São Paulo: Fundação Bienal de São Paulo, 5-6. Translated by Julia Manacorda.

For a Creative Criticism / Curating Exhibitions as Creation (Frederico Morais)

Morais. F. 1989. 'Por uma Crítica Criativa – a Curadoria de Exposições como Criação', 2nd ANPAP Encounter proceedings, São Paulo: 118-124. Translated by Julia Manacorda.

From the Body to the Ground (Frederico Morais)

Morais, F. 2006. 'Do Corpo à Terra'. In *Crítica de Arte no Brasil: Temáticas Contemporâneas*. Ed. Gloria Ferreira. Rio de Janeiro: Funarte, 195–202. Originally published in: *Do Corpo à Terra: um Marco Radical na Arte Brasileira*. 2001. Belo Horizonte: Itaú Cultural.

III Moving Images

Poets, Artists, Anarcho-Super 8-Filmmakers
(Rubens Machado Jr.)
   Machado Jr., Rubens. 2001. 'Poetas, Artistas, Anarco-Superoitistas'. In *Marginália 70: o Experimentalismo no Super-8 Brasileiro*. São Paulo: Itaú Cultural, 6–9. Translated by Julia Manacorda and Gabriel Menotti.

Some Ideas around Expo-Projection 73 (Aracy Amaral)
   Amaral, Aracy. A. 1973. 'Algumas Idéias em Torno à Expo-Projeção 73'. In *Expo-Projeção 73*. Exhibition catalogue. São Paulo: Centro de Artes Novo Mundo, 10–12. Translated by Gabriel Menotti.

(Audio-Visuals) (Frederico Morais)
   Originally published in *(Áudio-Visuais)*. 1973. Exhibition catalogue. São Paulo: São Paulo Museum of Modern Art, 12-23. Translated by Gabriel Menotti.

Block-Experiments in Cosmococa – A Program in Progress
(Hélio Oiticica)
   Originally published in 1973. Abridged Version.

The Early Days of Video Art in Brazil (Fernando Cocchiarale)
   Parts of this text were previously published in exhibition catalogues. Our version comes from: Machado, Arlindo, ed. 2000. *Made in Brasil: Três Décadas do Vídeo Brasileiro*. São Paulo: Iluminuras, Itaú Cultural, 61–68. Abridged version. Translated by Julia Manacorda and Gabriel Menotti.

Testimonial: Regina Silveira
   In Peccinini, Daisy (ed.). 1985. *Arte, Novos Meios/Multimeios: Brasil 70/80*. São Paulo, Brazil: Fundação Armando Alvares Penteado, 319-323. Translated by Julia Manacorda and Gabriel Menotti.

Testimonial: Anna Bella Geiger
   In Peccinini, Daisy (ed.). 1985. *Arte, Novos Meios/Multimeios: Brasil 70/80*. São Paulo, Brazil: Fundação Armando Alvares Penteado,

231-235. Abridged version. Translated by Julia Manacorda and Gabriel Menotti.

Videoart: The Brazilian Adventure (Arlindo Machado)
Machado, A. 1996. 'Video Art: The Brazilian Adventure', *Leonardo*, Vol. 29, No. 3: 225–231.

The Video Theatre Project (Otávio Donasci)
Originally published in the catalogue of the III Videobrasil Festival, in 1985. Translated by Julia Manacorda and Gabriel Menotti.

Video as a Utopian Television Project (Yvana Fechine)
Fechine, Yvana. 2000. 'O Video como um Projeto Utópico de Televisão'. In *Made in Brasil: Três Décadas do Vídeo Brasileiro*. Ed. Arlindo Machado. São Paulo: Iluminuras, Itaú Cultural, 85–110. Translated by Julia Manacorda and Gabriel Menotti.

Videobrasil and Video in Brazil: A Side-by-Side Journey (Solange Farkas)
Farkas, Solange. 2000. 'O Videobrasil e o Vídeo no Brasil: uma Trajetória Paralela'. In *Made in Brasil: Três Décadas do Vídeo Brasileiro*. Ed. Arlindo Machado. São Paulo: Iluminuras, Itaú Cultural, 219–223. Translated by Julia Manacorda and Gabriel Menotti.

Exploded Video and it Shrapnels Hovering Above Us (Lucas Bambozzi)
Bambozzi, Lucas. 2008. 'O Vídeo Explodido e Seus Estilhaços Pairando sobre Nós'. In *Video en Latinoamérica: A critical view*. Ed. Laura Baigorri. Special issue of *Revista Brumaria*, Spain. Excerpt. Translated by Julia Manacorda and Gabriel Menotti.

IV Personal Computers

Investigative Poetics (Christine Mello)
Excerpt from Mello's 2005 'Arte e Novas Mídias: Práticas e Contextos no Brasil a partir dos Anos 90', *ARS*, Vol. 3: 115–132.

DOI: 10.1590/S1678-53202005000100009. Translated by Pedro Neves.

Time Capsule (Eduardo Kac)
Originally published in 1997. CC BY-ND.

Itaulab Research: Paulista 1919, Abadia Virtual and Policarpo (Marcos Cuzziol)
Originally published in the catalogue of the exhibition *Memória do Futuro - Dez Anos de Arte e Tecnologia no Itaú Cultural*. 2008. São Paulo: Itaú Cultural, 66–73. Courtesy of Itaú Cultural Institute.

Technology and Contemporary Art: Bringing Politics into the Conversation (Arlindo Machado)
Machado, Arlindo. 2005. 'Tecnologia e Arte Contemporânea: como Politizar o Debate', *Revista de Estudios Sociales*, Vol. 22: 71–79.

Make Way for Tactical Media! (Ricardo Rosas and Tatiana Wells)
Manifesto published on the occasion of the Mídia Tática Brasil festival, held in March 2003 at Casa das Rosas, in São Paulo. Translated by Pedro Neves.

Gambiarra – Elements for a Reflection on Recombinant Rechnology (Ricardo Rosas)
Originally published in *Caderno Videobrasil-Arte Mobilidade e Sustentabilidade*. 2006. São Paulo: Associação Cultural Videobrasil. This essay is an abridged and modified version of an unpublished book by Rosas focused on 'technological *gambiarras*'. Translated by Pedro Neves.

Free Studios (Fabianne B. Balvedi, Guilherme R. Soares, Adriana Veloso and Flávio Soares)
Originally published on the Estúdio Livre website in 2006. Translation comes from Mansoux, Aymeric and Marloes de Valk (eds). 2008. *FLOSS + Art*. Poitiers: GOTO10. CC BY-SA-NC 2.5.

re:combo Full Use License (re:combo)
Originally published online and circulated on mailing lists in 2004.

Art Machines (Frederico Morais)
Morais, F. 1999. 'Máquinas de Arte'. In *Cotidiano/Arte. A Técnica.* Exhibition catalogue. São Paulo: Itaú Cultural, 4–10. Abridged version. Translated by Pedro Neves.

Works Cited

'3NÓS3/Interversão urbana'. 1981. *Arte em São Paulo*, No. 2, October.

'A Mágica de Palatnik: Luz no Lugar da Tinta'. 1951. *Tribuna da Imprensa*, São Paulo, November 5.

'MAC USP é pioneiro no Brasil na incorporação de NFT ao acervo'. 2022. *Artequeacontece*. March 8. https://artequeacontece.com.br/mac-usp-e-pioneiro-no-brasil-na-incorporacao-de-nft-ao-acervo

'MFAH Acquires Leirner Collection of Constructive Art'. 2007. *Artdaily*. March 17. https://artdaily.cc/news/19607/MFAH-Acquires-Leirner-Collection-of-Constructive-Art.

Amaral, Aracy. 1970. 'Art Abroad/São Paulo: The Bienal Boycott: Extension and Meaning', *Arts Magazine*, New York.

Amaral, Aracy. 2003. *Arte para quê? A Preocupação Social na Arte Brasileira (1930-1970)*. São Paulo: Studio Nobel/Itaú Cultural.

Arantes, Priscila. 2005. *Arte e Mídia: Perspectivas da Estética Digital*. São Paulo: Editora Senac.

Argan, Giulio Carlo. 1975. In *L'arte e la Città*. Lapud Ermanno Migliorini. Florença: Il Fiorino.

Arruda, Maria Arminda do Nascimento. 2001. *Metrópole e Cultura: São Paulo no Meio do Século XX*. São Paulo: EDUSC.

Asbury, Michael. 2013. 'Some Notes on Abraham Palatnik's Kinechromatic Device'. In *Abraham Palatnik: A Reinvenção da Pintura*. Eds. Felipe Scovino and Pieter Tjabbes. Brasília: Centro Cultural Banco do Brasil, 61-76.

Ascott, Roy. 2003. *Telematic Embrace: Visionary Theories of Art, Technology, and Consciousness*. Berkeley: University of California Press.

Azevedo, B. 2018. *Antropofagia: Palimpsesto Selvagem*. São Paulo: Editora SESI.

Barros, Geraldo de. 1976. Interview by Aureliano Menezes, FAU-USP, April.

Barroso, I. 1958. 'Cibernética', *Jornal do Brasil*, Suplemento Dominical, October 19.

Bastos, Oliveira. 1957. 'Por uma Poesia Concreta', *Jornal do Brasil*, February 3.

Baumann, R., ed. 2000. *Brasil: uma Década em Transição*. Rio de Janeiro: Editora Campus.

Beiguelman, Giselle. 2004. 'Admirável Mundo Cíbrido'. In *Cultura em Fluxo (Novas Mediações em Rede)*. Eds. Geanne Alzamora and Andre Brasil. Belo Horizonte: Puc Minas, 264-282.

Berger, René. 1977. 'Video and the Restructuring of Myth'. In *The New Television: Video After the Television*. Eds. Rachel Churner, Rebecca Cleman and Tyler Maxin. Cambridge, MA: MIT Press, 206-221.

Bloodstein, Oliver. 1943. 'General Semantics and Modern Art', *ETC: A Review of General Semantics*, Vol. 1, No.1 (Summer): 12-23.

Bongiovanni, Pierre. 'Parabolic People: el Manifesto de lo Maravilloso'. In *VideoCuadernos V. Textos sobre la Obra de Sandra Kogut*. Ed. J. Ferla. Buenos Aires: Nueva Librería.

Brett, Guy, ed. 2008. *Cildo Meireles*. Exhibition catalogue. London: Tate/D.A.P.

Brito, Ronaldo. 1999. *Neoconcretismo: Vértice e Ruptura do Projeto Construtivo Brasileiro*. São Paulo: Cosac Naify.

Britto, Jomard Muniz de. 1964. *Contradições do Homem Brasileiro*. Rio de Janeiro: Tempo Brasileiro.

Brown, Paul. 1996. 'An Emergent Paradigm', *Periphery*, No. 29. http://www.paul-brown.com/WORDS/EMERGPAR.HTM

Brown, Paul, Charlie Gere, Nicholas Lambert and Catherine Mason, eds. 2009. *White Heat Cold Logic: British Computer Art 1960-1980*. Cambridge, MA: MIT Press.

Burnham, J. 1980. 'Art and Technology: The Panacea that Failed'. In *The Myths of Information: Technology and Postindustrial Culture*. Ed. Kathleen M. Woodward. Madison, WI: Coda Press, 200-215.

Cacaso, Antônio Carlos de Brito. 2002. '*Orgulho', Beijo na Boca [1975]*. Rio de Janeiro: 7 Letras; São Paulo: Cosac & Naify.

Calvino, Italo. 1990. *Seis Propostas para o Próximo Milênio*. São Paulo: Cia. das Letras.

Campos, Augusto de. 1966. 'A Poesia Sólida de Wlademir', *O Estado de S. Paulo*, March 19.

Campos, Augusto de. 1979. *Poesia 1949-1979*. São Paulo: Duas Cidades.

Campos, Haroldo de. 1997. 'Depoimento sobre Arte e Tecnologia: O Espaço Intersemiótico'. In *A Arte no Século XXI: a Humanização das Tecnologias*. Ed. Diana Domingues. São Paulo, SP: Editora Unesp (Prismas), 207-215.

Candido, Antonio. 1973. *Literatura e Sociedade*. São Paulo: Companhia Editora Nacional.

Canongia, Ligia. 2010. 'Os Anos 80 e o Retorno a Pintura'. In *Anos 80: Embates de uma Geração*. Ed. Ligia Canongia. Rio de Janeiro, Brazil: Francisco Alves, 07-25.

Capparelli, Sérgio. 1982. *Televisão e Capitalismo no Brasil: com Dados da Pesquisa da ABEPEC*. São Paulo: L&PM Editores.

Carbonara, Corey and Michael Korpi. 1991. 'HDTV and Film: The Issues', *American Cinematographer*, Vol. 72, No. 8: 60.

Cateforis, David, Steven Duval and Shepherd Steiner, eds. 2018. *Hybrid Practices: Art in Collaboration with Science and Technology in the Long 1960*. Oakland: University of California.

Cavalcanti Simioni, A.P. 2013. 'Modernismo Brasileiro: entre a Consagração e a Contestação', *Perspective: Actualité en Histoire de l'Art*, Vol. 2. DOI: 10.4000/perspective.5539.

Chamic, Mario. 1961. *Instauração Práxis*. Volume 1. São Paulo: Edições Quíron.

Chamic, Mario. 1963. *Instauração Práxís*. Volume 2. São Paulo: Edições Quíron.

Cordeiro, Waldemar. 1957. 'Objeto', *Arquitetura e Decoração*, Winter.

Cordeiro, Waldemar. 1972. *Arteônica*. São Paulo: Editora das Américas. https://waldemarcordeiro.com/arteonica

Costa, Marcus de Lontra, ed. 2004. *Onde Está Você, Geração 80?* Rio de Janeiro: Centro Cultural Banco do Brasil.

De Certeau, Michel. 2011. *The Practice of Everyday Life*. Berkeley and Los Angeles: University of California Press.

De Ugarte, David. 2005. *El Poder de Las Redes*. Electronic book.

Dias-Pino, Wlademir. 1971. *Processo: Linguagem e Comunicação*. Petrópolis: Vozes.

Dias-Pino, Wlademir. 1972. 'SOLIDA', *Revista Vozes*, Vol. 7 (Summer): 49-54.

Dias-Pino, Wlademir. 1982. *Wlademir Dias-Pino*. Cuiabá: Edições do Meio.

Domingos de Lima, Juliana. 2021. 'Jaider Esbell Exigiu Presença de Mais Artistas Indígenas na Bienal', *Ecoa*, September 27. https://uol.com.br/ecoa/ultimas-noticias/2021/09/27/jaider-esbell-exigiu-presenca-de-mais-artistas-indigenas-na-bienal.html

Donati, Luisa Paraguai and Gilbertto Prado. 1999. 'Utilizações Artísticas de Imagens em Direto na World Wide Web'. In *Anais do 1º Encontro Internacional de Arte e Tecnologia*. Brasília: Universidade de Brasília.

Durand, José Carlos Garcia. 1989. *Arte, Privilégio e Distinção: Artes Plásticas, Arquitetura e Classe Dirigente no Brasil, 1855/1985*. São Paulo: Editora Perspectiva.

Dyson, F. 2006. *And Then It Was Now: Enduring Rhetorics*. Montreal: Daniel Langlois Foundation for Art, Science, and Technology.

Eisenstein, Sergei. 1968. *The Film Sense*. London: Faber & Faber.

Enguita, Nuria. 1995. 'Lugares de divagación: una entrevista con Cildo Meireles'. In *Cildo Meireles*, Valencia, IVAM Centre dei Carme, Generalitat Valenciana.

Fargier, Jean Paul. 1993. 'Poeira nos Olhos'. In *Imagem Máquina*. Ed. André Parente. São Paulo: Editora 34.

Faria, D. 2013. 'As Meditações Americanas de Keyserling: um Cosmopolitismo nas Incertezas do Tempo', *Varia Historia*, Vol. 29: 905–923.

Favaretto, Celso F. 1979. *Tropicália: Alegria, Alegria*. São Paulo: Kairós.

Fenollosa, Ernst. 1953. 'The Chinese Written Character as a Medium for Poetry'. In *The Little Review Anthology*. Ed. Margaret Anderson. New York: Hermitage House.

Ferrarese, Marco. 2021. 'Malaysian artists earn freedom to be creative with NFTs', *Aljazeera*, December 12. https://www.aljazeera.com/news/2021/12/12/malaysian-artists-earn-freedom-to-be-creative-with-nfts.

Ferreira Gullar. 1959. 'Da arte concreta & arte neoconcreta', *Jornal do Brasil*, July 18.

Ferreira Gullar. 1965. 'Opinião 65', *Arte em Revista*, Vol. 2 (Summer).

Ferreira Gullar. 1969. 'A Pesquisa da Contemporaneidade'. In *Dicionário das Artes Plásticas no Brasil*. Ed. Roberto Pontual. Rio de Janeiro: Civilização Brasileira.

Ferreira, Glória and Paulo Herkenhoff, ed. 2015. *Mário Pedrosa: Primary Documents*. New York: MoMA.

Flusser, Vilém. 1978. *Pós-História: Vinte Instantâneos e um Modo de Usar*. São Paulo: Duas Cidades.

Flusser, Vilém. 1983. *Für eine Philosophie der Fotografie*. Göttingen: European Photography.

Flusser, Vilém. 1985a. *Filosofia da Caixa Preta*. São Paulo: Hucitec.

Flusser, Vilém. 1985b. *Ins Universum der technischen Bilder*. Göttingen: European Photography.

Flusser, Vilém. 2002. *Writings*. Ed. Andreas Ströhl. Minneapolis: University of Minnesota Press.

Fonseca, Carlos Eduardo Corrêa da, Fernando de Souza Meirelles and Eduardo Henrique Diniz. 2010. *Tecnologia Bancária no Brasil: uma História de Conquistas, uma Visão de Futuro*. São Paulo: FGVRAE.

Fundação Bienal de São Paulo. 2022. 'Fundação Bienal anuncia equipe de curadores da 35ª Bienal de São Paulo', *Bienal de São Paulo*. March 8. https://bienal.org.br/fundacao-bienal-anuncia-equipe-de-curadores-da-35a-bienal-de-sao-paulo.

Gennari, A.M. 2002. 'Globalização, Neoliberalismo e Abertura Econômica no Brasil nos Anos 90'. *Pesquisa & Debate*, Vol. 13, No. 1.

Goodyear, Anne Collins. 2008. 'From Technophilia to Technophobia: The Impact of the Vietnam War on the Reception of "Art and Technology"', *Leonardo*, Vol. 41, No. 2: 169–173

Hayakawa, Samuel Ichiye. 1948. 'What is Meant by Aristotelian Structure of Language?', *ETC: A Review of General Semantics*, Vol. 5, No. 4 (Summer): 225-230.

Hayakawa, Samuel Ichiye. 1954. *Meaning and Maturity*. New York: Harper and Brothers.

Higgins, Hannah. 2002. *Fluxus Experience*. Berkeley: University of California Press.

Kac, Eduardo. 1986. 'The Brazilian Art and Technology Experience: A Chronological List of Artistic Experiments with Technosciences in Brazil'. *Leonardo Online*. http://leonardo.info/isast/spec.projects/brazilchron.html

Kac, Eduardo. 1996. 'Abraham Palatnik, Pioneer of Kinetic Art', *Leonardo*, Vol. 29, No. 2: 120–121. DOI: 10.2307/1576345.

Kane, Carolyn L. 2014. *Chromatic Algorithms: Synthetic Colour, Computer Art, and Aesthetics after Code*. Chicago: University of Chicago Press.

Khouri, Omar. 2004. *Revista na Era Pós-Verso: Revistas Experimentais e Edições Autônomas de Poemas no Brasil dos Anos 70 aos 90*. São Paulo: Ateliê Editorial.

Klüver, Billy. 1994. 'Artists, Engineers, and Collaboration'. In *Culture on the Brink: Ideologies of Technology*. Eds. Gretchen Bender and Timothy Druckey. Seattle: Bay Press, 207-219.

Krauss, Rosalind. 1978. 'Video: The Aesthetics of Narcissism'. In *New Artists Video: A Critical Ontology*. Ed. Gregory Battcock. New York: Dutton, 43-64.

Kutschat Hanns, Daniela. 2002. *Corpo-Espaço: Notas, Rotas e Projetos*. PhD Dissertation, University of São Paulo.

Kwastek, Katja. 2015. *Aesthetics of Interaction in Digital Art*. Cambridge, MA: MIT Press.

La Ferla, Jorge, ed. 1997. *Contaminaciones: del Videoarte al Multimedia*. Buenos Aires, Univ. de Buenos Aires.

Lafer, Celso. 1970. *The Planning Process and the Political System in Brazil/A Study of*

Kubitschek's Target Plan - 1956-1961. Ithaca, NY: Cornell University.

Lagnado, Lisette. 2005. 'O Malabarista e a Gambiarra', *Revista Trópico*.

Langer, Susanne Katherina. 1953. *Feeling and Form*. London: Routledge.

Lessig, Lawrence. 2005. *Cultura Livre*. São Paulo: Trama.

Lévi-Strauss, Claude. 1989. *O Pensamento Selvagem*. Campinas: Papirus.

Lima, Rita de Cássia G.B. 1997. *Todos os Tempos. Uma Intrepretação sobre o Trabalho de Sandra Kogut*. PhD dissertation. Programa de Comunicação e Semiótica - PUC-SP, São Paulo.

Machado, Arlindo. 1984. 'Perspectivas da Video Arte no Brasil', *Guia de Video no Brasil*, No. 1: 34-42.

Machado, Arlindo. 1985. 'Notas sobre uma Televisão Secreta'. *In Brasil: os Anos de Autoritarismo-Televisão e Video*. Ed. Fernando Barbosa Lima. Rio de Janeiro: Jorge Zahar, 58-66.

Machado, Arlindo. 1988. *A Arte do Video*. São Paulo: Brasiliense.

Machado, Arlindo. 1991. 'Inside Out and Upside Down: Brazilian Video Groups', *The Independent*, Vol. 14, No. 1: 30-33.

Machado, Arlindo. 1993. *Máquina e Imaginário: o Desafio das Poéticas Tecnológicas*. São Paulo: EDUSP.

Machado, Arlindo. 1996. 'Video Art: The Brazilian Adventure', *Leonardo*, Vol. 29, No. 3: 225. DOI: 10.2307/1576251.

Machado, Arlindo. 1997. *Pré-Cinemas & Pós-Cinemas*. Campinas: Papirus.

Machado, Arlindo. 1998. 'A Arte do Vídeo no Brasil'. In *Catálogo do XVI Salão Nacional de Artes Plásticas*. Rio de Janeiro: FUNARTE, 84-86.

Manovich, Lev. 1996. 'The Death of Computer Art', *Rhizome*, October 22. https://rhizome.org/community/41703.

Mattos, Sérgio. 1990. *Um Perfil da Televisão Brasileira*. Salvador: A TARDE/ABAP.

McCray, W. Patrick. 2020. *Making Art Work: How Cold War Engineers and Artists Forged a New Creative Culture*. Cambridge, MA: MIT Press.

McLuhan, Marshall and Quentin Fiore. 1967. *The Medium Is the Massage: An Inventory of Effects*. New York: Bantam Books.

Mello, Christine. 2002. 'A Experiência com a Poética de Philadelpho Menezes'. In *Mídias e Artes: os Desafios da Arte no Início do Século XXI*. Eds. Anna Barros and Lucia Santaella. São Paulo: Unimarco Editora, 27-31.

Miceli, Sérgio. 2003. *Nacional Estrangeiro: História Social e Cultural do Modernismo Artístico em São Paulo*. São Paulo: Cia das Letras.

Miceli, Sérgio. 2012. *Vanguardas em Retrocesso: Ensaios de História Social e Intelectual do Modernismo Latino-Americano*. São Paulo: Cia das Letras.

MoMA. 2022. 'Refik Anadol: Unsupervised'. *MoMA*. https://moma.org/calendar/exhibitions/5535

Monteiro, Adolfo Casais. 1957. 'Palavra, Letras e Poesia', *O Estado de São Paulo*, February 17.

Morais, F. 2004. 'Palatnik: Um Pioneiro da Arte Tecnológica'. In *Abraham Palatnik*. Ed. L.C. Osorio. São Paulo, SP: Cosac Naify, 163–175.

Mota, Regina. 2001. *A Épica Eletrônica de Glauber: Um Estudo sobre Cinema e TV*. Belo Horizonte: Ed. UFMG.

Motoyama, S. 2004. *Prelúdio para uma História: Ciência e Tecnologia no Brasil*. São Paulo: EDUSP.

Motta, R.P.S. 2014. *As Universidades e o Regime Militar: Cultura Política Brasileira e Modernização Autoritária*. Rio de Janeiro: Zahar.

Napolitano, Marcos. 2014. *1964: História do Regime Militar Brasileiro*. São Paulo: Contexto.

Novaes, Thiago, Francisco Caminati and Cláudio Prado. 2005. 'Sinapse XXI: Cultura Digital e Direito à Comunicação'. In *Mídias Digitais: Convergência Tecnológica e Inclusão Digital*. Eds. Andre Barbosa Filho, Cossette Castro and Takashi Tome. São Paulo: Paulinas.

Nunez, German Alfonso. 2016. *Between Technophilia, Cold War and Rationality: A Social and Cultural History of Digital Art*. PhD dissertation. University of the Arts London.

Nunez, German Alfonso. 2018. 'Between Worshipers, Priests and the Nuke: An Introduction to the Cultural and Social History of Early Computer Art'. In *Explorations in Art and Technology*. Eds. Linda Candy, Ernest Edmond and Fabrizio Poltronieri. London: Springer, 31-38.

Nunez, German Alfonso. 2019. 'Infomaré and Superinfovia; the sea and the highway: Brazilian imagination and the early commercial internet', *RESAW19: The Web that Was: Archives, Traces, Reflections*, University of Amsterdam. https://easychair.org/smart-program/RESAW19/2019-06-19.html.

Nunez, German Alfonso. 2020. '"Good for the Brazilian Ego": A primeira exibição de Computer Art no Brasil, A diplomacia cultural estadunidense e o envelhecimento social de Waldemar Cordeiro'. Filmed at *V Encontro de Pesquisas em História da Arte da UNIFESP*, Guarulhos, SP, 1h40. https://www.youtube.com/watch?v=Ohrp-Xx6iGM

Obradovic, Adelheíd. 1934. *Die Behandlung der Rämulichkeit im Spaeteren Werk des James Joyce*. Marburg.

Ortiz, Renato. 1988. *A Moderna Tradição Brasileira*. São Paulo: Editora Brasiliense.

Paes, José Paulo. 1977. 'Os poetas concretos, 20 anos depois'. *Revista Vozes*, Vol. 1 (Winter): 100.

Paros, F.M. 2014. 'O Mineiro e a Máquina: Vida e Obra de Erthos Albino de Souza'. In *SIIMI 2014*. III Simpósio Internacional de Inovação em Mídias Interativas, Goiânia: Universidade Federal de Goiás, 87–100. https://siimi.medialab.ufg.br/up/777/o/13_mineiro_maquina.pdf

Paros, F.M. 2015. 'De Engenharia e de Poesia... (Ou Algo da Vida e da Obra de Erthos Albino de Souza)', *Circuladô*, Vol 3, No. 3: 9–17.

Patterson, Z. 2015. *Peripheral Vision: Bell Labs, the S-C 4020, and the Origins of Computer Art*. Cambridge, MA: MIT Press.

Pedrosa, Mário. 1975. *Mundo, Homem, Arte em Crise*. São Paulo: Editora Perspectiva.

Pedrosa, Mário. 1996. 'The Chromatic Plastic Dynamism of Abraham Palatnik: An Introduction to the First International Biennial of São Paulo (1951)', *Leonardo*, Vol. 29, No. 2: 117–118, DOI: 10.2307/1576343.

Pedrosa, Mário. 1997. 'The Chromatic Plastic Dynamism of Abraham Palatnik: An Introduction to the First International Biennial of São Paulo (1951)', *Leonardo Online*. https://leonardo.info/isast/spec.projects/pedrosa.html.

Pereira, Gabriela de Gusmão. Non-dated. 'Sobreviventes Urbanos'. *Terreno Baldio*, http://www.terrenobaldio.com.br/

Pignatari, Décio. 1977. *Poesia Pois é Poesia*. São Paulo: Duas Cidades.

Pinto, M. I. M. B. 2001. 'Urbes Industrializada: O Modernismo e a Paulicéia como Ícone da Brasilidade', *Revista Brasileira de História*, Vol. 21: 435–455. DOI: 10.1590/S0102-01882001000300009.

Plaza, Julio and Mônica Tavares. 1998. *Processos Criativos com os Meios Eletrônicos: Poéticas Digitais*. São Paulo: Hucitec.

Prado, Gilbertto, Milton Sogabe and Yara Guasque. 2018. 'Breve História – Artistic Research in Brazil', *Journal for Artistic Research* [Preprint], DOI: 10.22501/jarnet.0010.

Prado, Gilbertto. 1994. 'As redes artísticas telemáticas', *Revista Imagens*, No. 3. Campinas: Unicamp.

Prado, Gilbertto. 2009. 'Breve relato da Pós-Graduação em Artes Visuais da ECA-USP', *ARS*, Vol. 7, No. 13, DOI: 10.1590/S1678-53202009000100006.

Rebãlo, P. 2002. 'Brazilians' Spin: Remix Music Biz', *Wired*, July 22. https://www.wired.com/2002/07/brazilians-spin-remix-music-biz/

Rocha, Glauber. 1965. 'The Aesthetics of Hunger'. In *Film Manifestos and Global Cinema Cultures*. Ed. Scott MacKenzie. 2014. Oakland: University of California Press.

Rouanet, S.P. 1997. 'Flusser em Praga', *Jornal do Brasil*, November 01.

Rotinwa, Ayodeji. 2021. 'Ayodeji Art X Lagos Puts NFTs by African Artists in the Limelight', *The Art Newspaper*, November 5. https://theartnewspaper.com/2021/11/05/art-x-lagos-puts-nfts-by-african-artists-in-the-limelight.

Ruesch, Jurgen and Weldon Kess. 1956. *Nonverbal Communication: Notes on the visual Perception of Human Relations*. Los Angeles: University of California Press.

Rush, Michael. 1999. *New Media in Late 20th-Century Art*. London: Thames & Hudson.

Salvo, Donna De. 2005. *Open Systems: Rethinking Art c.1970*. Exhibition catalogue. London: Tate Modern.

Santos Filho, G.M. dos. 2016. *Um Bit Auriverde: Caminhos da Tecnologia e do Projeto Desenvolvimentista na Formulação duma Política Nacional de Informática para o Brasil (1971-1992)*. São Paulo: Intermeios.

Santos, Laymaert. 2003. *Politizar as Novas Tecnologias*. São Paulo: Editora 34.

Santos, Milton. 1993. *A Urbanização Brasileira*. São Paulo: Hucitec.

Schaeffer, Pierre. 1952. *À la Recherche d'une Musíque Concrète*. Paris: Éditions du Seuil.

Schwarz, Roberto. 1978. *O Pai de Família e Outros Estudos*. Rio de Janeiro: Paz e Terra.

Silva, Jeremias Mariano Panichek da. 2019. *História, Alianças Estratégicas e Rede de Empresas da Itautec S.A.* MA thesis. UFPR.

Scovino, Felipe and Pieter Tjabbes, ed. 2013. *Abraham Palatnik: A Reinvenção da Pintura*. Brasília: Centro Cultural Banco do Brasil.

Shanken, Edward A. 2005. 'Artists in Industry and the Academy: Collaborative Research, Interdisciplinary Scholarship and the Creation and Interpretation of Hybrid Forms', *Leonardo*, Vol. 38, No. 5: 415–418.

Shanken, Edward. 2008. 'The Reception and Rejection of Art and Technology: Exclusions and Revulsions', *Leonardo*, Vol. 41, No. 1: 160–61.

Shanken, Edward. 2016. 'Contemporary Art and New Media: Digital Divide or Hybrid Discourse?'. In *A Companion to Digital Art*. Ed. Christiane Paul. Malden, MA: Wiley Blackwell, 463-481.

Sluckin, Walter. 1954. *Minds and Machines*. London: Penguin.

Smith, Clyde F. 2021. 'Beyond Hic et Nunc, Part 1: A Community Emerges', *nfts.wtf*. https://nfts.wtf/beyond-hic-et-nunc-part-1-a-community-emerges

Sterling, Bruce. 2005. *Shaping Things*. Cambridge, MA: MIT Press.

Sutcliffe, A. 2009. 'Patterns in Context'. In *White Heat Cold Logic: British Computer Art 1960-1980*. Eds. Paul Brown, Charlie Gere, Nicholas Lambert and Catherine Mason. Cambridge, MA: MIT Press, 175–190.

Taylor, Grant D. 2014. *When the Machine Made Art: The Troubled History of Computer Art*. New York and London: Bloomsbury Academic.

Torre, B.D. 2019. 'Modelos Críticos: Antônio Candido e Roberto Schwarz Lêem Oswald de Andrade', *Revista do Instituto de Estudos Brasileiros*, 178–196.

Turner, F. 2014. 'The Corporation and the Counterculture: Revisiting the Pepsi Pavilion and the Politics of Cold War Multimedia', *The Velvet Light Trap*, Vol. 73, No. 1: 66–78.

Valenti, Graziella. 2021. 'Talk Show Exame In: Daniel Peres, da Tropix, Destrincha o Metaverso', *E-Insight*. October 30. https://exame.com/insight/

talk-show-exame-in-daniel-peres-da-tropix-destrincha-o-metaverso/p

Viveiros de Castro, Eduardo. 2018. 'Que Temos Nós com Isso?' In *Antropofagia: Palimpsesto Selvagem*. Ed. B. Azevedo. São Paulo: Editora SESI.

Winston, B. 1998. *Media Technology and Society*. London: Routledge.

Zanini, Walter. 1997. 'Primeiros Tempos da Arte/Tecnologia no Brasil'. In *A Arte no Século XXI: a Humanização das Tecnologias*. Ed. Diana Domingues. São Paulo: Unesp (Prismas), 234–246.

Zanini, Walter and Eduardo de Jesus. 2018. *Walter Zanini: Vanguardas, Desmaterialização, Tecnologias na Arte*. Ed. Eduardo de Jesus. São Paulo: Editora WMF Martins Fontes.

Zielinski, S. 1999. *Audiovisions: Cinema and Television as Entr'actes in History*. Amsterdam: Amsterdam University Press.

www.ingramcontent.com/pod-product-compliance
Lightning Source LLC
Chambersburg PA
CBHW031604210526
45464CB00004B/1421